BORN TO SHOP
LONDON

THE BARGAIN HUNTER'S GUIDE TO NAME-BRAND AND DESIGNER SHOPPING

SIXTH EDITION

HarperPerennial
A Division of HarperCollinsPublishers

HarperCollins books may be purchased for educational, business, or sales promotional use. For information, please write: Special Markets Department, HarperCollins Publishers, Inc., 10 East 53rd Street, New York, NY 10022.

FIRST EDITION

Designed by C. Linda Dingler

ISSN: 1065-0563

94 95 96 97 ◆/RRD 10 9 8 7 6 5 4 3 2

Although every effort was made to ensure the accuracy of prices appearing in this book, please keep in mind that with inflation and a fluctuating rate of exchange, prices will vary. Dollar estimations of prices were based on the following rate of exchange: £1 = $1.50 U.S. Whenever possible, prices are quoted in pounds sterling (£) to show a more accurate reflection of local prices.

For Ian Cook
with love and thanks for all the pix

BORN TO SHOP LONDON
Editorial Director: Suzy Gershman
British Correspondent: Ian Cook
Executive Editor: Carol Cohen
Assistant to Executive Editor: Pat Bear
Associate Editor: Erica Spaberg
Manager, Publishing Reference Technology: John Day
Computer Production Editor: Douglas Elam

CONTENTS

2 MONEY MATTERS

3 SHOPPING NEIGHBORHOODS

4 LONDON RESOURCES

5 ENGLISH STYLE

6 HOME FURNISHINGS, DECOR, AND DESIGN

7 ANTIQUES, BOOKS, AND COLLECTIBLES

8 LONDON ON A SCHEDULE

PREFACE

I was sitting in a cafe in Beverly Hills recently and I suddenly realized that Beverly Hills is as foreign a city as Hong Kong to me, but that London is much more like New York, and like me.

Although, at home in the U.S., I do know which way to look first when crossing the street.

London is simply one of those cities where almost all Americans feel at home, even as they look down at the curb and see the words LOOK RIGHT written on the pavement. London is one of those cities that is always fun to come home to.

Indeed, London is not only my home away from home, but it is headquarters to my normal commuting scheme, since I use London as my hub city for travel to the Far East and many other international destinations. The overnight flight from the U.S. to the U.K. is such an easy commute that it's getting to be second nature to me.

The more business I do in London, the more my needs change.

You'll find this new edition reflects a change in those needs—there's more hotel and business resources (hairdressers, florists, etc.) as well as more ways to save money. There are tips for tourists and locals as well. I've used my shopping skills to find the fanciest meals in London at the lowest prices, as well as the best souvenirs and buys on home furnishings and clothes. I've eliminated listings for bespoke suits, handmade shoes, and anything else that averages £1,000 or more per item.

The book you are now holding has been totally rewritten and rechecked. I continue to use the same rules of *Born to Shop* fact-checking and research begun about a decade ago when Judith Thomas and I (and friends) started this series:

- The stores I visit have no idea who I am—all shopping and reporting is done anonymously.
- No store can buy a listing in this book or any other book in this series.
- I have personally checked every listing in this book. If the listing did not originate with me, it is credited to its source.
- All opinions expressed are my own—this is a very opinionated book. When a British point of view is called for, I attribute it to its source.

These books are updated and revised regularly, but if you catch a change before I do, please drop me a card or a note:

> *Born to Shop*
> HarperCollins Publishers Inc.
> 10 East 53rd Street
> New York, NY 10022

ACKNOWLEDGMENTS

London just wouldn't be London to me if it weren't for my local network of friends and colleagues. I offer up love, thanks, bouquets of balloons, and a huge debt for their continued help and support.

Ian Cook remains my best friend in London—he's always good for a pizza or an explanation of some cultural mishap I've just had. Ian has tested many of the stores and listings herein from a British perspective, and some of his tips are also seen in these pages.

Terry Holmes and Radha Arora have been hosts at my old home-away-from-home, The Ritz. I thank Peggy Adams at M. Silver in New York and Wolfgang Nitschke at the Regent in London, who let me try out a new location and write home about it. At the Dorchester, I thank Martine De Geus for tea and tips and Karen Preston in New York for helping to connect the two of us; as well as all my new friends on the Dorchester team. Hugs to Ricci Obertelli, the Dorchester's General Manager, who has spoiled me with his lavish hospitality. Alan Hancock, at Reception at the Dorchester, has won my heart with his help and hints. God bless.

At Bulldog, I've had help from Beverly Boyle, the North American rep, who faxed me pages and pages and found me Shirley Eaton. Thanks, Bev.

John Prothero at Michaeljohn and the adorable Kate Isaacs are my extended London/Beverly Hills family who take good care of me and always answer my London shopping and style questions; Kate also does my hair—just as well as her father does it, I might add.

Special thanks to the home team—John

Lampl and Lilla Santullo at British Airways, Pat Titley at BritRail and, last but not least, Douglas Elam, my computer guru who translates computer files into bookspeak.

Finally, love and thanks to Mike and Aaron Gershman, who either worked on sections of this book (Mike reported most of Chapter Seven) or stayed at home waiting for the phone to ring. Hi guys, I love you and miss you when I'm not there.

Thanks and love to all. Hail Britania.

INTRODUCTIONS

Welcome to London and a new edition of *Born to Shop*. I guess you could say that this introduction comes with a new twist. Both are new takes on an older form.

Since the beginning of the series, my father—the John from Michaeljohn—has been writing the introduction for *Born to Shop London*. Now that I've moved to London and started to work in the salon over here and Suzy has completely revised this edition for HarperCollins, we have teamed up for a fresh approach.

Everything inside this edition—not just my part—has been spruced up. When Suzy's in town, she always comes by for a wash and dry—and sometimes a whiff of aromatherapy. When she's here, I get to add the younger generation's take on shopping in London and put in my two cents (or is that twopence?) worth of shopping tips. Suzy gets to talk about how different I look from when I was six years old.

I have, in fact, known Suzy since I was six years old. We met the first week after my family moved to California. I have grown up with her watching and with the *Born to Shop* series as part of our lives, part of our bicoastal commute between London and L.A.

Now that I'm on my own in London, it's especially fun to hear Suzy talk about what she thinks is a good buy and to relate that to my years of living in America; it's just as much fun to have someone to share my own shopping secrets with. And believe me, if you're trying to make it on your own in London, you need a few shopping secrets.

So I welcome you to London. Stop by, say

hello, maybe even book a haircut, or at least a wash and dry. We like to think that Michaeljohn is Suzy's London office and that we are your *Born to Shop* headquarters. Come say hi, look me up, or ask if Suzy's in town.

There's just one thing: if you want any royal gossip, don't ask me. I'm not allowed to tell.

Kate Isaacs for
Michaeljohn

London certainly deserves the accolade as the 'most exciting city in Europe'. The point of entry into Europe for so many people, London is truly one of the most cosmopolitan cities in the world, with its rich variety of outstanding museums, tourist attractions, sophisticated shopping, historical sites and its famous theatre land.

Suzy Gershman is undoubtedly in an even better position to tell you about the wonders of London than I am. When I met her on her recent visit to London on behalf of *Newsweek*, she impressed me enormously with the breadth of her knowledge and it gave me some satisfaction to be able to point out to her something that she did not know about London. Namely, that a visitor to London can now expect to find true value for money in our top hotels and restaurants.

The Dorchester itself is a case in point. Suzy was certainly amazed to discover our £25 dinner plan in The Terrace restaurant, where our guests can dance to a live band every night after dinner. In addition, we offer exceptionally good value luncheons in The Grill Room (our British restaurant) and The Oriental (our Cantonese restaurant). If that were not enough, Suzy seems to have been seduced by our gorgeous linen sheets and our luxurious marble bathrooms and has now made The Dorchester her London home. A more delightful guest there could not be!

I hope you do not need much persuading to come to London. I am sure that just reading Suzy's book will make you want to jump into a plane. And when you get here, I can promise you a warm Dorchester welcome!

Ricci Obertelli
General Manager
The Dorchester

CHAPTER ONE

LONDON DETAILS

London Bridges

London Bridge is not falling down. In fact, last time I looked, it was closed for six months for repairs. The bridge is sort of a metaphor for all of London. Not that London is closed, but rather, it's just finished licking its wounds from the recession. People are hopeful, but there have been some major changes, just to make ends meet. London has changed forever.

- People are taking in boarders.
- The Queen has opened Buckingham Palace to visitors.
- Elegant, usually expensive restaurants now offer dining at less-expensive, fixed prices.

London has been hurt. A complete recovery is under way, of course; however, in the mean time, anyone with a little extra scratch can make out like a bandit.

There are quite a few special rates and cost-cutting tricks visitors can take advantage of. If ever you've wanted to hop the pond, now is the time to do it. All of London is just about on sale all of the time—not just in winter.

- Airfares (both transatlantic and, in some cases, from London to other European points) are actually lower than they were a few years ago. Even peak summer airfares average $500 per economy seat, round-trip.

- Hotels have rebates, promotional rates, deals in dollars, and all sorts of enticements to get you to come visit and spend a few of your hard-earned dollars.
- Package deals are becoming more flexible, so you can have the benefits of a fixed-price trip without being herded onto a bus and having to suffer through some first timer who wants to know who Big Ben was named after.
- The dollar has been stronger lately; the pound has been weakened by the German mark. At $1.50 to the pound, it barely pays you to stay home.

Between May of 1992 and 1993 alone, prices for Americans visiting Britain *dropped* an average of 21%. Anything can happen to the dollar and the pound at any time, but while the going is good—well, the good should get going.

The New London

The new London is deal city and will be until everyone gets fat and rich again.

Taxis are plentiful because locals are trying to save money. Fixed price menus are available at all the best places in town, including dinner and dancing packages at both the Dorchester and the Ritz.

The new London needs cash; the new London is still rebuilding.

- Sales begin earlier and last longer, although beware: you'll be fighting locals from all over Britain who have come to London to take advantage of these price breaks.
- People are taking in guests to their otherwise very private homes. . . and lives. They need to pay the mortgage; you get an opportunity to save on hotel rates and stay in the real London.
- Shabby chic has never been more stylish.

There is less emphasis than ever before on new clothes; everyone is flocking to the car boot sales and the secondhand dress shops.

- In the new London, when you latch onto a bargain you share it with everyone. Times are still tough. Recycle this book.

The Young Export/Import Scene

There's a whole generation of young English people who are struggling to get their first jobs, trying to make ends meet on very limited salaries, trying to find clothes and fashion statements and homestyles that work for them. They have come of age in a recession and are creative about how they spend their money.

- Vintage chic is an important part of the London fashion scene.
- OXFAM, a chain of charity shops, is considered an "in" resource for both worn threads and cheap imports.
- French and American designers have tried to move in with moderately priced clothing.
- Cheap Far Eastern imports bring ethnic looks into style (again).

Ferry companies advertise how much a young family can save by doing their grocery shopping abroad. In fact, bargain shoppers in London go to France to save money. Kids flock to Europe on the ferry to load up on groceries, wine, beer, and cheap clothes.

Meanwhile, French multiples are moving onto the British high streets in order to offer middle-class fashion at moderate prices. The English fashion industry fights back with its own new definitions aimed at these young people.

If nothing else, London serves as a great place to eyeball the youth market and the coming street trends. London is no longer a place to get dressed up in; it's a place to dress down in while observing street fashion in its move up from the street. And today's London scene is, like in the old days of Carnaby Street, very much on the streets.

Economics in Britain 101

Britain was much harder hit by the recession than the U.S. and is recovering at a slower pace, but is ahead of France and Germany. The turnover of stores in London has been rapid, which means lots of stores going out but very few new ones coming in. There are a number of "For Let" signs all over town, especially in the tony neighborhoods.

Many of the "high-street multiples" are reorganizing themselves to gain financial security. Some of them expanded too quickly in the shop-till-you-drop 1980s and have since closed down various branch stores. Others have had a change in design focus or management and are looking to merely hold on until money eases up.

Service businesses are desperately courting Americans because Americans tip well. If you go around flashing wads of dollars and spending like mad, you'll be looked down upon with great disdain by locals, merely because so many have had so little in London for quite some time now. You'll do better to dress down and book various promotional prices for meals. Shop in the streets for items that are unique to the market at home. Don't wear fur in the winter; don't speak in a loud American accent. Do share your bargain shopping secrets with all you meet, Brit and American alike.

Economics of British Shopping

While prices have gotten better for Americans visiting Britain just because of the fall of the power of the pound, things still aren't very well priced in London. In fact, I'm compelled to blurt this out loud and clear and I hope you're still standing when I finish: London is twice as expensive as any major U.S. city on every level of daily living and visiting.

At best, things in London cost the same as they do in the U.S., only the price is written in pounds sterling. If it costs $35 in the U.S., it costs £35 in Britain.

I say this to impress upon you the need for a bargain and prices guaranteed in dollars before you leave home, so that you will have money for shopping and for simply enjoying the town. I also say it to explain that you're going to have to let go of the notion of translating from pounds to dollars in the search for correlating value.

There isn't any correlating value.

London is more expensive than home.

To have the good time you deserve, you must understand the local prices and look for value only when comparing apples to apples. It won't do you any good to compare London prices to New York or St. Louis prices.

Your luxury hotel room may cost you $400 a night (not a week); a ride in the tube to a nearby sight (not across town) will cost you at least $1.50. The average taxi ride is £5, not $5. (A taxi from Gatwick to the Langham Hilton last year cost me over $100!)

You will find it counterproductive to compare prices and cross-reference what you can get at home compared to what you'll pay in London. It's smarter to select those special places you'd like to visit and the goods you'd like to buy carefully, so you return home with souvenirs and memories of great times. And you can, you just have to plan ahead.

The London Half-Price Rule

If London is twice as expensive as the U.S., then items that go on sale in London that are marked "50% off" are merely equal to the U.S. price. Let the buyer beware. Don't be fooled into a quick purchase because you thought you were getting a deal.

Pounds for Peanuts

It's actually unfair to yourself and your travel experience if you constantly convert British prices into U.S. prices and try to compare value. There is no comparison. You need to judge prices and value according to local standards.

That means that you have to know enough about the price structure to understand that anything that costs £10 or less is considered inexpensive. Ten pounds can be between $15 and $20 and yet in London it means little. To determine value, you've got to think in British terms. This may mean spending a few days on the streets absorbing and researching local prices before you buy anything.

In no time at all, you'll take up the local hue and cry: "And it only cost ten pounds!"

Peanuts for Pounds

Now that I've just about frightened you to death and sent your wallet into convulsions, let me assure you that there are plenty of things to buy in London and that you can still have a good time shopping. And yes, there are gift items to bring home that cost less than ten pounds. Less than ten pounds?

OK, everybody, let me hear that chorus:

"And it only costs ten pounds?"

Yes, and maybe less.

Try some of these sources for gifts in the £5–£10 range:

• THE BODY SHOP: If you're not familiar with

THE BODY SHOP, see page 126 for the run-down. Since there are almost a hundred Body Shop stores in the U.S., I assume you know about their line of environmentally friendly and politically correct cosmetics and health and beauty aids. Prices in London are 40%–50% less than in the U.S.

Therefore, you can find numerous gift items in the £5 range: gifts for men, women, and children. My favorite gift item is a tub of Mango Body Butter, which happens to be the Body Shop's best-selling item in the U.S. It costs $12.95 in the U.S.; £5 in London.

- AROMATHERAPY: Aromatherapy is techni-cally a form of alternative medicine based on the restorative powers of herbs and flow-ers. The concept has taken London by storm (see page 176), or at least by air. There are scads of products to scent up your life and bring you long life, peace, and happiness; most of them cost less than £10. You can buy aromatherapy gifts at HARRODS, THE BODY SHOP, CULPEPER THE HERBALISTS, various department stores (usually on the first floor in the toiletries department), and in many other shops and chemists (Brit-speak for drugstore).

  Here are a couple ideas: A tubular metal ring that sits on top of a light bulb costs less than £2 (it holds the scent and burns off with the heat of the light bulb). I'm enthusi-astic about CULPEPER THE HERBALISTS aromatherapy fan, which comes packaged with lavender oil for £12.50, because such fans are not available in the U.S. Scented candles are £4.

- TEA FOR TWO: For just under £2, you have your choice of various exotic blends of tea from the food halls of London's best depart-ment stores. Yes, you can buy teabags from

MARKS & SPENCER (St. Michael's brand only, my dear) and they do make an imaginative gift for the person with a sense of humor. Personally, I suggest splurging and paying £2 to come away with something like HARRODS' mango tea or HARVEY NICHOLS' black cherry tea. Both come in teabag or loose tea format. I might add that at the local yuppie grocery store where I live, mango teabags cost $9.50 for the same size box of 24. Don't forget FORTNUM & MASON for teas and foodstuffs as gifts and CHARBONNEL ET WALKER, a famous English firm despite the French-sounding name. They make a tin of cocoa that costs approximately $10 and makes a sensational gift. And, oh yes, WEDGWOOD also has tea tins for $10.

- THE JELLY WELLY: This is my all-time favorite inexpensive gift item. It's like a gummy bear, only it's in the shape of a Welly (see page 36 if you don't know what a Welly is). It's olive green just like a Welly and costs only 50p. I buy mine at THORNTON'S in Covent Garden; available only in spring. There are about ten million branches of Thornton's in Britain, so keep searching. You'll be hard-pressed to find another gift as good as this one for 50p.

- HARRODS: HARRODS logo merchandise does make a nice souvenir/gift. It's a tad obvious, but they have tons of choices. A key chain is fun, but to my mind, a little uninspired. For £6, I happen to like the phone message pad with the hole in it (for your Harrods pencil, sold separately, of course) or the potholders, also £6.

- ROYAL KITSCH: Royal memorabilia can be very expensive, especially if it's valuable. Royal kitsch is easy to find and rather inexpensive. You should have plenty to pick from in the under-£5 category. And no, all those wedding commemoratives from Chuck and Di's wedding are not going to be worth a fortune one day—there's simply too many of them on the market. My Charles-and-Diana tea cozy was still a steal at £3.

- BUTTONS: I happen to collect buttons, but I think that British military brass buttons with regimental insignias are a great gift—less than £5 for a full card. I buy mine on Saturdays at the markets on Portobello Road, but other markets sell them too.
- TABLOIDS: Trashy British tabs make great gifts for co-workers or casual acquaintances, especially if there's a royal scandal afoot. I look for *The Sun*, *The Mail*, and *The Express*; (*The Evening Standard* is one of my regular papers, so I just save those). At 50p a toss, I can buy four or five newspapers on a trip and not even gift-wrap them.

The Moscow Rule of Shopping

The Moscow Rule of Shopping is one of my most basic shopping rules and has nothing to do with shopping in Moscow, so please pay attention. Now: The average shopper, in pursuit of the ideal bargain, does not buy an item he wants when he first sees it, because he's not convinced that he won't find it elsewhere for less money. He wants to see everything available, then return for the purchase of choice. This is a rather normal thought process. If you live in an Iron Curtain country, however, you know that you must buy something the minute you see it, because if you hesitate, it will be gone. Hence the title of this international law: The Moscow Rule of Shopping.

When you are on a trip, you probably will not have the time to compare prices and then return to a certain shop; you will never be able to back-track through cities, and even if you could, the item might be gone by the time you got back, anyway. What to do? The same thing they do in Moscow: Buy it when you see it, with the understanding that you may never see it again. But, since you are not shopping in Moscow and you may see it again, weigh these questions carefully before you go ahead:

1) Is this a touristy type of item that I am bound to find all over town?
2) Is this an item I can't live without, even if I am overpaying?
3) Is this a reputable shop, and can I trust what they tell me about the availability of such items?
4) Is the quality of this particular item so spectacular that it's unlikely it could be matched at this price?

If you have good reason to buy it when you see it, do so.

Caveat: The Moscow Rule of Shopping breaks down if you are an antiques or bric-a-brac shopper, since you never know if you can find another of an old or used item, if it will be in the same condition, or if the price will be higher or lower. It's very hard to price collectibles, so consider doing a lot of shopping for an item before you buy anything. This is easy in London, where there are a zillion markets that sell much the same type of merchandise in the collectibles category. At a certain point, you just have to buy what you love and not worry about the price or the Moscow Rule of Shopping.

London's Best Buys

No matter what the dollar does, there will always be certain categories of merchandise that remain smart purchases in London. I'm not saying these things are cheap. I'm saying that merchandise falls into three categories: designer merchandise which is more expensive in the U.K. than the U.S., designer merchandise which is exactly the same price in the U.K. and the U.S., and designer merchandise which is actually less expensive in the U.K. Here's where you'll score:

English Big Names

If you are planning on a big British buy (such as a BURBERRYS raincoat), and you wanted to visit London anyway, do your shopping in January or July at the sale. Otherwise, check out prices at home before you assume a savings in the U.K. English-made ready-to-wear should be less expensive in England, but don't get caught assuming anything. Also remember the duty on ready-to-wear and stay within the $1,400 U.S. Customs limit, on which you will pay only $100 duty. After that, you'll get into higher duties on clothes, and your bargains may be tarnished. Generally speaking, you can save on U.S. prices if you buy British when it's on sale or if you get the VAT refund.

European Designer Fashions

There is a strange rule of retailing that generally only applies to sale times, but you can still score on European designer fashions at the end of the season and at big clearance sales. That's because everybody in Britain is broke. Regularly priced designer merchandise is surely no bargain in London, but even the sale prices on highfalutin' clothes may be too outrageously high for Sloane Rangers; so if other international jet-setters haven't beaten you to the punch, you can get lucky at a sale. Note that there are no bargains on regularly priced designer items, although you need to run the numbers carefully as there may be concessions due to VAT and state sales tax.

China and Crystal

Even with the cost of shipping to the U.S., you will save money on china and crystal if you buy it on sale or in outlet stores. Even plain old retail can offer a savings, if you don't ship.

Home Decor

More specifically on the home decor front: fabrics. If you crave the cabbage roses or the toile, the locally made fabrics cost less in London. Know your yardage and allow for the repeat. Few dealers will ship your order since they don't want to compete with their U.S. showrooms.

If you simply want some quick ideas or a way to spruce up a room, keep your eye on the major multiples (chain stores that seem to pop up everywhere). MARKS & SPENCER has a relatively new design department. Some British (and a few Scottish) cities have a free-standing M&S home furnishings store. BRITISH HOME STORES has some great-looking stuff at everyday low prices. LAURA ASHLEY remains a solid source for Americans who like bargains and the English look. It doesn't have to be John Fowler to be fabulous.

Needlecrafts

If you aren't already a Kaffe Fassett or Elizabeth Bradley nut, you will be when I finish with you. If you knit or do needlepoint, you should seek out Mr. Fassett's work in kit form in any London needlecraft shop, such as LIBERTY, where you'll pay a fraction of the U.S. costs. Other big-name knitting designers offer similar savings. Sweaters that cost $500 when made up cost $75 or less in kit form in London. Bradley Victorian-style needlepoint kits cost £55 in HARRODS and $250 in New York.

Books

Books are very, very expensive in Britain, but British publishing is so extraordinary that you have to consider new and used books as one of the city's best buys. You won't save any money on your favorite novel or paperback, but look at crafts, art, antiques, and travel books for a wider-than-usual selection than you'll find in the U.S. If you're only into fiction, buy used paperbacks. By the way, there's no VAT (see page 60) or U.S. duty on books.

Animals

If you are looking for the chichi gift of all time or a great gift for the person who has everything, London has something unique to offer. Through the London Zoo, you may adopt an animal. Or an animal part. For £20 you get a part of an animal and a certificate to mail out to the lucky recipient. Funds go for the upkeep of the animals. Write or call Animal Adoption Scheme, London Zoo, Regent's Park, London NW1 (71-722-3333).

Filofax

Prices are much lower in England. Even insert pages are half price. The basic leather set starts at $150 at Bloomingdale's. You can buy the whole works, top-of-the-line and complete, for less than $100 in London. Filofax items are sold in their own store, in the stationery departments of major department stores, in office supply stores, and even at the airport.

Doc Martens

Basically, shoes are a bad buy in Britain. That is, regular high-fashion shoes or even moderately priced high-fashion shoes, since the British don't know from moderately priced. In Britain they sell cheap shoes at high prices.

But wait, every rule has an exception. If you are the parent of a child twelve years old on the way to twenty, or are a 'tween-to-twenty yourself and you or your kin wouldn't be caught red or dead (you'll only get that reference if you're young and hip, so don't sweat it) without Doc Martens, here's the deal. These shoes are a good bit cheaper in London. If you get them on sale, you may even snag a pair for $50.

Bad Buys in London

- "Moderately priced" clothes are not moderately priced in England—they are downright expensive. If you expect to find both fashion and quality for less than $50 or so, forget it.

  Also check origin and quality: the £17 adorable handbag I bought on a recent trip in a middle-class department store (made in China) lasted exactly one week before the shoulder strap pulled out and snapped. Before that, I was prepared to tell readers to rush into this department store and snap up all the cheap handbags. Junk wears like junk. Don't waste your money.
- Although sweaters may be pushed at you from every direction, think twice. Unless you buy from a factory outlet, get seconds or discontinued styles, or get a big markdown, you may not find the savings you expected. You can count on finding a two-ply cashmere sweater in any big U.S. department store on sale for $129; maybe even $99. Take my word for it; Brits come to the U.S. to buy cashmere. British sale prices on a cashmere jumper are rarely below £99.
- American brand names. Clothes from THE GAP have their American price code on them and the price in dollars is merely translated into pounds sterling. Honest. I'm not making this up. Something on the sale rack for 19.99 means £19.99, or about $30.

The British Air Dare

I've made it my business to study London's two sale periods (January and July), and have come to the conclusion that the January sales are far, far better. Even though some of the stores are offering their July sales in June these days, January is actually worth flying over for, while summer sales are not that great.

The January sales are an event, especially in recessionary times when locals have held back on their Christmas shopping and have come from far and near to mop up the bargains. The sales are far more theatrical in January; the circus atmosphere is so much fun that it creates energy in the aisles. June/July sales last year merely had an air of desperation to them.

Years ago, British Airways asked me if it was possible to fly to the January sales in London and make back expenses in savings. I dubbed it "The British Air Dare." I've now been repeating the dare on an annual basis. Even when the dollar was at $2.06 per pound sterling, I was able to break even. This past year, with the dollar at $1.50, it was downright easy.

The costs:

Transatlantic Airfare: I bought a British Airways ticket for just $359 round-trip!

Lodging: I booked a room at the RITZ in London at a special promotional refundable rate offered at all Cunard Hotels.

Airport Transfer: I carried just a tote bag and took the tube to the hotel. On the return trip to Heathrow, with more luggage, I took the bus: £5.

Meals: I ate economically. One day I had high tea instead of dinner. Another night I ate a picnic from MARKS & SPENCER in my room. I ate at the Dorchester for my big night on the town for £25.

Entertainment: I went shopping. I watched movies on Sky Television (free). I laid out all my shopping triumphs and gloated. I read British *Vogue*, *Tatler*, and *Harpers & Queen*. I didn't go to the theater (at $50 a seat I'd rather have a new handbag), and I didn't visit Madame Tussaud's.

How much did I save? Beats me. Did I have a ball? You bet. In fact, if I could only go on one trip a year, I think I'd pick London in the first week in January. Why get the blues after Christmas when you can hop a plane? Why shop at the local mall's January sale when you can get a VAT refund? Why miss out on the fact that life is a cabaret and London is forever?

Look right.

The British Air Dare Deux

I wanted to take my son Aaron to London during his summer vacation, something I would normally never consider because of the high cost of peak travel. But travel to Europe, and London especially, is hot and heavy and airlines are offering deals galore these days.

So are hotels. To my utter amazement, I was able to book seats in the summertime for $500 round-trip and a Hilton hotel room with a Mayfair location for $200 a night. I could have gotten a suite for $150 a night at the CONRAD HILTON, but I didn't like the location.

It didn't take British Air to dare me to do this, I just opened my local newspaper one day, took a look at the airfares and said "Holy Cow."

While I am a big believer in out-of-season travel because you not only get better deals but you also have fewer crowds to contend with, please don't give up on in-season travel without making a few toll-free phone calls.

Furthermore, just to make an academic point

here—if my goal was a pleasant English vacation with my son and not specifically a trip to London, we could have flown into any number of other airports in England, bought a train pass, booked farmhouse overnights, and really saved a bundle.

London is a good 25%–30% more expensive than the rest of Britain.

Buying British

Once upon a time, Britain had an empire. I mention this because in those days, Britain manufactured goods and supplies, which were shipped to the colonies. And I'm not going back to the days of throwing tea into Boston Harbor. The reason Britain was rich was because its manufacturing business was first class.

The manufacturing scene has changed dramatically; offshore production has recreated the face of trade and distribution for all countries, not just for Britain. However, those goods still made in Britain continue to be recognized for their quality. While there are a lot of cheap imports on the shelves intended to appeal to a recession-weary local customer, you'll find that if you buy British when in Britain, you can't go wrong.

Value has always been related to quality. You'll do much better to invest in well-made British goods that will last for decades than to throw your money away on cheap or "moderately priced" items that won't cut the English mustard.

Sale Shops, Bargain Shops, and Big Sale Events

The British have perfected a most untraditional retailing method to move out their sale merchandise. It seems that designer shops will hoard their unsold sale merchandise and put it away until once or twice a year, when they will rent space and open up a sale shop. This sale shop will sell only markdowns. The shops are open for a matter of months and then they close. Word-of-mouth spreads among locals and good customers, the clothes are sold, and the shop closes—only to resurface again in another location a year or so later.

For two years, LIBERTY had what they called a "clearance zone" right off Carnaby Street; now it's gone. Recently, I spotted a WHISTLES markdown shop right on King's Road. I know it will be gone by the time you read this.

The number of available storefronts makes it easy for sale shops to come and go, so ask at your favorite multiple—you never know what a helpful salesperson might tell you.

There is no Loehmann's or Loehmann's-type of discount designer clothing store in London. They don't need Kmart because they have MARKS & SPENCER. There are a few "factory outlets" in Britain (with more coming), but they are outside London. There are an increasing number of resale shops, a few "designer" shops that sell bargains from designers you've never heard of, and a growing number of jobbers selling off odd lots. British *Vogue* lists resale shops in their back ad pages.

Special Sales

Imagine my delight when I casually picked up a card that announced a COLEFAX & FOWLER/ JANE CHURCHILL sale at the Royal Horticultural Society's Old Hall, where "slightly imperfect and discontinued chintzes, fabrics, wallpapers, furniture, and accessories" were for sale at "greatly reduced prices."

Very often, designers or shops hold on to their unsold beauties and donate them to a charity organizer who is holding a designer jumble sale. Rather than going the special shop route, they go for a special sale or charity event. You pay admission (which goes to charity) and enter a ballroom laid out like Loehmann's.

Among the most popular regular events of this nature are the Chelsea Designer Sale and the Kensington Cash 'n' Carry Fashion Fair. These events, and others like them, are usually held in January and August and are advertised in fashion magazines such as *Harpers & Queen*. They are most often held in a town hall with easy tube access.

Shopping Services

If you think you might need some help on the ground, if you have some corporate shopping to do, or if you want more specific help than I can offer, you may want to try a shopping service.

I found Shirley Eaton through THE BULLDOG CLUB—she is a hostess member and has a house that is to die for. With taste as fine as hers, you know you're in good hands if you sign up for her service. You can pay £25 for a half day (9:30 A.M.–1 P.M.) or £50 for a full day (9:30 A.M.–5:30 P.M.). She will shop with you and offer her suggestions for solving your immediate needs. As the former manager of one of the Designer Guild shops, Shirley's specialty is antiques and interior design, but she's also keen on fashion.

Contact her directly in London at 71-581-8429 (phone) or 71-584-9874 (fax).

Booking London

The number of guidebooks to London is staggering. I'll point you only to the ones I find essential.

- *London A to Z* (say "A to Zed"): This is a map guide that everyone, absolutely everyone, uses—locals and tourists.

Each page is an in-depth map. Look up the addresses you desire in the index in the back, turn to the map indicated, and find your spot. Tube stations are also indicated. No one can survive a serious stay without this gem, which is available in any bookstore or newsstand in London. There is a tube map on the back cover.

- *Fairs & Market Diary*: This is a little booklet that lists flea markets and jumble sales throughout Britain, divided into regions. Buy the London edition at the Monday flea market at Covent Garden, or write Peter Allbright, P.O. Box 30, Twyford, Reading, England RG10 8DQ. This guidebook now has a competitor, which you may prefer: *The Antique Trade Calendar*. The publisher is GP London, 32 Fredericks Place, North Finchley, London, England N12 8QE. I buy mine in Greenwich over the weekend.

- Filofax page insert of the London Underground. Even if you've got your A *to* Z, this is handy to have in your pocket.

- *Time Out*: This is a weekly magazine with cultural events and listings. Each edition also has a shopping column which is always worth checking out when you visit. I wouldn't suggest you buy the magazine just for the shopping column, but if you need theater listings and a complete run-down of goings-on about town, this is your bible.

Sleeping London

It's not hard to find a fabulous hotel in Mayfair—or anywhere else in London—but you may want to give some serious thought to what combination of location, price, and ease of making reservations suits your budget and sensibilities. I've found that a hotel is the single greatest factor in ensuring whether or not my trip has been a dream or a nightmare. I believe in luxury hotels, but I also believe in getting the most for my money.

- Prices in London for hotel rooms are pretty uniform, based on the rank of the hotel—all five-star hotels cost almost the same amount per night. Therefore one hotel with a fancier reputation is not necessarily more expensive than another.
- Many hotels have special promotions and rates. Almost every hotel discounts rooms in January when business is down, but they'll also discount during other time periods as well. When hotel rooms are empty, management gets creative. Use this fact to your benefit and don't be shy about places with hoity-toity reputations. It behooves you to spring for an international call to the hotel of your choice and to negotiate directly with them; it's unlikely that a computerized reservation service will have as much flexibility as a real live person smelling a deal.
- Look to the chains for promotions you might be able to qualify for. Cunard, Hilton, Meridien, Rank, Sheraton, and Forte all run price specials, even in the summer season. (See page 26 for specifics.) Often you can prepay for a room in U.S. dollars. Luxury hotels often have price breaks—the ranking of a hotel is controlled by official agencies, so there's no such thing as a dumpy luxury hotel. While no one can beat the prices offered in mass tourist hotels by package deals, if you crave the comforts of luxury hotels, you can still find some excellent packages and promotions.
- Weekend package deals are popular. Usually called "weekend breaks" in Britain, they are meant to generate business when business-

people and their expense accounts have not filled the ranks.

- Combination city-country deals are sometimes offered. If you are traveling around Great Britain, consider arranging your schedule so that you spend the first weekend in London at one hotel, travel during the week (rates are lower in the countryside and in Edinburgh), and then return to London for the second weekend—maybe even to a different hotel, depending on the deal. Forte has a good program for combining destinations.

Shoppers' Luxury Hotels

All hotels in London are expensive. Luxury hotels can cost $400 a night for a double. I once asked a London hotelier friend of mine why people would pay $400 a night. He explained that the room you get for $200 is frequently in such a bad hotel that you are delighted to pay twice as much and get what you want.

THE DORCHESTER

The bed. The bath. The spa.

It doesn't matter what they spent on the renovation, the spa alone is worth the price of admission. Actually, the spa is free when you book a room.

I met the Dorchester while writing an article for *Newsweek* on European value! One waltz through the lobby and I was hooked. That stationery with the embossed aubergine motto, "The Dorchester," makes you want to just swipe it. Indeed, even telling your taxi driver "The Dorchester" has a certain ring to it that's worth money. I'm wild about the little shopping neighborhood directly behind the hotel (see page 80) and I don't mean in the Marble Arch direction.

(See my write-up of the cheapest elegant dinner in town, page 42.) They greet you by name when you check in, and you may never check out. If you can't stay here, come for tea or breakfast. Order pancakes and coffee for £6.50 and have the time of your life.

A Leading Hotel of the World. For U.S. reservations, call 800-727-9820. Local telephone: 71-629-8888.

THE DORCHESTER
Park Lane, W1 (Tube: Marble Arch)

THE RITZ

The Ritz is a landmark, a nest of luxury, and a fabulous shopping hotel all wrapped into one. The location is one of its primary strengths—you're right at Piccadilly with a tube stop out the door (Green Park) and another (Piccadilly) down the block.

Part of the charm of the hotel is that it's drop-dead fancy but also intimately sized. With only 130 rooms, the Ritz is considered a small hotel. If you aren't staying here, you owe it to part of your London experience to come for a meal or for tea.

Prices vary tremendously; the Ritz offers a refundable program so that the more money you spend, the more money you get back. If your travel agent thinks you're nuts, spring for a call to London and ask the front desk if there are any special rates.

For reservations in the U.S., call 800-222-0939. Local telephone: 71-493-8181.

THE RITZ
Piccadilly, W1 (Tube: Green Park)

THE REGENT

If you're an old China hand and wouldn't stay anywhere else but the Regent in Hong Kong, you'll find that the Regent in London offers the same service, but no view. In fact, the hotel's location takes a little bit of getting used to. It's not that it's truly inconvenient, it's just that you are going to walk a bit further to get to the main shopping streets in Mayfair.

The best use of this location is to bring your kids here—the hotel is a block from Madame Tussaud's and Sherlock Holmes' house. You've got your pick of every fast-food eatery in town on Baker Street as well. And if your penchant runs to antiques, ALFIE'S ANTIQUES MARKET (see page 226) is just up the road in the other direction.

The rooms are large, the bathrooms incredibly spacious and luxurious, and there's a pool in the basement. Everyone on the staff, right down to the doorman, had learned my name by the second day of my last visit. Talk about impressive!

Because the hotel is new and still trying to woo regulars, there are some promotional rates.

For reservations in the U.S., call 800-545-4000. Local telephone: 71-631-8000.

THE REGENT
222 Marleybone Road, NW1 (Tube: Baker Street)

Hotel Savings Secrets

THE MAYFAIR
This is one of my better secrets, so get out your highlighter. The Mayfair is a luxury hotel, not in the same class as the palace hotels, but a find nonetheless.

This is a hidden hotel on a Mayfair back street, half a block from the RITZ and the Green Park tube station and unknown to most tourists. Furthermore, it is a member of the Intercontinental chain, but it does not use the Intercontinental name in its title. What this means is when you use airline miles or see a specially advertised rate offered by Intercontinental, you can book this hotel and get a charmer.

I've stayed here twice; one room was uninspired but large enough to hold a rollaway bed for my son Aaron. The second room was not only spacious and lavishly decorated in Edwardian style, but it had a full hot tub in the bathroom. You can sometimes book this hotel for $149 a night, guaranteed in U.S. dollars, under a special seasonal offer from Intercontinental. For U.S. reservations, call 800-327-0200.

THE MAYFAIR
  Stratton Street, W1 (Tube: Green Park)

HILTON HOTELS

Believe it or not, there are six Hiltons in London (and many more in the U.K.) and they are worth knowing about if you are on a budget. Granted, a Hilton will never offer you the same elegance the RITZ does, but their price breaks can be meaningful. Besides their big, flagship hotel skyscraper on Park Lane, there are several smaller, more intimate hotels, all in shopping neighborhoods, and many of them better priced than the large, somewhat glitzy Hilton. All are air-conditioned, which is a pleasant luxury in summer. They offer many promotional and week-end deals, making their prices moderate to expensive.

My two secrets are the LANGHAM HILTON, which has a fabulous shopping location one block from the intersection of Regent Street and Oxford Street, and the HILTON MEWS, which has the tiniest rooms you have ever seen but also some of the best rates I've ever found for a luxury hotel. The Mews is right behind the big Hilton, off Park Lane.

If you are with kids and need a suite deal, the CONRAD HILTON in Chelsea Harbour often has promotional deals at £99 for a suite, plus VAT. In the U.S., call (800) HILTONS.

HILTON PARK LANE
  22 Park Lane, W1 (Tube: Hyde Park Corner or Marble Arch)

HILTON MEWS
   2 Stanhope Row, behind Park Lane, W1 (Tube: Hyde Park Corner or Marble Arch)

LANGHAM HILTON
   Langham Place, W1 (Tube: Oxford Circus)

Hotel Chains

Hotel chains in the U.K. not only provide one-stop shopping for a visitor from the U.S. who may be booking rooms in several cities, but also offer the most competitive rates and promotional deals. Besides Hilton and Intercontinental, check out:

Cunard Hotels

Three of London's fanciest hotels are owned by the steamship company Cunard, which offers deals to those who cruise and stay or to those who book through the REFUNDABLE program, a promotion that is held only during certain times of the year. If you book one of the three Cunard Hotels—the RITZ, the STAFFORD, and DUKES—you are given a cash refund for expenses during your stay. You must book through their New York offices and ask specifically for this promotion. In the U.S., call: (800) 222-0939.

Forte Grand

Forte Grand is the new name given to a division of the old Trusthouse Forte. This chain has the group's more exclusive hotels in London as well as throughout the English countryside.

While not every Forte hotel reeks of charm, every member of the Forte Grand group is a winner. Most of them are rehabilitated hotels that have not been ruined or overrun with boring carpet. The WESTBURY, right in the heart of the Bond Street shopping district, is too modern for my taste, but couldn't be better situated for a real shopper or auction hound. I prefer the WALDORF, which is not nearly as convenient for shoppers, but has an old-fashioned feel to it that reminds me I am indeed in London. It's also cheaper. And they have a great tea (with dancing!).

There are also a few more posh addresses in London, such as BROWN'S HOTEL and the HYDE PARK HOTEL, but these are more expensive than the likes of the Waldorf.

For U.S. reservations, call 800-367-8352.

Rank Hotels

Rank has a number of large properties throughout London, ranging from the luxe ATHENAEUM at Green Park to the WHITE HOUSE, a large modern hotel at Regent's Park that has some of the cheapest four-star rooms in the city. Not all of the locations are great for shoppers; not all of the hotels are filled with Dickensian charm—but they are all clean. Rank is very promotion-minded and continually comes out with deals; they are the ones who often freeze the dollar and the pound at parity. In the U.S., call (800) 223-5560.

Edwardian Hotels

Most Edwardian hotels are four-star properties, but they do have one five-star in town, HAMPSHIRE HOUSE, right in the heart of the theater district. What Edwardian does offer is a whole lot of deal for your money. In most cases, not only do they freeze the dollar/pound ratio in your favor, but they throw in breakfast and—if you take the week-long package—sometimes a tube pass or a pair of theater tickets.

Their rates are better from January to April 15, but they have summer promotions as well.

Two of their smaller hotels, the MOUNTBATTEN and the MARLBOROUGH, are around the corner from Covent Garden, an excellent location for theater and shopping.

Please note that several airlines and package tour travel companies use Edwardian hotels as part of their package. Be sure to run the numbers and comparison shop to see which package offers you the best hotel at the best price. In the U.S., call (800) 447-7011.

B & B Breakthroughs

Things are so bad in London that many people are taking in boarders. Don't be shocked; be thrilled. While you may have your own personal connections (or follow up on ads in the back of *The New Yorker*), there is a service that links together private homes of elegance and taste and puts you right into a fantasy B & B with a London address that is guaranteed to be within a five-minute walk of a tube or bus stop. It's called THE BULLDOG CLUB, named after the British bulldog, and it has nothing whatsoever to do with Eli Yale.

Bulldog was the brainchild of a London woman with a gorgeous house and a need to keep it gorgeous. Taking in boarders has never been so glamorous.

I haven't tried this yet, but when you hear the details you'll be as intrigued as I am. There are some twenty houses in the group, all of which would be categorized as four- or five-star properties if they were hotels. Each private home is owned by a professional who is accustomed to entertaining (one of the hostesses even has a corporate shopping business; see page 19).

You receive your own key to the house and your room will be either on a separate floor from the family's bedrooms or in a separate part of the house, such as over the garage or in the coach house. There are tea and coffee-making facilities in the rooms, robes, toiletries, and amenities galore. The real charm of this find is that you will feel as though you are staying with a friend, yet you will still have privacy.

Full British breakfast is served in the private dining room, not with the family. Perhaps the best description of this unique service is the analogy Bev Boyle, Bulldog's North American representative, offered me: "It's the reverse of 'Upstairs, Downstairs.' "

To get acquainted with Bulldog, call Bev and chat with her yourself. Tell her what you're looking for and what your needs are. (You can even specify what kind of chintz you like best.) Within 24 hours she'll make your booking and fax the details to you. You have 48 hours to decide if it suits you. Provided it does, you'll need to join Bulldog, which costs £25 annually. They accept all major credit cards. After you're signed up, you receive a package from their London offices with information on your hosts, their home and its location, as well as bus and tube information and other London basics.

All rooms cost £73 a night (for two people!), including breakfast. Expect your hostess to have a name like Lavinia. In the U.S. or Canada, call 905-737-2798 or fax 905-737-3179. In the U.K., call 71-622-6935 or fax 71-720-2748.

Flat News

If you don't want to be anyone's guest at all, you may want to consider renting a flat, which not only works out cheaper on a nightly basis, but also gives you the option of cooking some of your meals. While prices vary tremendously, you can get a nice flat with two bedrooms and two baths in a slightly suburban London neighborhood in the £300-per-week range. Expect to pay £500 minimum for a small luxe flat with a fine location.

THE BARCLAY INTERNATIONAL GROUP is a U.S. firm that will book you into any of their apartments in London. A two-person studio starts at £220 for an entire week (including VAT). There are properties in Kensington and Mayfair; you can even arrange for their limo to pick you up at the airport. Their Grosvenor House apartments come with use of health club facilities. In the U.S., call (800) 845-6636.

THE APARTMENT COMPANY is a British firm that seems to work much like Barclay with similar properties. Their hottest locale is Dolphin Square because the Princess Royal (Anne) is a tenant. Draycott House is a prestigious address where flats are frequently rented by celebrities; you're looking at £700–£2000 a week (depending on size), plus VAT. In London, call 71-835-1144.

Home Sweet Home

While the real estate market is depressed, it's a good time to buy an apartment or a house in London. Just leaf through the opening ad pages of *Harpers & Queen* and *Tatler* for the drool of the week.

Getting There

There are a number of ways to get to England from the U.S., but since there isn't yet a tunnel which connects Boston with Britain, you'll probably be best off in an airplane. There are cruise ships that still make crossings, but the price wars are being fought in the air rather than the sea these days as both British and American carriers offer deal after deal. You'll find that prices from New York to London are particularly competitive because so many carriers want a piece of the action. If everyone has the same price, what do you base your choice on?

I say it's really simple: BRITISH AIRWAYS owns Heathrow. They've got their own terminal (Terminal 4) and a million amenities geared to their passengers in their private terminal. BA claims to be the world's favorite airline—they're certainly mine. Every trip finds new improvements; recently I discovered they now have express passport service, so you don't even have to stand in line at immigration in Heathrow.

In-flight amenities are extended to economy, which is not true on every other airline. They give you a free toothbrush and overnight kit, even in the "back" of the plane in the World Traveller section.

Prices vary with the seasons and the competition; it's frequently less expensive to fly from New York to London than from New York to Los Angeles. Winter prices are always the best deal. They also have complete package tours with hotel rooms—in and out of London—and many specials. My best secret: BA doesn't always advertise their rates. Watch for an American Airlines airfare war, then call BA. They will match the current lowest fares.

BA has almost a dozen U.S. gateway cities as well as the entire USAir fleet to help you make domestic connections. In the U.S., call (800) 272-6433.

Airport Value

When booking your tickets, pay attention to what airport you fly into and compare flights that go into different airports. Gatwick Airport is four times farther from London than Heathrow, and while there is direct train service from Gatwick, it is very difficult to get to if you are toting more than one suitcase and/or more than one child. A taxi from Gatwick to a West End London hotel will cost you at least $100.

If you have the free limo, you won't care. If you are a backpacker, you won't care. If you are a shopper and have three giant bags, you are going to care. Gatwick is a breeze for people who can manage their own luggage handily. All others should make certain they fly into Heathrow or have an unlimited budget for a car and driver.

Stansted Airport did not catch on the way it was hoped; few carriers use it for U.K.–U.S. traffic. Again, a taxi will be prohibitively expensive, but there is train service.

Heathrow offers many means of transportation to London: if you are footloose and fancy free, you can hop the tube. There's a station right there in Terminal 4, which is another of the many reasons to fly with British Air. My latest trick has been to take the bus. You can pay £5 as you get on the bus, or order a travelcard ticket package in the U.S. from BritRail before you leave: this provides you with a voucher for the bus.

There are two bus routes marked on the back of your voucher. The bus makes a good many stops before it gets to its final destination (always a major train station), so if your schedule is tight, you can always hop off at any point and hail a taxi, if necessary. When I stay at the LANGHAM HILTON, I get off at Marble Arch. The A1 goes to Victoria Station; the A2 goes to Euston Station.

Taxi fare from Mayfair to Heathrow with a tip (and no traffic) is about £35.

Getting Around

Thankfully, London is a great city for walking, so you can see a lot and be entertained every step of the way.

The tube does get you just about everywhere you need to go; some type of travel pass will be your best buy if you plan an active visit.

There are various tour cards and discount deals available in the U.S. that are not available in the U.K., so you must buy before you leave home. BritRail has recently been privatized, so there are deals offered to Americans that are not even known about in the U.K.

This is my rule of thumb:

- If you will ride the tube only once or twice a day and possibly not every day, pay for individual tickets as needed in London.
- If you are on and off the tube three or more times in a day, or going to Greenwich, buy a one-day travelcard for approximately £2.50.
- If you are spending a week in London and plan to explore it from dawn till dusk and don't really know what you're doing except that you want to do it all, purchase the London Visitor Travelcard. It costs approximately $50 (you can obtain it ahead of time in the U.S.) and gives you seven days of unlimited travel on tube and bus.

For more details on what's happened to good old BritRail, contact BritRail USA directly at 1500 Broadway, New York, New York 10036. Call 212-575-2667.

Taxis are plentiful in recession, even in the rain! If you ask the doorman of a hotel—not the hotel you are staying in—to get you a taxi, please tip him 50p. If you frequently get taxis from your own hotel, tip the doorman when you leave. (See page 58 for tipping guidelines.) The flag drops at £1 and escalates quickly; taxis are not cheap in London.

You do not want to rent a car in London.

Getting in Touch

I call home frequently and find that AT&T USA Direct service is great, but not necessarily the bargain I want. Please be aware of the actual charges incurred each time you use one of these newfangled access codes that have been marketed as bargain phone fares. Yes, you get U.S. phone rates which may be less expensive than British Telecom (BT), but you pay a per-call surcharge so that if you talk for only a minute, or get the answering machine of the party you are calling, you're paying a very hefty price for those airwaves. (AT&T surcharge is $2.50 per call; MCI surcharge is $2.00 per call.)

I now buy a £4 phonecard upon arrival in London (any news agent will sell you one). This card is good for calls placed anywhere in the world. To call a telephone number in the U.S., slide the card into the proper slot in any booth marked Phonecard and dial 010 plus the area code and the number. You pay 10p per unit for the card; the card sounds an electronic beep when you have used up most of your units. I spoke to my husband back home for several minutes for only 20 units and was quite pleased with myself and my savings.

To avoid hotel surcharges and the trek to a phonecard phone from your hotel room, do use the access lines. To call the U.S. from anywhere in the U.K., dial 0800-89-0011 to get USA Direct service. To use a similar service via MCI, call 0800-89-0222.

Translation, Please

There are a lot of British slang expressions that you can usually figure out from their context, but that's not always the case. When a friend's daughter once told me a store was "naf," I thought that meant "cool." It's the opposite. "Naf" can also be used as a verb, as in "naf off," a phrase Princess Anne was once quoted as saying to the English press corps. It's not an expression commonly heard from a princess.

Please note that there is a mine field waiting for you in the area of sexual slang expressions.

I'll leave you to chart this territory yourself, but here's a quick tip to give you an idea of what awaits you: a woman should never stop a male hitchhiker in Britain and ask him if he wants "a ride," as this is an offer of sexual favors.

Other Definitions

- *Access*: European firm which issues the equivalent of MasterCard
- *body*: bodysuit
- *boot*: the trunk of a car
- *braces*: suspenders
- *brolly*: umbrella
- *car boot sale*: a tag sale held in a field or parking lot where locals sell their precious valuables right from their cars
- *chemist*: a drugstore
- *chips*: French fries
- *crisps*: potato chips
- *deli*: gourmet food market
- *fringe*: bangs (hair)
- *jumble*: used clothing
- *jumble sale*: a tag sale
- *jumper*: a sweater
- *knickers*: underpants
- *loo* or W.C.: the bathroom
- *mall* (pronounced "mell"): shopping mall
- *nobs*: nobilities (experts)
- *pants*: underpants
- *pram*: baby carriage; stroller
- *spend a penny*: to go to the bathroom. As in "I have to spend a penny, excuse me."
- *suspenders*: garter belt
- *Switch*: British firm which issues the equivalent of a Visa card
- *tat*: used bric-a-brac; cheap goods
- *trousers*: pants
- *torch*: a flashlight

- *vest*: an undershirt
- *waistcoat*: a vest
- *Wellies*: waterproof boots or shoes

Shopping Hours

Shopping hours are downright unorganized in London, so try to pay attention to what day of the week it is when you are shopping. Tuesdays seem to have later openings in the morning while Wednesday, Thursday, or Friday have slightly later closings in the evening. Note that it can be all three of these days at some stores or only one or two of them.

If the store normally opens at 10 A.M., then on Tuesdays it probably opens at 10:30 A.M.

Very few stores in London open at 9 A.M. Those that once opened at 9 A.M. may have gone to 10 A.M., as did HARRODS. Almost all of the big department stores and multiples open at 10 A.M. now.

Note: If you have a beauty parlor appointment at a department store salon, do not panic. One of the store doors is open at 9 A.M. with direct access to the hair salon. Ask at the time you book your appointment.

Covent Garden stores may not open until 11 A.M. Very few stores close for lunch.

All stores close early in London. They do not know the meaning of late. To a British store, a late night means they are open until 7 P.M. or possibly 8 P.M.

Also, note:

London is filled with tourists during Christmastime. Many an unhappy shopper has written to ask me to warn you: Stores are closed for as many as three days in a row right at the Christmas season—they celebrate Christmas Eve, Christmas Day, and Boxing Day (the day after Christmas). Stores also close again for New Year's Day.

Bank holidays are celebrated at regular intervals in the British calendar; they seem to fall around the same time as the feasts of the Virgin, but ever since Henry VIII split from Rome, no one in England is big on feasts of the Assumption. Bank holidays will affect retail but in an odd way: banks and smaller stores will close; big stores and multiples are usually open.

Chemists' Hours

If you need an emergency prescription filled, or just have a late-night personal need, there is always a chemist or drugstore open somewhere in London on a later-than-usual basis. The BOOTS at Piccadilly Circus stays open until 10 P.M. and is also open on Sundays.

If your accommodations aren't anywhere near Piccadilly Circus, don't despair: there are a handful of all-night or late-night chemists dotted around town—just ask your concierge for the one closest to your hotel.

Condoms are sold in vending machines in most restaurants and in hotel gift shops.

Saturday Shopping

Stores and malls are jammed. Unless you like being surrounded by a sea of humanity and pushed into prams or hordes of desperate teens, you may want to avoid shopping on Saturdays entirely or choose your neighborhoods with care. Oxford Street on a Saturday is only for masochists.

Sunday Shopping

Flash: Stores may now open for six hours on Sundays!

Before, the only stores allowed to be open for business on Sundays are in designated "tourist areas," such as Covent Garden. There was much pressure from various retail organizations in specific neighborhoods of London to get themselves classified as "tourist areas"; finally, they changed the laws outright, so that anyone who wants to be open on Sunday can do so.

If you're looking for a Sunday destination that involves shopping, your best choices are Covent Garden (after 1 P.M.) and Greenwich (see page 92), where there are three flea markets and a crafts market. Petticoat Lane does have a market on Sunday, but it is really naf. Museum gift shops are open on Sundays. Hampstead (see page 92) is hot on Sunday afternoons; Windsor is also hopping on a Sunday, although Eton is not.

Royal Warrants

You may wonder where the Queen shops. She doesn't. Things are "sent round" to Buckingham Palace for her to consider. Money and price tags never touch her hands. However, she asks only certain stores and factories to send round goods—these stores have the royal seal of approval, which is called a royal warrant.

Holding a royal warrant demands total discretion. The warrant holder may not talk about the royals in any way—especially to the press or public—or he will lose his warrant. So if you walk into TURNBULL & ASSER and ask them what size pj's Prince Charles wears, you will be met by an icy stare and stony silence. Royal warrants are allowed to display the royal coat of arms and to use the words "by appointment." Since there is more than one royal family in Europe, and there are several members of the Windsor family, you may also see several coats of arms on the window of any given store—appointments from various royals.

A warrant is good for ten years and then must be renewed. If a merchant is dropped, he gets a sort of royal pink slip and has no means of redress. Every year about twenty to thirty new warrants are issued and the same number of pink slips are passed out. To qualify for a warrant, you must provide a minimum of three years' service to the crown.

There are warrants on everything from royal laundry detergent (Procter & Gamble) to royal china, and there can be several warrants in the same category. For china, HRH has as much trouble getting it down to one pattern as I do—she's got warrants at ROYAL WORCESTER, SPODE, and ROYAL DOULTON; the Queen Mother gets her bone china from ROYAL CROWN DERBY. (Say "darby," please.)

And yes, the royals are also in retail. Prince Charles has been trying to get a royal warrant for his Duchy of Cornwall products and Buckingham Palace has a small gift shop selling coffee mugs to tourists for $15 a pop. There goes the neighborhood.

Royal Hairdressers

Since it's unlikely that you're going to bump into the Queen while you are out shopping or touring the palace, I think it's time to tell you about my hairdresser. There's more on page 144, but if you feel that your trip to London will not be complete without a royal sighting, then you need to book a beauty appointment at MICHAELJOHN, a salon in Mayfair.

Talent aside, this happens to be the single best place in town for a bird's eye-view of the London social scene. You may even pass a princess or two in the bargain. Talk about tracing your roots.

Royal Mail—Shopping and Sending

News agents sell books of royal stamps in cute little red packages. When you purchase a book, you must specify if you want international stamps or not. There is a flat rate for all international postcards (33p), no matter where they are going. Stamps do not have denominations printed on them.

If you do decide to mail items home, you can buy jiffy bags in the stationery department of any department store or at an office supply store. Then head for any post office, or ask your concierge to do the deed. Mark your package "unsolicited gift" and place its value at $25. (Unless it's less, of course.) You may legally send one package per day home if its value is less than $50.

The Americanization of London

From a cultural standpoint, London hasn't been the city many Americans envision it being since the Yanks came over during World War II. After the war came American movies and television; now there are American-style shopping malls and multiples. Most aren't worth your time, so I only mention the few that are.

Brent Cross, NW3

Brent Cross is not a new mall, it's out in the suburbs a bit north of London and serves the local population quite well. Tourists can take a pass. The stores are open until 8 P.M. every weeknight; there's a ton of British multiples, and everything you could need is right here. Easily reached by car or public transportation. (Tube: Brent Cross)

Whiteleys of Bayswater, W2

Yes, yes, yes! Finally they got one right! Whiteleys was a huge department store built during Victorian times, complete with appropriate architecture. It's located in Queensway, a sort of ethnic neighborhood not far from everywhere. The mall is a rehab of the old department store (with additions), which takes up a city block. For retailing and architectural academics, not tourists. (Tube: Bayswater or Queensway)

Thomas Neals, WC2

London's newest mall is small and intimate, not overwhelming like most, and it's even open on Sunday afternoons. Located in a rehabbed warehouse one block from Covent Garden, this mall has a number of restaurants and several boutiques. You're gonna love it. Be sure to check out HK SPACE, a makeup store, and ARMAGANSETT, where the British buy the Southampton (Long Island) look. A nice addition to the scene. (Tube: Covent Garden or Leicester Square)

King's Walk Mall, SW3

Small, American-style, glitzy, modern mall, right there in the heart of King's Road. Mostly multiples inside with a good costume jewelry shop. (Tube: Sloane Square)

Lancer's Square, W8

I wouldn't even write up this American-style shopping square except that it houses EHRMAN'S, the knitting and needleworks supply store for the best British yarns and kits. It has a few other shops besides Ehrman's, including a TONI & GUY hair salon and OASIS, a hip version of Ann Taylor. (Tube: High Street Kensington)

Affordable, Elegant Meals

THE GAVROCHE

Le Gavroche is the single fanciest, best known and most written about French restaurant in

London; it's the kind of place I never thought I could afford to visit. Then I discovered their fixed-price meal. Le Gavroche has a fixed-price meal that includes tax and service. At £45 per person, it may be the single best deal in London.

Get dressed up, savor the stars (Michelin and otherwise), indulge in perfection but watch the cost of the wine...unless price is not a factor for you. Fax ahead your reservation; give Silvano as much notice as possible. Lunch is also served. If you splurge for one meal in London, this should be it.

LE GAVROCHE
43 Upper Brook Street, W1 (Tube: Green Park)

THE DORCHESTER

Don't think I've gone dotty for hotels; many of them happen to be offering fabulous deals. At the Terrace, one of several restaurants in the Dorchester, a fixed-price dinner is offered for £25 per person. I haven't stopped talking about since I tried it.

If you come on a weekend, cheek-to-cheek dancing is thrown in. Frankly, I think they should can the combo and concentrate on the food which was sensational when I was there.

You won't spend a better £25 in London; please note, however, that the crowd is mixed and can be touristy.

THE DORCHESTER
Park Lane, W1 (Tube: Green Park)

Tube and Train Shopping

Despite the recession and bust in building, London is still building train stations and renovating the existing ones. The latest is Waterloo Station, which was going to host the Chunnel traffic, but now isn't going to be on the Chunnel connection (leaving some architect with a Waterloo of his own); other restorations continue to search for tenants and a reason for being.

Since the privatization of BritRail, there are numerous changes being considered; watch this space. Of course, retail in train stations is already pretty sophisticated. People like to be able to grab what they need as they dash to and from the train, hence there are always florists, candy stores, bookstores, and even shoe repair or coffee bean stores. I've even seen branches of KNICKER-BOX, the lingerie chain, in several train stations. Duty-free stores are in stations that service the Chunnel; these are for non-EEC residents.

Museum Shopping

The Victoria and Albert Museum Shop

One of the very best museum retail outlets in the world, this shop is pretty big and has a gigantic selection of goods (and goodies). The Crafts Council shop is in the right rear; postcards are in the center, and gobs of gifts and publications are all around. A donation is suggested for admission; however, you can get into the gift shop without entering the museum. (Tube: South Kensington)

British Museum Shop

Don't miss the reproduction gifts and the gorgeous books. This is a huge museum, it's free, it's across the street from a great sweater store (WESTAWAY & WESTAWAY), and you can walk to Covent Garden from here if you're strong enough. This store is the perfect place for unique gifts and souvenirs if you aren't into kitsch and royal souvenirs. (Tube: Tottenham Court Road or Holborn)

The National Gallery Shop

Cards and calendars are the real finds, but the posters aren't shabby. The shop has been moved into the Sainsbury wing. Admission is free to this museum as well, and it's part of a perfect Sunday outing when teamed with a stroll around Covent Garden. (Tube: Charing Cross)

London Transport Museum

While Covent Garden is great on Sunday, this small museum is a treasure any day. Children will love shopping the gift area, which is also great for adults. There's a lot more here than you would expect; don't miss the thousands of postcards and posters of Transport Art (drawings which have decorated tube and train stations since the early part of the century). Actually, the museum happens to be fun too, but the gift shop is sensational. (Tube: Covent Garden)

Museum of the Moving Image

Part of the South Bank Arts Center at Waterloo, this is one of London's best. It's also great for kids weaned on TV and movies. Exhibits transport visitors from the earliest shadow plays to a 24-minute film that covers all of Hollywood's famous faces from Mickey Mouse to Mickey Rourke. The gift shop has a huge selection of books on movies, posters, videocassettes, notepads, postcards, Chaplin masks, movie-theme glassware, coasters, jigsaw puzzles, lamps, aprons, and other cinema tchotchkes. (Tube: Waterloo)

Design Museum

Sure the museum is neat, and the part of town where it's located (Butler's Wharf) is worth taking a look at to get a view of Thames redevelopment, but don't forget the gift shop or the restaurant. Products are featured heavily in the collections and are sold, along with the postcards and visual arts, in the shop. This entire complex, including the restaurant, is an example of Sir Terence Conran's genius; this is part of the New London. (Tube: Tower Hill)

Bramah Tea and Coffee Museum

You know I could never resist a teapot; this museum traces the history of both tea and coffee and features many novelty teapots, as does the small gift shop. Very close to the Design Museum. (Tube: Tower Hill)

Imperial War Museum

If you've got kids—especially boys—they will love this museum and the shop, which sells model airplanes, among other things. Don't knock the name of the museum or the concept: according to Aaron Gershman, it's a great place. Also note that you must pay an admission fee if you arrive in the morning, but the museum is free between 4:30 and 6 P.M. (Tube: Elephant & Castle or Lambeth North)

Attraction Shopping

Madame Tussaud's

Madame Tussaud's is outrageously expensive to visit and the lines out front can be thick. You can quit the scene and walk around to the side of the building, past the Planetarium, and gain access to the shop, but you'll have to knock on the door to be let in. The tour ends in the gift shop; they just aren't prepared for people who only want to shop.

The shop itself is rather large with several rooms. Much of the merchandise for sale is standard London destination souvenir stuff; however, there are some items which are unique to Madame Tussaud's. My favorite line is the group of items with the slogan "some of the people I met in London" with pictures, shirts and coffee cups of the famous, and infamous, as created in wax. (Tube: Baker Street)

Tower of London

Get there early because the lines are fierce. And you bet there are gift shops—we counted three on our last family visit; many of the gifts were historical or educationally oriented, such as color-your-self stained glass windows, etc. Don't ask me why they don't sell paste copies of the crown jewels—makes sense to me. (Tube: Tower Hill)

Souvenir Shopping

The best place to buy London, destination-specific souvenirs is from the street vendors who stretch across the "downtown" area—there are quite a few of them on Oxford Street from Marble Arch to Oxford Circle. There's another gaggle at Piccadilly Circus. The street vendors do seem to have the best prices in town. I priced those plastic bobby helmets at £1.50 in street stands and £1.99 in official souvenir shops. Just to hit the point home, the same hats were £3 at the news agent in Heathrow's Terminal 4!

Please note that if you are traveling out-of-season, you can bargain a little bit with the street vendors, except at Buckingham Palace, where souvenirs are about the most expensive in town.

Royal commemoratives also make good souvenirs, but be warned that some of these things become collectors' items and are frequently very, very expensive. At the time of a royal event (such as a wedding or a coronation), the commemoratives seem to be a dime-a-dozen, but once they dry up, they are gone forever and become collectors' items.

If you are buying for an investment, buy the best quality you can afford (branded ceramic versus cheap) and try to get something that was created in a limited edition.

On Saturdays, Portobello Road has several vendors selling souvenirs. Although some of the antiques vendors may have royal souvenirs, beware: most of what they're selling is the cheap and tacky kind that is not valuable.

Teatime

I am a longtime believer in the English custom of taking tea for two very simple reasons:

- After you've been shopping all day, you need to plop down, drop the packages and get off those feet.
- If you want to save money, you can eat a big tea and go light (or skip) dinner. Conversely, if dinner isn't until 8 P.M. or later, you'll never last without a sufficient tea break.

All the big fancy hotels have tea service; you can make it your job to try a different one every day. I have discovered, however, that there are several in's and out's to getting full value from teatime, so get out your highlight pen. If you're British, don't blush, but I'm going to talk about money.

Generally speaking, tea comes at a set price, per person, and includes the tea (or coffee) of your choice and a three-round selection of sandwiches, scones, and sweets. Sweets in British English means "a pudding;" in American English it means "pastry." Americans please note that British English calls for the word sweets to mean a candy; a pudding is any dessert, not just a gooey one.

Tea is usually served from 3–5:30 or 6 P.M. If sherry is served, it is called high tea. "Teatime," as a time of meeting someone or fixing your schedule, is usually meant to be 4 P.M.; by 5 P.M. it is socially acceptable to start drinking. I've never heard of anyone going to tea at 6 P.M.

Now for the tricky part: the finances of taking

tea. At grand hotels you pay a flat fee for the total tea service, and that price is not cheap. Expect to pay an average of £12 per person, although some are £10 and prices do go higher than £12.

It is very unusual, especially at a fancy hotel, for tea to be served a la carte. However, at a few addresses, you may buy the full tea service for one and a second (or even third) pot of tea a la carte, thus saving about $20. Furthermore, one or two hotels allow for total a la carte tea service. Since very few people can eat all of what is provided at teatime, this is a money-saving device. At the Dorchester, there is a fixed price for simple tea and scones.

THE RITZ

Tea at the Ritz is a Ritzual that few people want to pass up. While I recommend it as a once-in-a-lifetime thing to do, I have several Ritz secrets for you. Tea at the Ritz is so popular that management doesn't even like to publicize it— the place is packed. You may not even get to sit in the main court, but in one of the fancy halls, and you *must* have a reservation.

Tea is a lavish affair; if gentlemen do not have their ties on hand, they may borrow one from the cloakroom.

The trick at the Ritz is to come for either lunch in the Palm Court or breakfast. Breakfast is served in the most beautiful dining room in London (this is general knowledge, not just my opinion) and is not as crowded as tea, so you can really relish your surroundings.

THE RITZ
Piccadilly, W1 (Tube: Green Park)

THE STAFFORD

Guests may sit in the parlor, in front of the fire if so desired, and take formal tea (£10), or have one large scone, without ordering the entire tea service. This Georgian house is exactly my cup of tea.

THE STAFFORD
St. James's Place, SW1 (Tube: Green Park)

BROWN'S HOTEL

For years I've have been sending people to Brown's Hotel for tea: There's no question that it's one of the best teas in London and that their scones are among the best. You may request one setup (tea for one) and additional cups of tea, or you may request a platter of scones to replace the tea setup (but at the same cost) and individual pots of tea. Jackets and ties for the gentlemen; be prepared for a long wait if you aren't early. Next door to MICHAELJOHN.

BROWN'S HOTEL
Albemarle Street, W1 (Tube: Green Park)

Last Call for London

If you're leaving Britain via the fast train from one of the new train stations, the duty-free stores will be in place by 1994. If you're leaving via Heathrow, you're in for a shopping treat.

All terminals are cheek-and-jowl with stores; the prices are minus the 17.5% VAT, which saves you from doing the paperwork.

Terminal 1 has smaller boutiques and kiosks, including an area selling BUTLER & WILSON jewelry (bad selection) and a desk for THOMAS PINK, the shirtmaker.

Terminal 3 has its own mini-HARRODS department store.

Terminal 4 has a £4 million shopping mall that includes FERRAGAMO, HAMLEYS, SWATCH, and about a dozen others, as well as the usual duty-free for liquor and perfume. They do not carry size 10-1/2 shoes at the Ferragamo at Heathrow.

Parting may be sweet sorrow, but leaving London has never been so much fun for a shopper.

CHAPTER TWO

MONEY MATTERS

Paying Up

Whether you use cash, traveler's check, or credit card, you are probably paying for your purchase in a different currency than American dollars.

For the most part, I recommend using a credit card. Plastic is the safest to use and it provides you with a record of your purchases (for Customs as well as for your books). It also makes returns much easier. Credit-card companies, because they are often associated with banks, also give the best exchange rates.

It's even possible to "make money" by charging on a credit card. That's because the price you pay as posted in dollars is translated on the day your credit slip clears the credit-card company (or bank) office, not on the day of your purchase. Of course, you can conversely lose money.

If you're getting $1.50 for your pound in cash at the hotel desk, you may get $1.46 through your credit card. Or the pound can fluctuate in the two- to three-day period that it takes for your purchase to be officially posted to your account.

I don't like to remember this incident, but since it happened to me it could well happen to you—I did business on a specific day in Britain when the pound was trading at around $2. I went to bed. The next morning, the pound was at $1.70. Now then, this was a once-in-a-lifetime monetary accident (I hope) and I liken it to World War III—the Bundesbank forced the pound out of the EMU and England basically had to devalue. In this case, I lost hundreds of dollars.

However, if I'd bought something on a credit card on day one and they devalued on day two, I would have made thirty cents on the pound by the time the purchase was posted to my credit card.

Easy come, easy go.

Urrrrrrrrrgh.

The bad news about credit cards is that you can overspend easily, and you may come home to a stack of bills. The one extra benefit a credit card offers is the potential for delayed billing, since it may take a month or two for the London charges to appear on your bill.

Traveler's checks are a must, however, for safety's sake. Shop around a bit and compare the various companies that issue checks. I happen to use American Express traveler's checks, but they are not the only safe game in town. Just make sure the checks you use are issued by a firm that has many outlets for cashing them, so you do not have to pay an additional fee.

I like to buy American Express traveler's checks in the U.S. at the AAA Motor Club near my home. Membership has its benefits alright: there's no additional fee for buying in pounds sterling. Again, whenever you deal in two currencies, there are chances to win and to lose. I began buying pounds at $1.70; I put every extra bit of spare cash I had into traveler's checks in sterling at $1.70. Needless to say, I'll have to sit on those traveler's checks for a long time to even break even.

You can make yourself nuts over the pros and cons of the foreign money market, and I'm an expert at making myself crazy. But if you travel to England a lot, you may want to follow the rates and buy low.

Certainly, these days, with the dollar rather stable against the pound at $1.50, you can use a combination of credit cards, traveler's checks in pounds sterling, and common sense and come out a winner. As the dollar gets closer to $2 to the pound, you might want to rethink your spending patterns.

In my travels, I've found that $1.70 is fair, $1.50 is a bargain, and $2 is disgusting. Hoard accordingly.

Currency Exchange

As already mentioned, currency exchange rates vary tremendously. The rate announced in the paper (it's in the *Herald Tribune* every day) is the official bank exchange rate and does not particularly apply to tourists. Even by trading your money at a bank you will not necessarily get the same rate of exchange that's announced in the papers.

- You will get a better rate of exchange for a traveler's check than for cash, because there is less paperwork involved for banks, hotels, etc.
- The rate of exchange can be fixed if you buy traveler's checks in the U.S. in sterling. There will be no fee for cashing them anywhere in Britain and shopkeepers are happy to take checks in sterling, whereas they rarely know what to do with checks in U.S. dollars—or simply won't touch them.
- Expect a bank to give you a better rate than your hotel, although it may not. I've found the best rate of exchange at the American Express office. Usually they give as close to the bank rate as is humanly possible, and they do not charge for changing traveler's checks or personal checks.

American Express

American Express offices in London:

- 6 Haymarket
- 89 Mount Street

Thomas Cook

I took American Express traveler's checks to a Thomas Cook bureau for change one day and had to pay a fee—a very hefty fee! I was furious. When you choose a check brand, you'd do best to match up checks to offices.

Thomas Cook Bureaux de Change in London:

- 43 Berkeley Street
- 4 Henrietta Street (Covent Garden)
- King's Cross Railway Station
- Victoria Railway Station
- 1, Marble Arch
- 196 Oxford Street
- 156 Regent Street
- 90 Baker Street

Here are some tips for your monetary transactions:

- Don't change money (or a lot of it, anyway) with airport vendors, because they will have the worst rates in town—yes, higher than your hotel.
- If you want to change money back to dollars when you leave a country, remember that you will pay a higher rate for them. You are now "buying" dollars rather than "selling" them. Therefore, never change more money than you think you will need, unless you stockpile for another trip.
- Have some foreign currency on hand for arrivals. After a lengthy transatlantic flight, you will not want to stand in line at some London airport booth to get your cab fare.

Your home bank or local currency exchange office can sell you small amounts of foreign currency so that when you arrive in London you have enough change to take care of immediate needs. There are usually foreign exchange booths at international airports as well. No matter how much of a premium you pay for this money, the convenience will be worth it.

Do keep this money readily available on landing—you don't want to have to undress in the taxicab to reach your money belt, nor do you want the money packed in a suitcase in a very safe place.

If you are arriving at London Heathrow and plan to take a taxi into "town," have £50 minimum on hand. If you are taking the bus or the tube, £20 will be sufficient for transportation and immediate tipping at the hotel.

If you are arriving at Gatwick and plan to take a taxi into London, have a minimum of £100 on hand. If you take the bus or train, £20 will be quite sufficient.

- Keep track of what you pay for your currency. If you are going to several countries, or if you must make several money-changing trips to the cashier, write the sums down. When you get home and wonder what you did with all the money you used to have, it'll be easier to trace your cash.

- Make mental comparisons for quick price reactions. Know the conversion rate for $50 and $100 so you can make a judgment in an instant. Also know them in reverse: can you cope with an item priced at £10, £20, or £50? Have your reflexes honed to know where your price barriers are. If you're still interested in an item, then slow down and figure out the true and accurate price.

- Expect to pay a commission—often hidden—each time you change money. Even at banks. That commission is commonly £3, but can be £5 per transaction! Compare the cost of the commission (if you have to pay one) with your hotel rate; sometimes convenience is the lesser of two evils. There is no commission for cardmembers at American Express or for Barclaycard holders at Barclays.

Changing Money at Hotels

Every guide book I read tells you not to change money at hotels, that banks offer a better rate. Having now worked this job for about a decade, I find this isn't great advice for a businessperson or someone in a hurry.

You have to go out of your way to visit a bank, even if you happen to pass by one in a convenient tourist spot. You have to stand in line. You have to pay a commission.

At your hotel, the rate may be marginally worse than at the bank, but you won't have to pay a commission and you won't have to go out of your way or disrupt your day to cash in.

How to Get Cash Overseas

Bank holidays, weekends, and late nights are not good times to be without funds. If you think you can sail into your deluxe hotel and present your credit card to the cashier for an instant injection of cash or the redemption of a personal check from your U.S. bank, think again.

You can go to American Express for additional cash (in dollars or sterling) if you are a cardmember. It's all a relatively simple transaction: You write a personal check at a special desk and show your card, it is approved; you go to another desk and get the money in the currency you request. Allow about a half hour for the whole process, unless there are long lines. Usually you get the credit advance on your card at the same desk.

Bank cash machines are also used all over London and offer one of the best ways to change money. (See the "Cashpoint" section below.)

Make sure you know your PIN number (don't laugh—I can remember my own trick numbers, but when the number is assigned by the bank, as some are, I have no idea what they are. The last time I was in London I brought my international bank card and the address of the corresponding banks in London, but not the PIN number!).

Cashpoint, Please

Electronic banking machines exist everywhere—some are outside on the street, and some are in lobbies of banks, which means that they are only open during specific hours of the day. Do not count on 24-hour access to a bank machine, even in London.

If you have a U.S. bank card, check with your bank at home before you go to London and find the corresponding banks.

If you have a U.K. bank card but are unfamiliar with London, I have tried to put a few addresses of cashpoint machines into various neighborhood listings. The biggest banks in the U.K. are called "high-street banks" (like high-street multiples) because they invariably have a branch on the high street of any town.

Make sure you are aligned with one of these for convenience's sake:

- Barclays
- Lloyd's
- NatWest (National Westminster)
- Midland

Personal Checks

It's unlikely that your hotel will take your personal check, unless they know you very, very, well and you are (a) famous, or (b) rich, or (c) *both*. Be prepared to cry, whine, or go to extraordinary lengths to get your hotel to provide this service. But carry your checkbook anyway, because all sorts of places will take your old-fashioned American check. In fact, *never travel without your checkbook*.

You will also most likely want to write a check to U.S. Customs for the duty you owe. I happen to pay my duty with a credit card so that I get mileage credit, but Uncle Sam has only recently begun to take plastic, and having a checkbook is a good safety net.

Send Money

You can have money sent to you from home, a process that usually takes about two days. Money can be wired through Western Union (someone brings them the cash or a certified check and Western Union does the rest—this may take up to a week) or through an international money order, which is cleared by telex through the bank where you cash it. Money can be wired from bank to bank, but this really only works simply with big-city, major banks that have European branches or sister banks. Banks usually charge a nice, fat fee for doing you this favor. If you have a letter of credit, however, and a corresponding bank that is expecting you, you will have little difficulty getting your hands on some extra green. . . or pink or blue or orange.

In an emergency, the American Consulate may lend you money. You must repay this money. (There's no such thing as a free lunch.)

Tipping

One of the most difficult things for Americans to do when they travel is to lose the concept of translating everything into dollars. Not only do you like to know what things cost, but you probably figure your tips based on your system at home.

When you travel, it works better if you plug into the local rules and denominations for tipping, because the amounts are pegged to local coins.

If you normally tip $1 per suitcase at a hotel, you are not going to stand there with your calculator and tip 73p in London.

Also, please note that Americans are known throughout the world as big tippers. Taxi drivers in particular, but people in all service businesses hope for American clients because they anticipate bigger tips from them.

On the whole, British people find the subject of money distasteful and do not even want to talk about it. Tipping is embarrassing—on both the giving and receiving end.

- In restaurants, ask if VAT and service are included in the bill. In most cases it is clearly stated on the bill. I had a dreadful experience whereby I made an expensive miscalculation and lost £20. Never be embarrassed to ask. (I was, and it cost me.)
- You tend to tip more generously and more frequently in London than in the countryside.
- You become more judgmental about tipping because you realize that the local custom is to not tip, or to tip 10%, whereas you might've been brought up to believe that 15% constitutes the minimum for a tip.

Here are my basic London tipping rules:

IN RESTAURANTS
If service is not included in the dinner price, I

tip between 10% and 15% but never over 15%, and frequently at whatever number handily falls between the two, according to the sum of the bill. I do not tip maitre d's. I guess I don't hang out at the right places.

AT THE HAIRDRESSER

At the hairdresser, I tip a total of 15% on the whole—that usually means £1.50 for the shampoo person and £3.50 to whoever did my hair, up to a maximum of £5 total. Please note that in Edinburgh I was told service was included. When I insisted on giving the stylist £1, which was 10% of my bill, she was thrilled but very flustered. (See page 144 for more on hairdressers.)

IN TAXIS

I round up the bill to the nearest number that is somewhere around 10%. If the driver has been particularly helpful, I round up a bit more.

IN HOTELS

- I tip 50p to a hotel doorman for getting me a taxi, if it is not my hotel. If I have been at a hotel for several days and used many taxis, I tip £5 in an envelope on which I write my name, my room number, and my thanks. I address the envelope to "front door staff."
- If the concierge staff has been helpful, I tip another £5—more if they have been incredibly helpful.
- I tip the bellhop 50p per suitcase.
- On departure, I again tip the bellhop 50p per suitcase in person when he or she comes to pick up my bags.
- I do not tip the valet who automatically brings ice or turns down the bed. If I call down for a small but specific service—bring me a vase, please—I tip 50p when said vase arrives. I do not tip when a fax is brought to the room. I say "thank you."

AT THE AIRPORT

They have free trolleys at London airports. Should you need a skycap, there is a fixed price of £5. I always considered that highway robbery until I needed one; he more than earned his keep!

Export Tax Scheme (VAT)

When you bring an item to a cash register in the U.S., sales tax is added to the sticker price of your purchase. In Europe, the tax is added before the item is stickered, so that the price on the sticker is the total amount you are charged.

This system is called value-added tax. It's known in Britain as VAT. Businesses that make over £37,000 a year must pay VAT. The cost is therefore passed onto the consumer.

If you are not a British subject and if you take the goods out of Britain, you are entitled to a refund on the VAT. You may also get a refund on VAT for hotel rooms and car rentals, but that's another subject.

The VAT is 17.5%.

In the scheme of things, you should be getting a 17.5% refund on purchases; however, that is a major oversimplification of the system.

The basic value-added tax system works pretty much like this:

- You are shopping in a store with prices marked on the merchandise. This is the true price of the item, which any tourist or any national must pay. (I'm assuming you are in a department store with fixed prices, not a flea market.) If you are a national, you pay the price without thinking twice. If you are a tourist who plans to leave the country within six months, you ask a salesperson, "What is the minimum expenditure in this store for the export refund?"

The rate varies from shop to shop—usually touristy neighborhoods and drop-dead, chichi stores have a higher quota. The law states that a refund can come your way with a minimum expenditure of £50. However, in some shops you may be asked to spend £75–£100 before you qualify. Or more!

- More and more stores, especially the fancy ones, charge a commission for issuing the VAT refund. Expect to lose £5 of the refund.

- There are now three different companies paying out VAT refunds for shop subscribers. All three have different types of forms, but the system works the same way. One of these companies works out your refund on a chart—although I spent almost £100 at Culpeper the Herbalists, according to the chart my refund was £3.50! I was outraged. For $5, it wasn't worth my trouble to show those goods to the Customs officer in London and schlep them on the plane with me. Check out the size of the refund before you see stars (or discounts) in your eyes.

- Once you know the minimum, decide accordingly whether you will make a smaller purchase, or come back another time for a big haul. Only you know how much time your schedule will permit for shopping. Remember that on a $100 purchase, the 17.5% minus a £5 fee may mean the saving is too little to make the VAT meaningful.

- Judge for yourself if you are certain the store you are about to do business with will actually give you the refund after the paperwork is done. If you are dealing with a famous department store or a reputable boutique, there never should be a problem. I have had considerable problems with several big-name boutiques in both London and in the English countryside.

- If you are going to another European country, consider the VAT or *détaxe* policy there. It may be smarter to wait until you get to France to purchase the same item.

1) Sometimes the only savings you get when shopping abroad is the VAT discount. Don't knock it if you can afford it.

2) If you go for the VAT, budget your time to allow for the paperwork before you leave the country. It takes about five minutes to fill out each form, and you must have them filled in when you present them upon exiting the country.

3) Along with the VAT forms you will be given an envelope. Sometimes the envelope has a stamp on it; sometimes it is blank (you must provide the postage stamp before you leave the country). Sometimes it has a special government frank that serves as a stamp. If you don't understand what's on your envelope, ask.

4) When you are leaving the country, go to the Customs official who serves the VAT papers. *Do this before you clear regular Customs or send off your luggage.* The Customs officer has the right to ask you to show him or her the merchandise you bought and are taking out of the country. He may not even look, but by law you are supposed to have the goods with you.

If you have too much stuff to carry on board, you must allow plenty of extra time, as you'll have to exit immigration with your baggage while a security guard stands by, then get rid of your checked luggage. I dare say 17.5% just isn't worth this kind of aggravation.

Right after you've done passport control in Heathrow, you go to the VAT desk (to your right if passport control is to your back) to show your goods—see there, you can carry them on board after all—and get your paperwork taken care of. All of the paperwork takes some preparation (filling in your name, address, passport number, etc.) which you are expected to have completed *before* you stand in the VAT line. It really gums up the works for everyone else if the officer has to explain to you that you should have already done the fill-in-the-blanks part and would you please step over to one side.

Whether the officer sees your purchases or not, he or she will stamp the papers, keep a set (which will be processed), and give you another set in the envelope. You then mail the envelope (which usually is preprinted with the shop's name and address, or will have been addressed by the shop for you). There is a mailbox next to the officer's desk.

5) When the papers get back to the shop and the government has notified the shop that their set of papers has been registered, the shop will then grant you the discount through a refund. This can be done on your credit card or through a personal check, which will come to you in the mail, usually three months later. (It will be in a foreign currency—your bank may charge you to change it into dollars.) If you are smart, you will indicate that the refund should be credited to a bank card or American Express so that you will end up with a refund in dollars.

If It's Tuesday...

If you are travelling to several EEC countries on one trip, you do the VAT for all purchases when you depart your final destination. Allow time for this, especially if you have a connection to make.

Protection Plus

In these days of recession and depression, charge cards and bank cards are cutting back on their perks and amenities. American Express barely has any Purchase Protection plan in place.

If you are making a big purchase—especially if you are planning to make this purchase before you leave home—you might want to call your various bank and charge-card companies and check on what kind of free and extra insurance and purchase protection you have. Then pick the best card for the purchase.

In the old days, American Express offered Purchase Protection automatically to all card-members and Optima holders so that if a purchase was lost, stolen, or broken within ninety days of purchase, it would be replaced or refunded. Many bank cards came out with similar plans. With bank cards you may have to register in order to be covered; ask.

Because these plans are being phased out and may exist only on premium cards or not at all in the future, it pays to check it out rather than assuming that you are covered.

U.S. Customs and Duties

To make your reentry into the U.S. as smooth as possible, follow these tips:

- Know the rules and stick to them!
- Don't try to smuggle anything.
- Be polite and cooperative (up until the point when they ask you to strip, anyway. . .).

Remember:

- You are currently allowed to bring in $400 worth of merchandise per person, duty-free. Before you leave the U.S., verify this amount with one of the U.S. Customs offices. Each member of the family is entitled to the deduction; this includes infants. You may pool within a family. You count into your $400-per-person everything you obtain while abroad—this includes items bought in duty-free shops, gifts for others, the items that other people asked you to bring home for them, and—get this—even alterations.

- You pay a flat 10% duty on the next $1,000 worth of merchandise. This is extremely simple and is worth doing. We're talking about the very small sum of $100 to make life easy—and crime-free.

- Duties thereafter are based on a product-type basis. They vary tremendously per item, so think about each purchase and ask store-keepers about U.S. duties. They will know, especially in specialty stores like furriers or china shops.

- The head of the family can make a joint declaration for all family members. The "head of the family" need not be male. Whoever is the head of the family, however, should take the responsibility for answering any questions the Customs officers may ask. Answer questions honestly, firmly, and politely. Have receipts ready, and make sure they match the information on the landing card. Don't be forced into a story that won't wash under questioning. If they catch you in a little lie, you'll be labeled as a fibber and they'll tear your luggage apart.

- Have the Customs registration slips for your personally owned goods in your wallet or easily available. If you wear a Cartier watch, be able to produce the registration slip. If you cannot prove that you took a foreign-made item out of the country with you, you may be forced to pay duty on it!

- The unsolicited gifts you mailed from abroad do not count in the $400-per-person rate. If the value of the gift is more than $50, you pay duty when the package comes into the country. Remember, it's only one unsolicited gift per person for each mailing. Don't mail to yourself.

- Do not attempt to bring in any illegal food items—dairy products, meats, fruits, or vegetables (coffee is OK). Generally speaking, if it's alive, it's *verboten*. We don't need to tell you it's tacky to bring in drugs and narcotics.

- Antiques must be 100 years old to be duty-free. Provenance papers will help (so will permission to export the antiquity, since it could be an item of national cultural significance). Any bona fide work of art is duty-free whether it was painted fifty years ago or just yesterday; the artist need not be famous.

- Dress for success. People who look like "hippies" get stopped at Customs more than average folks. Women who look like a million dollars, who are dragging their fur coats, have first-class baggage tags on their luggage, and carry Gucci handbags, but declare they have bought nothing, are equally suspicious.

- Laws regarding ivory are new and improved —for elephants, anyway. You may not import any ivory into the U.S. Not to worry, there is little new ivory for sale in London; antique ivory should have provenance or papers to be legally imported.

- The amount of the Customs allowance is expected to change or be modified into a different type of declaration. If you are a big shopper, check before you leave to see if there's any news.

One Last Calculating Thought

Unless you have a Ph.D. in mathematics from MIT, I suggest you keep a calculator in your purse at all times. Furthermore, it should be the kind that uses batteries. Solar-run calculators are very cute, but your purse is dark inside, and many shops are, too. There's nothing worse than trying to do a bit of hard negotiating when your calculator won't calculate. If you use your calculator frequently, or if your children like to play with it as a toy, buy new batteries before you leave on the trip. Unless the pound is trading at exactly $1.50 or exactly $2, you will probably need help figuring exact prices.

CHAPTER THREE

SHOPPING NEIGHBORHOODS

Yours in a Zip

Zip codes in London are called postal codes. They are made up of two sets of letter and number combinations. The first set actually indicates the precise part of town where the address is located, and makes a good indicator for shoppers who want to organize themselves by neighborhood. As a matter of fact, pretty soon you'll see a postal code and have an immediate association—"Ah, there's my old friend WC2."

If you'll study the map below, you'll see that the metropolitan area is divided into quadrants and that these have a few subcategories, such as southwest and southeast, and so on. There is a central core; those central zones have the letter C in them for—you guessed it—"central." You can look up the general area of a store or shopping neighborhood just by using this map.

As you get more sophisticated at using this method, you'll learn the few overlapping places. For instance, Mayfair is W1, but Jermyn Street, at the edge of Mayfair, is in SW1. Practice, practice, practice.

London by Neighborhood

London is one of the best cities in the world in which to pick a neighborhood and wander without specific goals. Each neighborhood is dis-

London Postal Codes

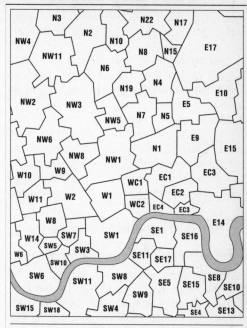

SELECTED POINTS OF INTEREST

SE1:	London Bridge
SE10:	Greenwich
SW10:	South Kensington, King's Road
SW3:	Chelsea, Knightsbridge, South Kensington, King's Road
SW1:	Westminster, Belgravia, Jermyn Street, Sloane Street
SW7:	South Kensington, Knightsbridge
EC1:	Islington, Angel
EC3:	Tower of London, City of London
EC4:	Fleet Street, Old Bailey
N1:	Islington, Angel, King's Cross
NW1:	Camden, Chalk Farm, King's Cross, Euston
NW2:	West Hampstead
NW3:	Hampstead, Kentish Town
NW5:	Kentish Town, Highgate, Camden, Chalk Farm
NW6:	Hampstead, West Hampstead, St. John's Wood
W1:	Mayfair, Soho
W2:	South Kensington, Portobello Road
W8:	Kensington High Street, Earls Court
W10:	North Kensington, Portobello Road
W11:	Portobello Road Market
WC1:	Mayfair, Soho, The West End, Savile Row, The Strand, Oxford Street
WC2:	Covent Garden, Trafalgar Square, Charing Cross Road, Piccadilly

tinctive because of the way the city grew out of many individual cities. Some famous names overlap (Chelsea and Knightsbridge); some are actually separate cities.

Do note that it is inappropriate to refer to London or the portion of London an American might deem to be "downtown" as *The City*. In Britspeak, The City truly means The City of London, which is a teeny-tiny one-mile area; it is where the financial institutions have their offices and the banking people—and insurance people and the suits—do their business.

You might want to learn a few basic London neighborhoods before you arrive, just to be safe.

Sightseeing and Shopping by Neighborhood

The marketing nobs in London always say that the McDonald's people didn't have to spend any money on market research when they came into Britain—they simply looked for a high street with a MARKS & SPENCER on it and bought space as close by as possible.

You'll note that much retail in Britain is coordinated by the same type of marketing plan—it's as though a hundred years ago some Victorian marketing genius said, "Let's find a tourist attraction and then build a store right next to it." As a result, many tourist attractions are in shopping districts, or vice versa. This makes it easy to combine neighborhoods, culture, and credit cards in one fell swoop.

The only major exception to the shop-and-see theory is that the Tower of London is sort of in the middle of nowhere. Also note that The City offers very little retail, just a few shops to serve the needs of local businessmen and women. Furthermore, entrance to The City is restricted because of terrorist bombings.

Banking by Neighborhood

If you are not from London, you may find yourself in a certain neighborhood and in need of a bank either to exchange currency or just pick up some extra scratch.

Your best bet, of course, is to know what kind of bank you are looking for and to look it up in the phone book or ask your concierge as you plan your day's schedule. I've heard sorry tales of tourists wandering in desperation, spending entire afternoons searching vainly for a Lloyd's bank.

American Express and Thomas Cook offices are listed on page 53; here are some bank offices by neighborhood, just to get you started.

NatWest (National Westminster)

Neighborhood	Address
Mayfair	1 Berkeley Square, W1 (Tube: Green Park)
Camden Town	166 Camden High Street, NW1 (Tube: Camden High Street)
Charing Cross	10 St. Martin's Place, WC2 (Tube: Covent Garden or Leicester Square)
Covent Garden	34 Henrietta Street, WC2 (Tube: Covent Garden)
Chelsea	300 King's Road; 224 King's Road, SW3 (take bus)
Baker Street	69 Baker Street, NW1 (near Madame Tussaud's) (Tube: Baker Street)
Islington	3 Upper Street, N1 (near antique market) (Tube: Angel)
Knightsbridge	69 Knightsbridge, SW1 (near Harrods) (Tube: Knightsbridge)
Oxford Street	358 Oxford Street, W1 (near Marks & Spencer) (Tube: Bond Street)

Oxford Circus   40 Oxford Street, W1
                (Tube: Oxford Circus)
Piccadilly Circus   19 Shaftsbury Avenue, W1
                (Tube: Piccadilly Circus)
Piccadilly   63 Piccadilly, W1 (near the Ritz)
                (Tube: Green Park or Piccadilly
                Circus)
Sloane Square   14 Sloane Square, SW1
                (Tube: Sloane Square)

Lloyd's

Neighborhood	Address
Mayfair	Berkeley Square, W1
	(Tube: Green Park)
Camden Town	140 Camden High Street, NW1
	(Tube: Camden High Street)
Kensington	112 High Street
	(Tube: High Street Kensington)
Knightsbridge	79 Brompton Rd., SW3
	(Tube: Knightsbridge)

Barclays

Neighborhood	Address
Camden Town	193 Camden High Street, NW1
	(Tube: Camden High Street)
Covent Garden	5 Henrietta Street, WC2
	(Tube: Covent Garden)
Hyde Park Corner	27 Knightsbridge, SW1
	(Tube: Hyde Park Corner)
Kensington	35 Notting Hill Gate, W11
	(Tube: Notting Hill Gate)
Knightsbridge	1 Brompton Rd., SW3
	(Tube: Knightsbridge)

Connect the Dots by Neighborhood

If you work with a daily schedule or list of shopping goals, you'll soon see that certain neighborhoods lead directly to each other, usually by foot, but often by bus. The tours in Chapter

8 are organized to move you through London in an orderly neighborhood sequence.

I have tried to organize this neighborhood section by interconnecting neighborhoods related to a larger area. To me, a person who listens to the vibes of the sidewalk, a shopping neighborhood may only hold that specific mood for two or three blocks before changing into something else. I've tried to indicate the changes and segues.

The West End

The West End is the name for a large portion of real estate; a W1 address is very chic—for a store or a residence.

The major shopping areas in the West End are Oxford Street, Oxford Circus, Regent Street, Bond Street (Old and New) and Piccadilly.

OXFORD STREET

Most of the time I walk on Oxford Street, I hate it: it's always mobbed and it's just too real-world for my tastes. To enjoy Oxford Street, you have to settle into the right frame of mind (or be twenty-two) and begin to groove on the street vendors selling Union Jacks, the fruit and flower stands, the locals in search of a bargain, and the street fashions that pass by in hurried profusion.

The beauty of Oxford Street is the fact that most of the moderately priced big department stores, including the flagship MARKS & SPENCER, are lined up in a row between Marble Arch and Regent Street. The high-rent department stores are on Regent Street, just around the corner, but a million miles away. You can also expect to find a branch store of many popular multiples such as BODY SHOP and a number of inexpensive shoe shops. There is a small BOOTS and, oh yes, there are outposts of the big record shops such as VIRGIN MEGASTORE and HMV.

Saturdays are downright zoo-like. Weekdays

West End/Soho/Covent Garden

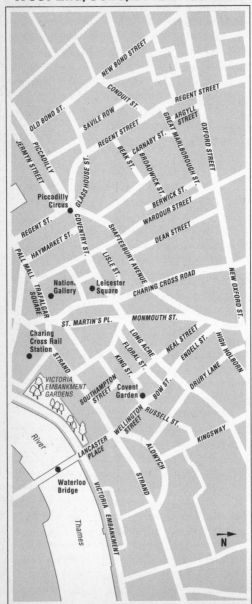

are quite bearable. Many teens and 'tweens shop the multiples here, so just walking down the street may give you a chance to study London countercultural fashion like an academic. If you have a non-shopping husband, do not bring him to Oxford Street.

OXFORD CIRCUS

To me, Oxford Street is the stretch of Oxford Street from Marble Arch to Regent Street. End of story.

Oxford Circus, and it *is* a circus, begins at Regent Street and continues along Oxford Street for a block or two toward Tottenham Court. In Romanspeak, a circus is a circle. In the new London, this is more of a zoo.

Oxford Circus has a decidedly more hot and hip atmosphere to it. The stores are still cheap, but they are selling high-fashion street looks to young people on the cutting edge of the cutting edge. These shoppers will segue over to Carnaby Street from Oxford Circus—it's just a few blocks away.

There are more multiples here, including a branch of MARKS & SPENCER that is not as big as the Marble Arch flagship and does not sell cashmere sweaters, but does have a good grocery store in the basement. You'll also find record shops such as HMV, the mini-mall OXFORD PLACE, and my favorite multiple, MOTHERCARE, artfully placed between the teen fashion places and record stores to remind all of Britain's teens that safe sex is smart.

X, also known as DEPARTMENT X (although you'll only see the big X and not the rest), is a branch of the multiple NEXT. It's for teens and it's so hot that you must go out of your way to explore it. Even if you aren't a teen, or the parent of a teen, check it out: it's the kind of store that inspires ideas and creative dressing with a look that combines jeans, casualwear, and street fashion.

Speaking of NEXT, there is a small store in this neighborhood that sells whatever NEXT hasn't sold in their stores—it's a sort of permanent sale shop called NEXT TO NOTHING. I've never found the prices to be next-to-nothing or the merchandise terribly spectacular, but NEXT is a great store and while you're in the neighborhood you should stop by briefly (129 Oxford Street).

REGENT STREET

I love to walk Regent Street from Piccadilly to Oxford Circus. It's a little less than a mile in distance and each side of the street is packed with stores, but only one side of the street appeals to me—the HAMLEYS side (if Oxford is to your rear, you're on the left-hand side of the street toward Piccadilly). If I only have one hour in London, this is where I'll spend my hour.

You can spend a full day shopping these stores, of course, but even non-shopping husbands and kids alike will enjoy the walk to just soak up the best of the London shopping scene. If you do happen to be with kids, note that both HAMLEYS, Britain's largest toy store, and the DISNEY STORE are in this stretch of Regent Street. And Carnaby Street (see page 78), is directly behind, so there's something for everyone in the family.

Bored husbands, please note that LAURA ASHLEY has a sofa by the front door. Plop yourself down there if you need a rest.

Regent Street hosts the British institutions that make London retail so glorious. If there's only one store on your tour, it's got to be LIBERTY. But there's also everything from THE GAP to JAEGER to LAWLEY'S (china) to even the REJECT CHINA SHOP. Also BURBERRYS, AQUASCUTUM, and the BRITISH AIR TRAVEL STORE, where you can confirm plane reservations, buy travel books and products, change money, and use the medical clinic.

BOND STREET

While Regent Street is big department stores with big names, Bond Street is small boutiques with big names. This is where you'll find everything from CHANEL to KARL LAGERFELD. The incredible GIANNI VERSACE store is worth a tour; they should sell tickets to the place—it's far more interesting than Buckingham Palace. You won't find any bargains in these stores, but do remember that most of them have prices that will automatically qualify you for a VAT refund.

Bond Street is divided into two parts: Old Bond and New Bond. Both are chockablock with big-name designer boutiques from all over the world.

PICCADILLY

Piccadilly Circus is a little bit tacky with its TOWER RECORDS store, the TROCADERO mall, and a whole lot of traffic, but if you cut over onto Piccadilly itself and begin to walk toward the RITZ, you'll find retail heaven. This is part of the Regent Street experience to me, with some special British institutions that are the reason you came to London in the first place—such as FORTNUM & MASON, BURLINGTON ARCADE, and HATCHARDS, the bookstore.

Soho

Traditionally speaking, Soho is a seedy neighborhood known for its porn shops. But here and there among the tattoo places and the massage parlors there are some hip stores. The most expensive hip stores are strung together in order to improve the real estate and make shopping easier for the customers. Newburgh Street is such a venue—it's chockablock with places such as GAULTIER JUNIOR. WORKERS FOR FREEDOM on Lower John Street looks small and uninviting, but has a reputation for high-fashion clothes that set trends.

CARNABY STREET

Carnaby Street itself has artistic banners and flags to welcome you to the rebirth of this tourist trap; there are a number of head shops selling black leather clothing (much with studs), funny, floppy hats, T-shirts, and imports from India—with and without tie-dye. You get the picture. The teens hang out in droves.

If I haven't made it clear that I loathe these shops, let me go on to explain what I do like about the neighborhood:

- The kids and the people are fabulous to stare at.
- There's a lot of energy here—and a sense of being in a foreign destination, which is exactly what you want from a trip to Europe.
- There are lots of postcard shops.

For my own shopping taste, there's a branch of BOOTS, there's a BODY SHOP, and there's MUJI—a Japanese store that is known for the sublime look and feel of all their goods. There are many branches of SHELLY'S SHOES, the shoe shop for Doc Martens and hip London looks; there's a china shop with a good selection of novelty teapots called CHINA WARE HOUSE [sic], and then there's the back street Newburgh Street, where the expensive new-wave designer shops of Soho are located.

I like to walk the alleys, streets such as Foubert's, Marlborough (where Body Shop, Muji and others are located), and Ganton.

JERMYN STREET

These few short blocks of a shopping neighborhood run one block from Piccadilly and end at St. James's. Most of the stores here are small, with the exception of ALFRED DUNHILL and FORTNUM & MASON, the back of which is on this street. Jermyn Street represents a world that has almost ceased to exist—most of the stores

St. James's and Mayfair

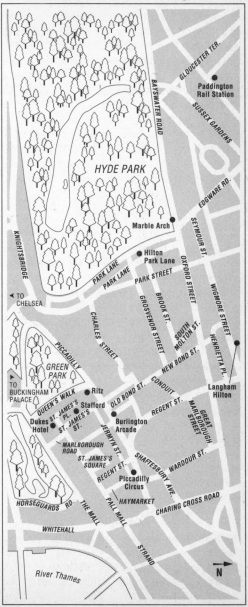

are devoted to the private world of serving the upper-crust London gent. It's the home of exclusive shirt shops such as TURNBULL & ASSER, HILDITCH & KEY, and HARVIE & HUDSON.

Press your nose against the glass of all the shops, take in the dark wood and the aroma of old money. There are several famous stores for toiletries from CZECH & SPEAKE to TRUMPER'S (which is in Simpson's and is actually a place for m'lord to have a shave and a haircut for more than two bits), and there's DAVIDOFF for the right smoke. Cuban cigars cannot legally be brought into the U.S., but it is not a crime to smoke them in London.

St. James's

St. James's Street stretches from St. James's Palace near Pall Mall to Piccadilly, and is lined with some of London's most famous stores, many of which are a hundred years old. Or more. It all adds to the charm of the stroll.

Most of the stores have their original store fronts or have been restored to make you think they are original. Don't miss JOHN LOBB (No. 9) for bespoke shoes (you can look, you needn't plunk down a thousand bucks), JAMES LOCK & CO. (No. 6), a hatmaker for men and women, WILLIAM EVANS GUN & RIFLEMAKER (67A St. James's Place), and D.R. HARRIS (No. 29), an old-fashioned chemist whose brand of toiletries is considered very chic. My son Aaron keeps boxes of the quill toothpicks, which are individually wrapped in paper and quite the last word; I buy the "skin food" moisturizer. With a name like that, how could I resist?

Dorchester

There's a private part of Mayfair that you will never find unless you prowl the streets or happen to be staying at the DORCHESTER, or possibly the CONNAUGHT. South Audley Street is the main drag of this niche to good taste and fine retail, but you will also want to wander Mount Street and end up at Berkeley Square before taking Bruton and connecting to Bond Street.

Mount Street and Bruton are known mostly for their very fancy antique stores. South Audley has a hodgepodge of delectable goods from one of London's better spy shops (honest) to KENNETH TURNER (corner of Brook Street)—a florist whose work is so sensational I suggest you take a look—to THOMAS GOODE, London's most exclusive address for china and tabletop. GOODE now runs a museum service so that you can bring your coat of arms out of retirement and have it painted on your next set of dishes. Yes, it's that kind of neighborhood.

This is a part of town only frequented by rich people, which is just what makes it so much fun. Don't miss SHEPHERD MARKET, which is closer to Curzon Street—it's a hidden medieval alley with a few shops and pubs that looks like it hasn't changed in 300 years.

Knightsbridge

Fashionable and "with it," Knightsbridge crosses into a few different neighborhoods and borders Chelsea to such an extent that it can be confusing for a tourist to grasp the difference.

Once you've passed Hyde Park and are headed toward HARRODS, you'll be on a street which is first called Knightsbridge and then changes its name to Brompton Road. This makes it especially confusing if you are watching addresses or street numbers because Knightsbridge doesn't really change its name, it just disappears into a nowhere turn. Chances are you won't realize that you've turned a corner at Sloane Street and ended up on the beginning of Brompton Road. Never mind. Pay no heed to street names and you'll be fine.

South Kensington and Chelsea

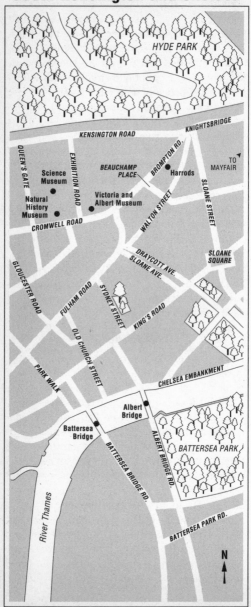

HYDE PARK

KNIGHTSBRIDGE

KENSINGTON ROAD

QUEEN'S GATE

EXHIBITION ROAD

Science Museum

BEAUCHAMP PLACE

BROMPTON RD.

Harrods

TO MAYFAIR

Natural History Museum

Victoria and Albert Museum

WALTON STREET

SLOANE STREET

CROMWELL ROAD

DRAYCOTT AVE.

SLOANE AVE.

SLOANE SQUARE

GLOUCESTER ROAD

FULHAM ROAD

SYDNEY STREET

KING'S ROAD

OLD CHURCH STREET

PARK WALK

CHELSEA EMBANKMENT

Albert Bridge

Battersea Bridge

ALBERT BRIDGE RD.

BATTERSEA PARK

BATTERSEA BRIDGE RD.

River Thames

BATTERSEA PARK RD.

N

The part around HARVEY NICHOLS is decidedly different than the part that comes after HARRODS. At the Harvey Nichols end, aside from wonderful Harvey Nichols itself, there are branches of all the multiples and a number of high-end retailers as well, such as RODIER and SCOTCH HOUSE. The closer you get to Harrods, the less tony the retailers become.

Harrods and Harvey Nichols are only a few blocks apart, so we're talking chockablock shopping here. Also note that Sloane Street (which has its own atmosphere and tempo, see below) leads off from Brompton at the corner where Harvey Nichols is standing. So you have to be organized and know where you're going because there are many directions and many, many choices to make.

SLOANE STREET

On its own, well, Sloane Street just ain't what it used to be. When the economy was better, Sloane Street was two blocks of cheek-and-jowl designer chic. You could glance down the street and just rattle off an international who's who in big-name retailing from CHANEL to VALENTINO.

Many of these shops are still holding on; there's a rather well-known shoe shop, GINA, which I find overrated but locals seem to like, and there's a new KENZO here, proving that someone still believes in the neighborhood.

KING'S ROAD

If you continue along Sloane Street you will end up at Sloane Square. Here, surrounding the square, are numerous stores. On your way to the square, make sure you take a look at JANE CHURCHILL and GENERAL TRADING COMPANY. The focal point of Sloane Square is the medium-sized department store, PETER JONES.

Just as Sloane Street dead-ends and disappears, you have two choices for two different retail experiences: Pimlico (see page 85) and King's Road.

For King's Road, put General Trading Company at your back and make a right at Sloane Square. You're now on King's Road. King's Road became famous (or is that infamous?) in the 1960s as the hot street for the bell-bottom people. It was groovy. Now King's Road is mostly a congregation of multiples, but it still has its own distinct flavor and charm, predominately design-oriented businesses. It also possesses a few of London's best antique arcades.

The worst thing about King's Road is its lack of transportation, since there is no convenient tube station along the way. You can either go up one side and down the other and end up back at Sloane Square, or put on your hiking boots and march all the way up into the 500 block—it is kind of interesting all the way up.

Upper Knightsbridge

From HARRODS, if you stay on Brompton Road, you'll see a branch of PAST TIMES, which is worth crossing the street for if you have never seen this multiple (they sell historical reproductions commonly carried in museum shops). In a block, assuming Harrods is at your back, you'll arrive at Beauchamp Place. If you stay on Brompton Road, you'll pass EMPORIO ARMANI and then soon you'll be at Museum Row on a street now called Cromwell Road. Brompton goes off on its own to become yet another neighborhood (Brompton Cross, see page 85).

BEAUCHAMP PLACE

Whether you're going on to museums and culture or Brompton Road and yet more shopping, please take some time to explore Beauchamp (say "Beechum") Place, which is only one big block with stores on both sides of the street. There's been a great deal of turnover here because of the recession, but JOHN BOYD has moved in and SARAH SPENCER has her headquarters here. KANGA (a shop carrying the line of clothes made by Lady Dale Tyron, Prince Charles' former best friend) is here, as well as SAN LORENZO, the luncheon hotspot where Princess Di hangs out when she can do lunch, and three different branches of REJECT CHINA SHOP. If you decide to splurge on lunch at San Lorenzo, make sure you have booked a reservation and have asked for the front room.

Naturally, you are dressed to kill. Hats optional.

BROMPTON CROSS

Brompton Cross was, until yesterday, one of the hottest parts of London for retail. Hard hit by the recession, this neighborhood is certainly worth the trip, but is no longer the glory spot it once was. Maybe next week.

The showpiece of the whole area is MICHELIN HOUSE, a Conran rehab which houses THE CONRAN SHOP, truly a good store for design ideas, home and tabletop, gift items, and even luggage. There are a few JOSEPH stores in this area and an interesting small street which leads back to HARRODS—Walton Street.

Walton Street is a narrow street with tiny shops, many of which are devoted to interior design. (NINA CAMPBELL, one of London's biggest names in interior design, is here.) There's a marvelous resale shop (PAMELA'S), where I purchased a John Boyd hat for £23 (see page 150).

PIMLICO ROAD

This is not the neighborhood of Pimlico as laid out in your A to Z, but rather a street called Pimlico Road (SW1) which comes right before the real Pimlico district. To reach it by tube, use the Sloane Square stop.

For those interested in interior design, this street is filled with shops of trimmings, fabrics, and antiques. Working designers or those with a need should find some useful resources here.

From the Sloane Square tube, if the station is to your back and you are facing toward PETER JONES, make a left on Holbein Place. This will lead you to Pimlico Road within a block; there are some shops here along the way. When you do both sides of Pimlico Road, return to Sloane Square via Lower Sloane Street, which runs parallel to Holbein Place.

Kensington

This neighborhood is a must if you are in the fashion business, want to see the young hip looks, or have teens and 'tweens. It's also a must for those interested in antiques.

KENSINGTON HIGH STREET

Like any other high street, the thoroughfare which stretches before you as you emerge from the Kensington High Street tube station is chockablock with multiples and real-people stores. There's the architecturally interesting BARKERS OF KENSINGTON department store, KENSINGTON MARKET for the black-leather-and-tattoo generation, and HYPER HYPER, for the with-it fashion crowd. A sneeze behind the high street is LANCER'S SQUARE, a mini-mall which houses EHRMAN'S for needleworks, tapestry, sweater kits, and wools.

Town Hall, around the corner from the high street, frequently hosts antique shows and events. Eat lunch in the adorable train car cafe in Hyper Hyper.

KENSINGTON CHURCH STREET

Leading up the hill from the high street (therefore meeting it in a perpendicular fashion) is Kensington Church Street, a curvy little road that is only three or four blocks long. It leads directly to Notting Hill. It hosts a few multiples, but more importantly is home to many, many antiques shops of the high-end, but not so high-end that they are too stuffy to enjoy. Many of these dealers do the big shows, so watch out for the month of June—the stores may be closed or are only open at weird hours.

NOTTING HILL GATE

I can't quite get into Notting Hill Gate as a neighborhood; it's more like a sigh between Kensington Church Street and Portobello Road, but there are a few multiples here as well as a good bookstore. This is your tube stop if you are going to Portobello Road.

PORTOBELLO ROAD

There is indeed a Portobello Road and it is the home of the Saturday market; it is also the home of many genuine antiques dealers who are open during the week. To think that Portobello Road is *just* a Saturday event is wrong. It's easier to enjoy the shops during the week when the Saturday throngs, the tour buses, the German tots, and the organ grinder are not in place.

Considering how famous Portobello Road is, it's not that easy to find. Please note that on Saturdays there is a chalkboard at the stairwell inside the Notting Hill Gate tube station giving specific directions how to get to Portobello Road (see page 221). The fun starts as soon as you turn right onto Pembridge Road from Notting Hill Gate and continues as you wend your way to Portobello Road. Follow the crowd.

Covent Garden

The area I call Covent Garden is actually a parcel of real estate that includes Covent Garden among a handful of other neighborhoods. This part of town begins at Trafalgar, but actually backs up on one end at Mayfair and at the other, Soho.

COVENT GARDEN

The entire area around Covent Garden is filled with fabulous little shops and pubs, which makes the whole place a super shopping area. It's also an officially designated tourist area, so stores are open on Sunday (please note that not all are open, but unlike in other parts of London, many are).

Prowl everywhere, not just the festival marketplace. Include the two buildings of Covent Garden—a rehab of the old marketplace—and make sure you also see the three different markets that are more or less attached to Covent Garden (between the two buildings; out the back building; and to the side of the two buildings).

Several multiples have branches in the red-brick mall stores; one of the most interesting entries is TWILIGHT, a division of MONSOON and ACCESSORIZE (which is technically also a division of Monsoon), that specializes in dress-up clothes for evening, hence the name. I will admit that I flipped out when I discovered that a mere wisp of nothing but Thai silk and wire to wrap around the hair was selling for £18, but the clothes themselves are more moderately priced.

While I've probably done business in every THORNTON'S candy store in London, it was at the Covent Garden branch that I found the Jelly Welly (50p), one of the great gift items from London (see page 8) and it was June.

NEAL STREET

Walk out the front end of Covent Garden, pass the Covent Garden tube; you are on Neal Street, a pedestrian area that is one of the few places in London that is actually booming. A new mall (THOMAS NEALS, Earlham Court) adds to the excitement; there are pubs and people and stores galore with a funky, friendly feeling that makes the whole Covent Garden adventure more complete. The stores here are mostly open on Sundays as well; don't miss it.

LEICESTER SQUARE

Get here—to the heart of the theater district and not much of a shopping district—via New Row, so you can take in a few more cute shops. New Row is only a block long, but there's something very charming, very Old World about it and the combination of bookstores, antiques stores, and crafts stores that makes you thrill with discovery.

THE STRAND

This is a so-so tourist area where there are branches of the big-name shops (CHINACRAFT, NEXT, etc.), but where everything seems to have been in its prime in 1960. The Strand begins at Charing Cross and stretches along in the direction of St. Paul's Cathedral and The City. The Strand actually changes name in a few blocks and becomes the infamous Fleet Street, but no matter.

The heart of The Strand as a shopping district is near Charing Cross and Covent Garden; here you've got the SAVOY HOTEL, SIMPSON'S IN THE STRAND for roast beef, and a handful of multiples. Stamp collectors know the area well because several famous dealers are located here; there are also a lot of sporting-goods stores here. You can connect to Covent Garden or Charing Cross (by walking), so the location can't be ignored, and it's certainly not intimidating here as it may be in Mayfair.

If you are here anyway, don't miss THE RUSSIAN SHOP, 99 The Strand, where Russian folk arts are sold at somewhat reasonable prices.

Other Neighborhoods

Fulham Road

Fulham Road can't make up its mind what it is, as it stretches around King's Road and closer to Sloane Square and the Sloane Ranger state of being. If you have some time on your hands, you'll be startled by the contrast between the up-and-coming and the more traditional neighborhood shops.

Consider RITVA WESTENIUS (#153) for incredible wedding gowns; THE SLEEPING COMPANY for the English version of French bed linens; DIVERTIMENTI for stylish housewares; OGGETTI for the hard-line Italian/Memphis look in watches, knives, and teakettles; and THE WATCH GALLERY, which is just plain fascinating for the variety of fun watches they have. All these shops stand together on Fulham Road.

If you've been a fan of PIERRE DEUX in the U.S. and have been frustrated by the fact that they are closing stores right and left, get over to SOULEIADO (#171), the French distributor for Pierre Deux, where you can still buy the famous Provençal prints and goods. Also note that a competing store, LES OLIVADES, is in Brompton Cross—so you have two different opportunities for Provençal prints.

Camden Town

I'd just as soon ignore the fact that Camden Town exists, because, well, it's not exactly my cup of tea. That's because I am over forty. If you are over ten and under thirty (hmmmm, maybe you need to be under twenty)... you just may adore it here. And so, mothers of teens and preteens, grit your teeth. This is an entire neighborhood dedicated to buying used clothes and black T-shirts and having your nose pierced. It's particularly busy on Saturday, as this is the day to shop and socialize among the many markets that line the high street.

You may have the urge to hold on to your handbag and to take a bath after you've been here, but your kids will consider this a very awesome part of town. Take the tube to Camden Town, and walk to your right.

Islington

The tube stop for Islington is Angel and you will be in heaven, especially on a Wednesday or Saturday, when you wander for a while through fair Islington. You see, Wednesday and Saturday are market days and there's an alley filled to overflowing with vendors—talk about charm galore. There's an indoor antiques market open every day, but the extra street (alley) action is what makes this fun.

I also like the city market, which is for real people and is no different from any other market, except that this is where I buy my ARSENAL team luggage. If you are looking for anti-status luggage, you too may want to stock up on the lines offered by the football vendors.

All of these marvels are within walking distance of the tube, so go and take cash. You're gonna love it.

The Docklands

My heart is breaking when I think of the Docklands. If I had a spare billion dollars in the bank, surely I'd buy the whole neighborhood, just to stop it from falling into decay. Without adequate public transportation and with CANARY WHARF busted, the pride of east London redevelopment has become a sad disaster.

The term "the Docklands" has come to refer to all development along both sides of the Thames, below Tower Bridge and stretching to Greenwich. However, the development on the south side of the river, where the Design Museum is located, is not in the thick of what is generally known as the Docklands.

I used to like to drive around here just to gawk. Now it merely breaks my heart. At this point, no one would go to the Docklands to shop. In fact, people don't even go to the Docklands any more. Sad, sad, sad.

The best way to see it all is to go to the Design Museum, eat lunch at one of the several restaurants or cafes there (take your choice— they are all CONRAN establishments and something to behold), then take a boat and see the rest from the water.

Hampstead

To the north, and in a totally different frame of mind from the Docklands, is the wealthy suburb of Hampstead, charmingly located right off its own heath. For those who want to see what upper-middle-class London suburbs (with good shopping) are like, and for those who might be browsing for just the perfect neighborhood to move to, Hampstead is a must.

Even though McDonald's has just been allowed to build in town, Hampstead still has the feel of an English country village.

The tube station is very deep and sort of ugly; I have found it frightening. You'll only fall in love once you get to street level. Trust me on this.

After all, if it was good enough for Blake and Keats, it'll probably have something to please you, too. Beyond the immediate shopping area lies the famous Hampstead Heath, where a number of famous folk are buried.

The High Street has its share of famous multiples, but it also has an American-style 1950s diner, some good food shops, and a few specialized boutiques. There is an antiques center near Louis.

Greenwich

How do I love Greenwich, let me count the ways. There's mean time and in-between time, and then there's Sundays. If you want the perfect Sunday in London, you can hightail it to Greenwich.

Greenwich is more a suburb than a neighborhood, but please don't ignore it. The town of

Greenwich is not beautiful; I find it charming, but that's because I love the combination of flea markets, crafts fairs, and historical sights, and it has special family memories for me from one perfect summer when Mike, Aaron, and I lived in Greenwich.

The village is on the regular tourist beat because the *Cutty Sark* is anchored here and there are other significant sights—like the Old Royal Observatory, the National Maritime Museum, and the one-time royal residence the Queen's House, designed by Inigo Jones and restored rather recently.

If you're as interested in the culture as the shopping, you may want to buy a Greenwich Day Passport, which is a combined admission ticket that saves you money if you're doing the whole lot. (The Royal Naval College does not charge admission.)

A more significant sight, if you ask me, is the crafts fair held in the Victorian covered market in the center of town. There is a High Street (it leads from the train station into town), but there is no regular high-street shopping, no branch stores of any multiples. . . no, there's not even a BOOTS or an M & S. Nada. Locals have to go to Blackheath to shop, and they don't even have a lot of multiples there. Greenwich is simply a string of dealers who sell crafts and vintage clothes and junk and used furniture and more junk, and I adore it.

Take the train from Charing Cross; the price of the ride is included in your Travelcard (see page 33). Please note that there is much talk about extending the tube to what is called "East Greenwich" and if that ever happens, or when that happens, you may want to try that alternative to the train. You can also do as I do: take the boat from Charing Cross pier. It docks beside the *Cutty Sark* in the heart of downtown Greenwich.

CHAPTER FOUR

LONDON RESOURCES

The British Big Names

Buying British is the very essence of shopping in London; buying British that's on sale and comes with a VAT refund borders on genius—if you can manage without going too far over your U.S. duty allowance.

Those British big names with stores all over the world may have altered prices to be the same in all venues; check prices before you leave home. Those brands without U.S. distribution stand to offer the best bargain.

Note that due to the recession, various big-name designers have given up their boutiques. Those who are featured in department stores are not listed below. Also note that the scene changes dramatically: one day Victor Edelstein closes, another day Roland Klein goes back into business. You need a scorecard to keep the players straight.

AQUASCUTUM

The "other" BURBERRYS, Aquascutum offers an alternative to cream, beige, red, and black plaid. Established in 1851, Aquascutum has grown from a tiny cottage industry to a major international name. Most people who go to London for the first time want to come home with an Aquascutum or Burberrys raincoat. The Aquascutum line includes skirts, sweaters, and any accessory you could imagine. Instead of a plaid like Burberrys, Aquascutum is known for their checkered pattern.

AQUASCUTUM

100 Regent Street, W1 (Tube: Piccadilly Circus)

ASPREY

Asprey isn't a designer name, but is nonetheless one of the big names of London. Essentially, they sell expensive *tchotchkes*—pens, leathergoods, some luggage, little this-and-thats for wedding presents and presentation gifts. Just your average blue-blood, British version of Tiffany & Co. without the seriously big-time jewels, although they certainly do have jewels.

They have a store in New York, with prices to match—so if you're looking for a elegant gift, Asprey is the place to go while in London. Even if you buy zip, go just to gawk.

Since any gift you buy from Asprey has a high-status message, you may do very well here for the kind of business gifts that have to look like money, but you hope to get a good buy on. On a recent visit, I found something that might fall into this category: a small magnifying glass that rotates in and out of its own leather case (£30).

ASPREY

165–169 New Bond Street, W1 (Tube: Green Park)

LAURA ASHLEY

Ashley has had a lot of ups and downs in the past few years, partly due to Lady Laura's death, but they are very much back on track. Americans who love the Laura Ashley look, unite and spend your money here. Those who loathe it, please reconsider with a visit to the Regent Street store. Much of the line is made up of pure country classics and has nothing to do with little flowers.

Regular prices at regular retail in London are substantially less than in the U.S. Some of this stock is not sold in the U.S.

The line encompasses everything that has to do with the home and also a complete line of dresses, kids' wear, and sleepwear. Oh yes, they even have hats.

The home furnishings department is the best. Chintz fabrics cost less per meter here, but bed linens from U.S. makers can be cheaper at home. Each store has its own close-out policy—you may see baskets filled with discontinued wallpapers (these are sold in double rolls, for added bargains) that sell for £5. Usually there is enough of one or two patterns to paper a small room. This is one of the world's best deals.

Two extra thoughts:

- In the Regent Street store, which is the single best store Ashley has in London, there is a sofa by the front door. Feel free to park your husband or kids here or just take a break if you're pooped.

- The Regent Street store has clothing on the street level and home furnishings upstairs; the store on Harriet Street (right off Sloane Street, around the corner from HARVEY NICHOLS) is devoted entirely to home furnishings. Other branch stores do not have as good of a selection of home furnishings.

LAURA ASHLEY

7–9 Harriet Street, SW1 (home furnishings only) (Tube: Knightsbridge)

35–36 Bow Street, Covent Garden, WC2 (Tube: Covent Garden)

256–258 Regent Street, W1 (Tube: Oxford Circus)

MacMillan House, Kensington High Street, W8 (Tube: High Street Kensington)

449–451 Oxford Street, W1 (Tube: Marble Arch or Bond Street)

120 King's Road, SW3 (Tube: Sloane Square)

BETTY BARCLAY

Hip, hip, hooray! for Betty—she's made the breakthrough from department stores into her own shop; to do this during hard times tells you just how talented she is. Barclay is one of the Brit Brat Pack of young, hip designers who made it: her clothes are spicy without being too outré to wear.

BETTY BARCLAY
99 New Bond Street, W1 (Tube: Bond Street)

BURBERRYS

A Burberrys purchase sums up the British fashion consciousness: the style is classic, the product is well-made, and it will last a lifetime (if you don't leave it on the train).

There are actually two shops in Mayfair; the line is also sold at zillions of sources and is readily available in the U.S., and even at the London airport. The big Regent Street shop is multilevel, and if you love the signature cream, camel, red, and black tartan plaid that has become a status symbol to some, you will be in heaven.

If you are expecting bargains, you can tour the store quickly and find your way out. (There is a factory outlet in Woodbury Common near Harriman, New York).

Should you be ready to make the big raincoat purchase, please come prepared with numbers (style and price) from home and, if you are really serious, come to London specifically during the sale season. With a sale and a VAT refund, you may save money. But you will also have to pay duty, so go figure. You can also purchase sweaters, hats, shawls, umbrellas, scarves, and luggage to match your trench coat. There is even a special mini-trench for the five-and-up set. If you're looking for the last word in Burberrys logo merchandise, note that they have sunglasses patterned in their traditional check to match the raincoat at a mere £60. (For the sunglasses, not the raincoat.)

You can get traditional English fashions here as well as bespoke suits. Some items in the store, such as the umbrella, seem to be outrageously expensive ($50), while others seem quite reasonable.

The Haymarket Street store is smaller, more intimate, sort of more British, and it possesses a large children's department. It's conveniently located a few doors away from an American Express office.

BURBERRYS

165 Regent Street, W1 (Tube: Piccadilly Circus)

18–22 Haymarket, SW1 (Tube: Piccadilly Circus)

CAROLINE CHARLES

Think taffeta and silk and dress-up and Princess Diana and veddy-veddy-but-still-gorgeous, and you've got the edge on Caroline Charles. Think Ascot and The Season and just the right hat-and-suit combination. You're back at Caroline Charles. There is an unwritten rule with British women that you can't go wrong with Caroline Charles, so if you're trying to impress the natives, one-stop shopping will do it.

CAROLINE CHARLES

55 Beauchamp Place, SW3 (Tube: Knightsbridge)

JASPER CONRAN

One of the more inventive of the young set of designers, with lines that vary tremendously from season to season, but always show a creative touch and a distinctive style. For the woman who doesn't want to look ordinary. He always does a range of simple, drop-dead chic black dresses with various necklines to flatter any figure.

JASPER CONRAN

303 Brompton Road, SW3 (Tube: South Kensington)

ALFRED DUNHILL

This is the largest and most extensive collection of Dunhill products in what I would call the mother store, but with the heavy-duty masculine image of the store, I guess I have to call it the father store.

The shop actually looks a little more like a Dunhill museum than a retail store. Nevertheless, the merchandise is absolutely top-of-the-line as far as quality goes. Note that people in Britain (and continental Europe) still smoke, so those wonderful Dunhill lighters are still quite an item. Americans have been concentrating on pens instead. There's also a complete line of ready-to-wear goods and leathergoods and, of course, cigars.

In fact, Dunhill is probably most famous as a tobacconist. Once again, the quality is aimed at the top of the market. The cigars are stored in a climate-controlled room to ensure freshness; pipe tobaccos are available for sampling. Dunhill also has a beautiful line of humidors, or will convert your prized antique box into one for you. *Remember*: It is illegal to bring Cuban cigars into the U.S.

ALFRED DUNHILL

30 Duke Street, SW1 (Tube: Piccadilly Circus or Green Park)

NICOLE FARHI

Don't let this foreign-sounding name throw you off the track: Farhi has arrived on the scene as a very acceptable designer to provide your clothes for a British fashion statement (almost an oxymoron) that still works for the horse-and-hedge set. This British designer does the elegant-working-woman look with New York panache and would fit well into the American scene. The tailored clothes are rich and simple, always elegant but with sporty comfort. Branch stores are popping up so frequently that she may soon be considered a multiple.

NICOLE FARHI

25–26 St. Christopher's Place, W1 (Tube: Bond Street)

193 Sloane Street, SW1 (Tube: Knightsbridge)

27 Hampstead High Street, NW3 (Tube: Hampstead)

12 Floral Street, WC2 (Tube: Covent Garden)

MARGARET HOWELL

Margaret Howell offers—to me—the epitome of British casual classy dressing. The clothes are expensive but so chic and elegant, so much the real subtext of what Ralph Lauren has always been able to capture and recreate. There are London dress-up clothes, but this resource is best for more casual everyday clothes and for weekend chic—casual sweaters (hand-knit), twin sets, jackets, coats. One of the best in Britain for the right stuff.

MARGARET HOWELL

29 Beauchamp Place, SW3 (Tube: Knightsbridge)

BETTY JACKSON

Known for wearable clothes, especially separates, Betty Jackson was in the forefront of the wave of hip, young London designers who could sell to U.S. department stores. Now she's made a name for herself with clothes that real people want to buy. She likes longer skirts and snappy designs that speak loudly but don't shout.

BETTY JACKSON

311 Brompton Road, SW3 (Tube: South Kensington)

JAEGER

Jaeger is a basic, classic British resource— sold in their own shops and in many department stores. They have a way with wools in particular and stride the fine line between boring English clothes and high fashion. For quality, you can always trust Jaeger. I like to buy the women's wear when I can afford it; the men's clothes usually leave me cold. . . they're for thin men with European bodies.

The shop on Regent Street is almost a department store. Not only is this shop easy to find, it also has everything, including hats and accessories. One of the good things about the Jaeger line is that it is totally color-coordinated each season, so you can buy a complete wardrobe of interchangeable pieces (great for travel); the bad news is that if you don't like the color palette for a season, you're out of luck. I've seen some summer combinations that I would categorize as too British for my taste or for continental European taste.

But you'll never go wrong when they do navy and white, or with their blacks, reds, and neutrals. Many items are good travel basics.

The most Jaeger fun you'll ever have is during the January sales when you can hit department stores (HARRODS has a good selection) and Jaeger boutiques. One warning: Jaeger may cost less in the U.S.! Shop carefully. There's a Jaeger boutique in the mall near where I live; sometimes I get better prices there, although not as big a selection.

JAEGER

204 Regent Street, W1 (Tube: Piccadilly Circus or Oxford Circus)

JOSEPH

Joseph Ettedgui is now holding his own after big changes with some of his Joseph lines. I must confess that I feel old and battered, hit hard by the financial tides, when I realize that the Joseph Tricot line and stores have bitten the dust. JOSEPH POUR LA MAISON and various other Josephs around town survive. The man is incredibly inventive and creative; his nest of stores in Brompton Cross can still give you a visual stimulation that defines the best in hot British fashion.

Joseph's look is rich, casual, inventive, and usually layered.

JOSEPH

21 Sloane Street, SW1 (Tube: Knightsbridge)

88 Peterborough Road, SW6 (Brompton Cross flagship store. Tube: South Kensington)

130 Draycott Avenue, SW3 (near Brompton Cross. Tube: South Kensington)

MULBERRY

Mulberry has a small shop of their own (right off Oxford Street, don't let the address throw you); they also have boutiques in many department stores and wide distribution of their clothes throughout Britain. Although first known as a leathergoods resource (see page 136), Mulberry now has clothes for men and women to complete the look. Indeed, this is a look in much the same vein as Ralph Lauren's country chic, and it is rich and fabulous. It's also expensive.

MULBERRY

11/12 Gee's Court (off St. Christopher's Place), W1 (Tube: Bond Street)

BRUCE OLDFIELD

The Princess of Wales brought Bruce Oldfield into the spotlight, but he has been a British social secret for many years. He is most admired for his fabulous ball gowns and luxurious evening wear, which are anything but plain or simple. Most of his designs flow and rustle, and if they are black, there is always something glistening attached. Located in the heart of Sloane Ranger chic, Oldfield offers both a retail and a bespoke operation.

BRUCE OLDFIELD

27 Beauchamp Place, SW3 (Tube: Knightsbridge)

EDINA RONAY

First known for her small sweater shop on King's Road and her famous last name, Ronay began designing a full line of clothing a few years ago and hasn't looked back. The clothes are rich, lush, somewhat dramatic, and on the crease between what you would call hot London fashion and hot Milano fashion.

EDINA RONAY

141 King's Road, SW3 (Tube: Sloane Square)

PAUL SMITH

One of the kingpins of Covent Garden retail, Paul Smith is also one of the purveyors of the Witty Britty look in menswear. What makes these conservative clothes work so well is the marvelous array of colors they are made in. You can find a great selection of tweed suits, sports coats, corduroy pants, and shoes. Prices are moderate to high; free-standing store in Manhattan pales when compared to the wonders of Londers.

PAUL SMITH

41 Floral Street, WC2 (Tube: Covent Garden)

EMMA SOMERSET

Emma Somerset does not really belong in a list called British Big Names, but I have no list for British Medium Names. She is well-known to a small segment of the population that has money and likes to overdress. The look is what is socially acceptable for The Season and more. If you are American and are buying to impress a British audience and want advice on dressy affairs, you may want to begin here and see if you can make a match with your own style and Emma's.

EMMA SOMERSET

69 Knightsbridge, SW1 (Tube: Knightsbridge)

TOMASZ STARZEWSKI

OK, so he's got a Polish name, but he's British and he's very hot. For those in England who still have money, this is where to spend it. Princess Di helped make the man's reputation by buying into his beaded couture; there is also a ready-to-wear line. British *Vogue* calls him "the darling of the ballroom." The reason he's such a hit, aside from his talent, is the fact that his couture costs 60% less than everyone else's. A dress that would cost $15,000 elsewhere is a mere $5,000 here. You can get a dinner suit to swoon for in the £500 price range. And you'll wear it for twenty years.

TOMASZ STARZEWSKI

15–17 Pont Street, SW1 (Tube: Sloane Square or Knightsbridge)

VIVIENNE WESTWOOD

When American fashion lion John Fairchild made up his list of the most influential and important designers of our time, Vivienne Westwood headed it up. Fairchild calls her the designer's designer because more mainstream designers are influenced by her bright and fresh ideas. She invents shapes, moods, and concepts of dressing and produces slightly way-out clothes that age well, though they are more for the young and monied.

VIVIENNE WESTWOOD

60 Davies Street, W1 (Tube: Bond Street)

Hip & Hot

WORKERS FOR FREEDOM

Although they have a reputation as the wild kids on the block, this Soho house actually makes very chic and wearable clothes that are not cheap. They may be on the cutting edge, but they are not too outré to be worn well by middle-aged matrons wanting to make a fashion statement. After all, the designers Graham Fraser and Richard Nott used to work for VALENTINO. This is not particularly a teen resource; the prices are very high. I think it's more for movie and rock stars.

WORKERS FOR FREEDOM

4 Lower John Street, W1 (Tube: Piccadilly Circus)

RED OR DEAD

This is a teen and 'tween resource and is so popular that it's on the way to becoming a multiple. They also influence other designers with their big contribution to street fashion. My fourteen-year-old friend Serena, queen of a Manhattan prep school, used to send to Red or Dead for her Doc Martens before they were available in New York.

Red or Dead has a range from expensive to inexpensive clothes that are considered on the cutting edge. The Kensington High Street shop is virtually next door to HYPER HYPER and across from KENSINGTON MARKET, making this the only place in town you need bring your teen or 'tween. Actually, all store locations are in precisely the right place for the market—there's one near Covent Garden and another near my least favorite place in London, Camden Town. Shoes, accessories, and items that kids call clothes. Ahem.

RED OR DEAD

36 and 49 Kensington High Street, W8 (Tube: High Street Kensington)

33 Neal Street, WC2 (Tube: Covent Garden)

186 Camden High Street, NW1 (Tube: Camden Town)

STIRLING COOPER

This is a cheapie multiple, but they sell top-dog looks for teens and prices are conducive to throwaway fashion: black leather and studs. A little more mainstream than RED OR DEAD.

STIRLING COOPER

Westone Mall, Oxford Street, W1 (Tube: Bond Street)

MISS SELFRIDGE

Alright, alright, so my middle-aged, middle-class roots are showing. There is nothing truly young, hip, or imaginative about Miss Selfridge.

It is a copycat store and a mass merchandiser at that. It is the Limited Express for the Doc Marten set. But surely I've got to give the devil his due. This is a fabulous store; it's a marvelous resource and I suggest that every women in Britain, no matter what her age, check it out.

The clothes are cheap (mostly, anyway)—they're not well-made, but they are cutting-edge copies. There's a line of makeup and accessories; there's the whole look in a box. I'd like to open a chain of these stores in the U.S. and laugh all the way to the bank.

Miss Selfridge is a multiple; it is a branch of the SELFRIDGES department store. There are free-standing Miss Selfridge stores on every high street in Britain and all over London. The best one is attached to the side of the Selfridges department store on Oxford Street. You may enter through the store's front door on Oxford Street and work your way to the right from inside the store if the front doors are to your back. Or simply enter Miss Selfridge directly from Duke Street, which is the side street.

If you go into a branch store, you may not get the whole range the way I want you to. . . and then you might think I'm nuts to rave the way I do.

MISS SELFRIDGE
40 Duke Street (flagship store), W1 (Tube: Bond Street)

75 Brompton Road, SW3 (Tube: Knightsbridge)

42 Kensington High Street, W8 (Tube: High Street Kensington)

HYPER HYPER
Whether you like avant-garde fashion or not, this is like a trip to a museum of visual delights on Mars. Take teens and adolescents with you. . . and your camera. Street fashion is blooming in London and is rapidly being absorbed into

the American culture and the mainstream. The big New York department stores estimate that over 50% of their merchandise comes from London now.

The best buys in London are on unknown designer goods. Many of these unknowns sell their work for $500 a pop—so not everything is a steal. But if you are the kind of person who seeks a unique design before a well-known brand name, check out some of the up-and-coming stars and get yourself over to Hyper Hyper.

These clothes are not just for twenty-year-olds, by the way. I saw plenty of things suitable for people like me. Hmmmm.

Clean restrooms: in the rear of the first floor near the cafe. A great pit stop, by the way. Not the toilets, the whole place.

HYPER HYPER
26–40 Kensington High Street, W8 (Tube: High Street Kensington)

X
Sometimes referred to as Department X, this store is best recognized by the big X in a circle on the front window. . . which might not be that easy to spot because so much else is going on in the front window. Never fear. Your teens will pick up the vibes from down the block and march you right in the door. This is a member of the NEXT chain, and there are a few of these 'tweenage stores around the U.K.; whether or not you or yours wear these clothes, you owe it to history to take a look. This is the hip video look par excellence, and it is truly fabulous, in sort of a rock-and-roll way. Don't miss it.

X
189 Oxford Street, W1 (Tube: Oxford Circus)

ACADEMY
One of the best shops on King's Road is Academy, which isn't large but does have a wide

selection of up-and-coming English designer fashions. There's also a Soho branch.

ACADEMY

188A King's Road, SW3 (Tube: Sloane Square)

15 Newburgh Street, W1 (Tube: Oxford Circus)

RITVA WESTENIUS

Perhaps she should win a prize for her unusual name as well as her unusual wedding designs. If you are looking to become Cinderella in your next life or are planning the wedding to end all weddings, you'll find old-fashioned elegance as well as poufs of net attached to satin tops in a look that no one back home can duplicate. The clothes offer tiers of skirts with fairy-tale embroideries and details. I find these clothes too sophisticated for a teenager; you need to be a middle-aged teenager to really appreciate them.

RITVA WESTENIUS

153 Fulham Road, SW3 (Tube: Fulham Broadway)

DAVID FIEDLEN

If you have been ambivalent about a trip to see the hotshot designers of King's Road, but you crave the best and the brightest, hop right on the tube and repeat after me: David Fiedlen, David Fiedlen, David Fiedlen. The shop is small, the talent is huge.

Fiedlen does wild clothes and swirling hand-painted nonsense in high-fashioned statements that will make your jaw drop open. Not for your mother or the Queen Mother.

DAVID FIEDLEN

137 King's Road, SW3 (Tube: Sloane Square)

ANNE HIGGINS

The thrill of my last visit to London was discovering Anne Higgins' out-of-the-way (but not inconvenient) shop. Because she is right around the corner from the PORTOBELLO ROAD MARKET, Saturday is as good a day as any to visit her.

Higgins makes hand-knits that have a medieval feel to them. There's sweaters, coats, and tunics—each is truly a piece of art. Considering what you are buying, the prices (starting around £150) aren't bad at all.

There's no question in my mind that she will become one of the best-known designers in London.

ANNE HIGGINS
118 Kensington Park Road, W11 (Tube: Notting Hill Gate)

GEORGINA VON ETZDORF

Right in the heart of Sloane Square shopping, von Etzdorf's shop is no bigger than a sneeze, but is filled with her hand-painted silks and accessories that will label you as an original.

GEORGINA VON ETZDORF
149 Sloane Street, SW1 (Tube: Sloane Square)

International and American Big Names

No shopping mecca is more international than London; no international resource can consider itself in the big time if it doesn't have a London address listed on a glossy shopping bag. But there are very few bargains here in international merchandise, unless you hit a big sale and can then get the VAT refund. Most likely you'll find a small savings of less than 10%. (But, of course, don't forget the VAT, which often makes large expenditures more worthwhile.)

While American retailers and chain stores are opening right and left in London, this is to take a piece of the British market—these stores offer merchandise that is much more expensive in Britain than in the U.S. I go to GAP stores all the time, just to laugh. The prices in pounds are exactly the same as at home in U.S. dollars. (If you want to bring a gift to someone in Britain, buy it at the Gap in the U.S.)

Now then, I had tea with my British friend Martine, who goes to New York a few times a year on business. She told me many sagas of hunting down American brands in the U.S. in order to save money, only to find the items were *exactly* the same price in London. The items she priced at exactly the same in New York and London were Ralph Lauren wallpaper and a DKNY blazer.

I must also report that in the Adrienne Vittadini nook in HARVEY NICHOLS, I saw merchandise I'd never seen in a U.S. store. Granted, I don't live in the shipping department of a major mall—but it seemed incredible to go to London to fall in love with an Adrienne Vittadini outfit. (At full British retail, no less.) Academics may want to note that one of the ways Harvey Nichols likes to differentiate itself from other London department stores is that they are heavily committed to American designers and American brands.

International Big Names

GIORGIO ARMANI
    178 Sloane Street, SW1 (Tube: Knightsbridge)

AGNÉS B.
    111 Fulham Road, SW3 (Tube: South Kensington)

BENETTON/STEFANEL
    328 Oxford Street, W1 (among many) (Tube: Oxford Circus)

BLEYLE
    40 Sloane Street, SW1 (Tube: Knightsbridge)

PIERRE CARDIN
    20 Old Bond Street, W1 (Tube: Bond Street)

CÉLINE
    28 New Bond Street, W1 (Tube: Bond Street)
    27 Brompton Road, SW3 (Tube: Knightsbridge)

CERUTTI 1881
76 New Bond Street, W1 (Tube: Bond Street)

CHANEL
26 Old Bond Street, W1 (Tube: Bond Street)
31 Sloane Street, SW1 (Tube: Knightsbridge)

DESCAMPS
197 Sloane Street, SW1 (Tube: Knightsbridge)

ADOLFO DOMINGUEZ
57 South Molton Street, W1 (Tube: Bond Street)

ESCADA
67 New Bond Street, W1 (Tube: Bond Street)

FENDI
37 Sloane Street, SW1 (Tube: Knightsbridge)

LOUIS FÉRAUD
73 New Bond Street, W1 (Tube: Bond Street)

FERRAGAMO
24 Old Bond Street, W1 (Tube: Bond Street)

GIANFRANCO FERRÉ
20 Brook Street, W1 (Tube: Green Park or Bond Street)

FOGAL
36 New Bond Street, W1 (Tube: Bond Street)

GENNY
19 South Molton Street, W1 (Tube: Bond Street)

GUCCI
33 Old Bond Street, W1 (Tube: Bond Street)
17–18 Sloane Street, SW1 (Tube: Knightsbridge)

HERMÈS
155 New Bond Street, W1 (Tube: Bond Street)
179 Sloane Street, SW1 (Tube: Knightsbridge)

JACADI
473 Oxford Street, W1 (Tube: Marble Arch)

KENZO
   15 Sloane Street, SW1 (Tube: Knightsbridge)

KARL LAGERFELD
   173 New Bond Street, W1 (Tube: Bond Street)
   201 Sloane Street, SW1 (Tube: Knightsbridge)

LALIQUE
   162 New Bond Street, W1 (Tube: Bond Street)

LLADRÓ
   194 Piccadilly, W1 (Tube: Piccadilly Circus)

LOEWE
   130 Old Bond Street, W1 (Tube: Bond Street)

MAX MARA
   153 New Bond Street, W1 (Tube: Bond Street)

ISSEY MIYAKE
   21 Sloane Street, SW1 (Tube: Knightsbridge)
   270 Brompton Road, SW3 (Tube: Knightsbridge)

OILILY
   10 Sloane Street, SW1 (Tube: Knightsbridge)

OLIVER
   55 South Molton Street, W1 (Tube: Bond Street)

RODIER
   106 Brompton Road, SW3 (Tube: Knightsbridge)

YVES SAINT-LAURENT
   135 and 137 (men) New Bond Street, W1 (Tube: Bond Street)
   33 Sloane Street, SW1 (Tube: Knightsbridge)

SOULEIADO
   171 Fulham Road, SW3 (Tube: South Kensington)

TRUSSARDI
   50 South Molton Street, W1 (Tube: Bond Street)

VALENTINO
   160 New Bond Street, W1 (Tube: Bond Street)
   174 Sloane Street, SW1 (Tube: Knightsbridge)

GIANNI VERSACE
   34-35 Old Bond Street (flagship store), W1
(Tube: Bond Street)
   80 and 92 Brompton Road, SW3 (Tube:
Knightsbridge or South Kensington)

LOUIS VUITTON
   149 New Bond Street, W1 (Tube: Bond Street)
   198 Sloane Street, SW1 (Tube: Knightsbridge)

ERMENEGILDO ZEGNA
   37 New Bond Street, W1 (Tube: Bond Street)

American Big Names

COACH
   8 Sloane Street, SW1 (Tube: Knightsbridge)

CRABTREE & EVELYN
   6 Kensington Church Street, W8 (Tube: High
Street Kensington)

THE DISNEY STORE
   140–144 Regent Street, W1 (Tube: Oxford
Circus)

ESPRIT
   6 Sloane Street, SW1 (Tube: Knightsbridge)

THE GAP
   208 Regent Street, W1 (among several) (Tube:
Oxford Circus)

GAP KIDS
   146 Regent Street, W1 (among several) (Tube:
Oxford Circus)

TOMMY HILFIGER
   18 South Molton Street, W1 (Tube: Bond
Street)

KEN LANE
   66 South Molton Street, W1 (Tube: Bond
Street)

POLO/RALPH LAUREN
143 New Bond Street, W1 (Tube: Bond Street)

ORVIS
27 Sackville Street, W1 (Tube: Piccadilly Circus)

TIFFANY & CO.
25 Old Bond Street, W1 (Tube: Bond Street)

TIMBERLAND
72 New Bond Street, W1 (Tube: Bond Street)

Department Stores

American department stores are mostly patterned on British ones, so you will feel right at home at just about any department store in London. All are in big, old-fashioned buildings and offer the kind of social security that enables you to know you could live in them. Most of them have several restaurants or tearooms. They all have clean bathrooms.

During the Christmas shopping days, department stores are open later than usual, which may mean until 7 P.M. Whoop de do. They are rarely open until 9 P.M. Other than at Christmastime, department stores have one night a week—either Wednesday or Thursday—during which they stay open until 7 P.M, or possibly 8 P.M., and just maybe—this is wild and unusual—9 P.M., but that's more than likely to be some kind of a counterculture, alternative retailing source and is hardly ever a traditional department store.

All department stores have export desks that will help you with the VAT forms; all department stores allow you to collect your receipts over a period of time to qualify for the VAT. Some may charge £4–£6 for administrative work on a VAT form. The minimum amount of money spent needing to qualifying for a VAT refund varies dramatically from department store to department store.

When you go to the VAT desk in any given department store, allow some time for not only the paperwork, but also (if it's in season) the line of others waiting to do the same thing. If you can move right through, the process will take about ten minutes. Do have your passport on hand or know your number by heart.

HARRODS

Quite simply, I have a love/hate thing with Harrods. There is no question that this store is a landmark and that it offers one hell of a lot of merchandise. The china department and the food halls are what becomes a legend most; the children's toy department is almost as good as HAMLEYS.

What I hate about Harrods is that I think they've just stopped trying to be innovative; they just keep on keeping on. HARVEY NICHOLS, which isn't anything like Harrods in reality, is at least young and alive and changing with the times. Harrods is plain old dependable vanilla ice cream.

Upon entering Harrods, you may find it hard to imagine that Henry Charles Harrod began his store as a little grocery business in 1849. From a small family business with a staff of two, Harrods has grown to be the most complete department store in London. You probably read the Jeffrey Archer book all about it.

The food halls, located on the ground floor, are internationally known, with seventeen departments in all. The department store itself covers four-and-a-half acres of land and has fifteen acres of selling space. This is good to remember when your feet are telling you to stop, but you don't even feel that you have made a dent in the store.

Ground floor: food halls, men's fashions, fabrics, perfume and cosmetics, fashion accessories, jewelry, stationery, and clocks; *one*: designer clothing, a definite must-stop; *two*: china, glass, books, records, housewares; *three*: furniture; *four*: toys, several stops for tea, and a shop for teens called WAY IN, which is fabulous. (This is where I bought the banana toothbrush to send Aaron at camp; £5.) *Five*: sporting goods, hair and beauty.

There's a large selling salon on the lower level, near the gifts for the home and the theater ticket office, featuring just Harrods merchandise and souvenirs. You've never seen so many choices. Some are too expensive for what they are; there are many, many items selling for £10 and less. There's another small souvenir salon on the fourth floor, but it's not spacious or well-displayed; hit the basement via the escalator in the middle of the store.

Don't forget that Harrods prides itself on being a full-service department store. Because of that, on the lower level, you will find a complete travel agency, export department, London Tourist Board, bank, and theater ticket agency. There is a hair salon upstairs on five, which opens at 9 A.M., even though the store opens at 10 A.M.

When you need some refreshment, Harrods has five restaurants, three of them on the fourth floor. I was offended by just how tacky the main "Regency"-style room is—it's called the Georgian Restaurant—if I had children and thought I was bringing them to Harrods for tea as a treat, I would have cried right into the teapot. But then, there is the all-you-can-eat rule, so it is something to think about.

If you need a food hamper to complete your Season, order ahead from Harrods. Prices begin around £20 per person; kids' menu available at £12.50. There is a deposit on the traditional wicker basket, the dishes, and the cutlery. Call 71-730-1234, extension 2058.

HARRODS
   Knightsbridge, SW1 (Tube: Knightsbridge)

SELFRIDGES

There was one brief shining moment when you could almost compare Selfridges to HAR-RODS as the place where you really could get everything. If Harrods has stood still on the time line to modernity, Selfridges has gone downhill. Except for the fabulous MISS SELFRIDGE business (see page 105), this store is a big yawn.

But wait! They do carry many of the same basics of life that aren't flashy but may be on your shopping list, and the requirement for a VAT refund is £75, not £150 like at Harrods.

Harry Gordon Selfridge was an American who believed that the European market could benefit from a full-service department store. He was unable to convince his employers at Marshall Field's in Chicago of that fact, so in 1909 he opened his own version of the American department store. Now Selfridges covers an entire city block. Like Harrods, the store is filled with concessions of big names; there are branches of the multiples within the store itself—such as THORNTON'S, the candy chain, which has its own counter; HOLLAND & BARRETT, the health-food chain, has its own department, etc.

Basement: housewares; *ground floor*: food halls (not as interesting as Harrods, but OK if you want picnic supplies), cosmetics, some accessories, some men's accessories, MISS SELFRIDGE; *one*: export bureau, men's clothing; *two*: women's clothing (designers); *three*: kids' clothing; *four*: sportswear.

Selfridges has three restaurants, four coffee shops, and a juice bar. At 3:30 P.M., a gong is rung and teatime is on. It's sort of like that Colombian coffee commercial we watch on the telly: Attention Selfridges shoppers—Tea is now being served.

SELFRIDGES

400 Oxford Street, W1 (Tube: Marble Arch or Bond Street)

LIBERTY

I have a simple motto that repeats itself in the back of my brain each time the Tudor-style Liberty building comes into my line of sight: "Give me Liberty or give me death."

You haven't been shopping in London if you haven't visited Liberty, and I mean the mother store on Regent Street, not a branch store.

Originally opened in 1875 by Arthur Lazenby, who did not play James Bond no matter what you remember, Liberty is a topsy-turvy department store with nooks and crannies and salons and other parts of the store hidden up and down staircases and around corners and through glass-leaded doors.

Liberty is known worldwide for its Liberty prints, which are sold as fabrics or made up as gift items. Indeed, a basic souvenir or gift item from London is *something* made in a Liberty print. I've got scads of pairs of earrings; the little snapper doodads that hold on your mittens are one of my faves. Liberty boxer shorts are chic, but expensive.

What Liberty is best at is first drama and charm, then fabric.

The store is a visual feast and is surely the best department store in London. Don't miss it. Be sure you are in the "Tudor Building" part of the store—memories are made of architecture like this! Also check out the ready-to-sew skirts and dresses on the second floor; fabrics and needleworks are on three; linens and housewares are on four; antiques on five. The basement has the housewares, china, and exports from the Far East on which the original Liberty rep was based; there's also a bookstore on the street level *behind* the Tudor store, and then an accessories shop through a door behind that where hair bands and things like that are sold.

LIBERTY

210–220 Regent Street, W1 (Tube: Oxford Circus)

HARVEY NICHOLS

Although Knightsbridge's other department store is much smaller than HARRODS, it makes up for size with quality. Harvey Nichols does not try to be everything to every person. They concentrate their energy on the latest of high fashion for men, women, and children. They are, frankly, a *real* store—not a tourist trap trading on an old reputation. Styles are always the latest, and most of the major design houses are represented; there are lots of American designers.

I must admit that no trip to London is complete for me if I have not gone to the back part of the street level and spent a half hour in the hat department, trying on hats. If you're looking for weird and wonderful hats for Ascot, you may be disappointed. These hats go from bland to sophisticated, but do not pass the weird or wonderful category. Prices range from £50 to £500; the selection is as good for The Season as it is in the fall, which is the best commentary and recommendation I can give anyone. I have worked the hat department of every department store in London and this is the single best one. It's not huge and it's not overly dramatic—it's simply solid.

I like the home decor floor with its own NINA CAMPBELL boutique; the fifth floor—named The Fifth Floor—has the new food hall and a hotshot restaurant called, get this, The Fifth Floor. There is also a place for coffee, a snack, or quick lunch between the fancy eats and the food halls, also on the fifth floor.

I wish I could tell you what all the fuss about the food halls is. Harrods' food halls are a genuine emotional experience; this is like a trip to Zabar's in Manhattan. This is not much more than a trip to your local deli or grocery store; SAINSBURY'S (a big British grocery chain) is just as much fun. But then, it's a practical grocery store. There are ready-made-up foods that made for *le picnique*; there are exotic-blend housebrand teas (black cherry) for £2 a box—a perfect gift for someone at home.

Lower level: men's; *one*: hats, cosmetics, accessories; *two and three*: women's fashions; *four*: home furnishings; *five*: food hall and restaurants.

HARVEY NICHOLS
Knightsbridge (corner of Sloane Street), SW1 (Tube: Knightsbridge)

FORTNUM & MASON

Your visit to Fortnum & Mason actually begins before you enter the store—the clock outside is very, very famous, so stand back and take a look. Then go through the revolving doors into a food emporium of fun.

Like many of the old department stores, Fortnum & Mason began (in 1707) as a grocery store; its founder, William Fortnum, was a footman in the household of Queen Anne. He collected and traded the used candle ends from the palace, and saved his funds until he could open his own shop. He persuaded Hugh Mason, who owned a small shop in St. James's Market, to become his partner, and thus began Fortnum & Mason.

The firm's great success during the empire's reign had to do with supplying goods not only in London, but also to the British families overseas. In the Victorian era, Fortnum & Mason also became famous for their fine-quality preserved fruits, jellies, and hams. Their hampers are a must for a status Christmas gift or for the picnics that you must eat (in the car park, no less) when you attend Royal Ascot or any of the events of The Season. Order ahead!

After World War I, Fortnum & Mason became

a full department store with clothes and handbags and normal merchandise. That is not what I
go there to buy, but you can wardrobe yourself as
well as your pantry. I often eat at the Fountain,
although singles beware: parties of two or more
are seated more quickly, so it may behoove you
to get friendly with another single in the line.

There are food tastings and various promotions; there is a midsummer sale and a January
sale; there is sometimes what they call an
"Account Customers Preview Day"—it's an
evening event that allows you a first go at the
sale goodies. You must buy a ticket to this event
(£25); call 71-734-8040, extension 572 or 431.

Lower level: china, glass, silver; *ground floor*:
foodstuffs; *one*: ladies' fashions, perfume; *two*:
children's, nursery, toys; *three*: gentlemen; *four*:
antiques.

FORTNUM & MASON
181 Piccadilly, W1 (Tube: Piccadilly Circus)

LILLYWHITES

Lillywhites is a department store for sporting
goods. All brand names (of sportswear and
equipment) are sold, including America's and
Europe's finest. The sport shoe selection is flab-
bergasting. There aren't any bargains in this
store, but the selection is enough to keep your
head spinning at Olympic speed. There is also
equipment and outfitting for sports that are not
played in the U.S., so you can get quite an educa-
tion. Snooker, anyone? Do stop by the "Outdoor
Department," which is housed in what used to be
a ballroom. Golf nuts may want to move into the
newly renovated golf department.

Ground floor: track suits; *one*: shoes; *two*: gym;
three: books, video, ski; *four*: racket sports; *five*:
darts, snooker, water sports, shooting, riding.

LILLYWHITES
Piccadilly Circus, W1 (Tube: Piccadilly Circus)

DEBENHAMS

Of the few look-alike department stores on Oxford Street (there are three or so of them, all of which are virtually indistinguishable from each other), this one is the best and the most American. Debenhams was remodeled a few years ago; it's one of House of Fraser's better middle-class department stores and has enough space around the displays so that you can see the goods and enjoy your spree.

There's a KEITH PROWSE office for theater tickets on the ground floor; VAT desk is downstairs.

Lowest level: restaurants; *ground floor*: cosmetics, accessories; *one*: kids, ladies, Jaeger; *two*: home furnishings; *three*: furniture.

DEBENHAMS

334-338 Oxford Street, W1 (Tube: Oxford Circus)

D.H. EVANS

Just like the old Macy's, or the large department store of your coming-of-age, Evans has a good selection of their own private-label items and many designer names. The ceilings are low and the store is more dense, so it's not as glamorous as other stores.

You'll see things here that you just won't find in other shops (but they are in other House of Fraser stores, such as BARKERS OF KENSINGTON); you'll also find that they billboard midrange designers who can get buried in glitzier stores. It's not the fanciest store you'll find in London, but if you like bread-and-butter clothes, you may want to give it a try. JAEGER boutiques on two floors.

To make themselves stand out in the world, D.H. Evans has teamed up with the computer generation and opened a Computer Superstore on the fifth floor.

Ground floor: cosmetics, accessories, men's

wear; *one*: women's fashions; *two*: kids' clothing,
designers; *three*: fabrics, linens, bath shop; *four*:
silver, kitchen; *five*: computers.

D.H. EVANS
318 Oxford Street, W1 (Tube: Bond Street)

JOHN LEWIS

By the time you get to John Lewis, your eyes
are beginning to cross and you have no solid idea
of why there are so many look-alike department
stores on Oxford Street. I'm not much of a fan of
John Lewis, except they have a good fabric
department and this has always been a source for
me to find high-fashion Alice bands (hair bands)
at very moderate prices—£4–£5.

JOHN LEWIS
278 Oxford Street, W1 (Tube: Bond Street)

BRITISH HOME STORES (BHS)

This is a big department store geared toward
young families on a budget; it's snazzier than
Kmart, but the fashion for career women is from
hunger. The kids' clothes are cute; the home furnishings items are worth a look-see for real-people products.

The main store is on Oxford Street, but there
are branches around London and around U.K.
Tourists can take a pass.

BRITISH HOME STORES (BHS)
252 Oxford Street, W1 (Tube: Bond Street)

DICKINS & JONES

Dickins & Jones is the high-end House of
Fraser entry; because it is on Regent Street it is a
world away from D.H. EVANS, even though there
is some overlap of merchandise. But they sell
YSL earrings for £50 a pair at Dickins & Jones,
whereas this isn't a big item for the D.H. Evans
shopper.

The store specializes in big-name designers
and snazzy clothes. Here you'll find the Yves
Saint-Laurent Variations line as well as the

bridge lines from other designers that may not sell to the U.S. They have two hat departments: both are disappointing!

Ground floor: accessories, cosmetics; *one*: designers; *two*: executive woman; *three*: coats, British collections.

DICKINS & JONES
224 Regent Street, W1 (Tube: Oxford Circus)

FENWICK
With the recession biting into my wallet, I have new respect for Fenwick (say "Fennick"). In fact, I almost count it as my favorite stop on Bond Street. I've shopped Fenwick top to bottom and am happy to say this is a great source for affordable designer bridge lines, cheap-junk fashion looks, and yes, hats.

I found the hat I wore to Aaron's bar mitzvah right here at Fenwick; the hat of my dreams, on sale for £20. That's my kind of price, especially for an important hat. I had to add my own ribbon to the hat (bought in Manhattan for $12, but still. . .), but this one purchase convinced me that I love Fenwick.

I've also bought Betty Barclay here (she does have her own shop now; see page 96) and John Smedley women's knits. The store is not overwhelmingly large, they have clean bathrooms, you can get a coffee or tea or a bite to eat, and the location is yummy.

FENWICK
63 New Bond Street, W1 (Tube: Bond Street)

GENERAL TRADING COMPANY
I guess this is a department store, but it doesn't sell clothes. It's more an old-fashioned emporium—it sells a little of everything in a series of town houses that are strung together into one big funhouse dedicated to the art of whimsy. You go up and down sets of stairs here and there as you wander in and out of connected

salons, finding cute gifts and some souvenirs, imports from Bali, silk flowers, botanical-print wastepaper baskets, pretty umbrellas, etc. The store has anything and everything, including a bridal registry and an interesting tabletop department.

Princess Diana did indeed register here; you have a good memory. This store, by the way, is not in the Sloane Street grouping of big-name boutique branches—don't let the street address throw you—it is very close to PETER JONES, a great department store, and King's Road. You may also have breakfast or lunch here.

GENERAL TRADING COMPANY
144 Sloane Street, SW1 (Tube: Sloane Square)

PETER JONES

I really like Peter Jones for the trimmings, fabrics, and bed linens. That may sound like a strange combination, but these three departments are all strung together and make a great half-hour stop before you tackle King's Road or after you've shopped Sloane Street.

Although this is a full-service department store, I don't shop ready-to-wear here, but I love the sheets and the duvet covers.

The sheets (and duvet covers) come in colors we simply don't get in America—solid colors, but high-fashion solid colors with a range simply not seen in America. There must be five or six different shades of green alone.

PETER JONES
Sloane Square, SW1 (Tube: Sloane Square)

British Multiples

A few successful chain stores dominate British retail. There's one of these shops in every high street, every main shopping neighborhood, or the next new mall. That's why they call them multiples. In the British business press, these stores are referred to as "high-street multiples," because they are usually found on the high street of every town.

Some stores have a hundred (or more) branches; those listed below are either my favorite branch of the store or the ones in the most frequently shopped neighborhoods. Please note that there is some crossover with British Big Names; obviously LAURA ASHLEY is a high-street multiple. I've tried not to duplicate any listings, but there is a thin line between these two categories of merchandise and stores.

AUSTIN REED

A chain of stores selling men's and women's traditional (read: boring) British clothing from the big makers—the place to shop where you know you can't go wrong if the Brit Look is your need. Branch stores tend to be in need of renovation. All the sturdy and steadfast British big names are sold through these stores; you can sometimes bump into something fashionable.

If you have been invited to partake in The Season, if you are going to a social or business function in which you must look British, this is an excellent resource—you can't go wrong. You will find clothing that you will enjoy wearing and which will help you "fit in."

Please note that some branches of Austin Reed open early in the morning for the business crowd running an errand or two on the way to the office.

AUSTIN REED
103-113 Regent Street, W1 (Tube: Piccadilly Circus)

THE BODY SHOP

After a period of disinterest (I found the "green" philosophy of these stores a little too precious), I am now smitten with The Body Shop, especially since I've learned that their products are much cheaper in Britain that in the U.S.

I am particularly fond of their Mango Body Butter (the single best-selling product in the U.S., coincidentally). My friend Olive likes the Avocado Body Butter (same song, different tune).

Olive's husband Barry buys his personal toilet products and skin care items at The Body Shop, relying on a line called Mostly Men. As Barry explains, he's not going to buy a men's product from a fancy cosmetic company, but he wants something better than he could pick up at the local chemist or drugstore.

The shops are easily recognizable by their dark green painted exterior. Inside is a world of environmentally and politically correct soaps, scents, and other beauty products; some aromatherapy products; and a full line of men's products and baby products. Condoms too.

THE BODY SHOP
Covent Garden, WC2 (Tube: Covent Garden)

BOOTS

In the Queen's English, Boots is a chemist. To Americans, Boots is a drugstore. To me, Boots is a way of life. No day in London is complete without a dose of Boots.

What a drugstore: They carry just about everything, although some stores are bigger and better than others. The best thing about Boots is that they have a huge selection of health and beauty aids, usually at reasonable prices. Their house lines offers choices in many pharmaceuticals and beauty products.

There is always a pharmacy, sometimes an optical shop, and always a selection of small appliances such as hair dryers, should you discover that your French model will not work in England. (It won't—different plugs.) You can buy pantyhose here, film, some costume jewelry, or just about any brand of makeup or perfume. Sometimes there are promotions—once I got a free train voucher for a BritRail ticket just for spending £5.

There is a Boots in almost every city in England and Scotland, most often located on the high street. In London, there's a store in every major trading area, although old London hands please note that the great Boots on Regent Street has closed.

BOOTS

Piccadilly Circus, W1 (Tube: Piccadilly Circus)

CRABTREE & EVELYN

It's American; it's American; it's American. Think old-fashioned English and you've got the wonders of Crabtree & Evelyn, a firm that has been successfully selling old-timey packaged soaps, shampoos, shortbreads, potpourri, and teas seemingly for centuries. All of the shops are wood-paneled, with the feel of yesteryear; the firm is so large that there is now a multiple not only in every British city but in every American city as well. The shops are a pleasure to browse; the prices are about the same in the U.K. as at home. I have listed the stores here and not in the American big-name section to help you understand that this is merely a marketing ploy.

CRABTREE & EVELYN

6 Kensington Church Street, W8 (Tube: High Street Kensington)

CULPEPER THE HERBALISTS

Despite the popularity of THE BODY SHOP and CRABTREE & EVELYN, Culpeper the Herbalist has found its niche selling the same kinds of things in a very different manner. The Body Shop and Crabtree & Evelyn are "loud"— they shout their cutie-pie looks and style. Culpeper shops are not as elaborately decorated as the competition, so the stores feel more low-key and down-home.

They offer soaps, essences, and oils, as well as other beauty products. They are very big in aromatherapy. Culpeper sells a wide range of oils

(£2–£15, depending on size and rarity) as well as means to distribute the scent—little pots, rings that sit on top of light bulbs (also sold in the U.S., but less than £2 at Culpeper) and what I consider to be the best-of-show: a small, white, plastic, flat, battery-operated fan which holds a paper pad (extra pads, three for £1) on which you drip a few drops of essential oil. Turn on the fan and *voilà*, the scent lasts for six hours.

You choose the scent based on what aromatherapy techniques you need to accomplish (see page 176); I bought orange because I love the notion, but when I gave Olive the lavender and she told me how nice it was to sleep with the lavender scent, I got hooked. It's fabulous for jet lag.

Back to the fan itself: you can buy the fan for about £8; provide your own AA batteries. You can buy a gift package of fan, lavender oil, and paper scent pad for £12.50. I've never seen anything like this in America; I think it's the single best gift you can give anyone who has everything. I've sent these packages to people in the hospital; they are a marvelous get-well gift.

You can also buy fresh herbs in little pots in season; they have a line of spices and cooking products. Also a range of scented candles; try 'Relaxing' for £4.50 in a clay pot.

CULPEPER THE HERBALISTS
Covent Garden Market, WC2 (Tube: Covent Garden)

HOBBS
An excellent shoe chain for well-made, sporty, and dressy shoes at the top end of the moderate-price range, but not so over-the-top that you can't afford them. Always reliable for fashionable, but not overly chic, footwear. Also handbags.

HOBBS
Convent Garden, WC2 (Tube: Covent Garden)

JANET REGER

If you've ever wondered what the True Brit woman wears under her rather safe and standard clothing, you might be shocked to discover how frilly and fancy her underthings can be. Janet Reger is the Victoria's Secret of the British underwear crowd: more sophisticated than many (and more expensive), but not so pricey and fancy that it's totally out of your range.

JANET REGER

2 Beauchamp Place, SW3 (Tube: South Kensington)

JIGSAW

One of the best examples of what a British multiple can (should) be, Jigsaw is a fashion chain selling hip-but-wearable fashion for women. The line is such that a lot of merchandise is on the cutting edge (which means good, frequent sales) and much of it is for women under forty. Prices are moderate; the stores are always high-tech chic; there's always something to see and be impressed with—even if you are just sizing up the hot looks. This chain is just beginning to move into the international market.

JIGSAW

Covent Garden, WC2 (Tube: Covent Garden)

KNICKERBOX

The Knickerbox business is one of the major success stories in recent retail history: The underwear buyers from MARKS & SPENCER—famous throughout the land—went out on their own and opened Knickerbox. Almost immediately, it became a gigantic multiple with shops in every mall; kiosks in every train station, and even high-street stores in high-rent districts. The underwear (bras, panties, camisoles, etc.) comes in cotton and silken varieties and in jazzy and even risqué styles. Prices are not dirt cheap.

KNICKERBOX
189 Regent Street, W1 (Tube: Oxford Circus)

MISS SELFRIDGE
There is a Miss Selfridge department in the main SELFRIDGES store, but there are numerous free-standing Miss Selfridge stores all over London. Their specialty is the young, kicky look at inexpensive prices—this is a find for teens or those who want to dabble in a trendy look without spending too much money. I go on at great length about this store on page 105.

MISS SELFRIDGE
40 Duke Street, W1 (Tube: Bond Street)

MONSOON
A chain of low-to-moderate-priced women's fashions made in India in current styles but of fabrics inspired by the mother country (India), and therefore gauzy, colorful, sometimes ethnic (but not always), and very distinctive. The look is very popular in the 'tweens-through-twenties set. The business is so gigantic, and so popular during hard times, that there are now spinoffs such as a chain of small stores selling only accessories called ACCESSORIZE and a small chain for dress-up clothes named, appropriately, TWILIGHT.

MONSOON
67 South Molton Street, W1 (Tube: Bond Street)

MOTHERCARE
A gigantic chain of stores selling maternity and brand-new-baby needs as well as kids' clothes and things like strollers and plastic dishes. Well-designed; good quality; moderate prices. There are some stores in the U.S., but they pale compared to even a branch store in the U.K.

MOTHERCARE
461 Oxford Street, W1 (Tube: Marble Arch)

NEXT

Every city in Britain has a handful of Next shops—some sell women's clothes, some sell men's clothes, some sell home furnishings, some sell kids' clothes, some sell accessories to go with the above. Next is a force for the yuppie consumer, selling a total-lifestyle look that is modern, as opposed to the Laura Ashley sweet-flowers routine.

Don't miss their X stores for the teenage set; very avant-garde and hip, with sort of wild architecture. OK, it's not Lloyd's of London, but it's architecturally interesting.

NEXT
160 Regent Street, W1 (Tube: Piccadilly Circus)

JUMPERS

A jumper is a sweater in Britspeak, so this chain just sells sweaters. The look is mass-merchandise, but not on a cheap level. This is not the store for a cashmere twin set; it is where you'll find a solid crew neck in this season's colors or a pictorial knit. Wools in winter; cottons in summer. The James Street address is exactly in front of Covent Garden.

JUMPERS
31 James Street, WC2 (Tube: Covent Garden)

DOROTHY PERKINS

Petite clothes are sold in specialty parts of some of the major department stores, but this high-street multiple is devoted to the smaller sizes and sells clothes for the professional woman at low-to-moderate prices (for Britain, anyway).

DOROTHY PERKINS
311 Oxford Street, W1 (Tube: Oxford Circus)

PRINCIPLES

Hot, with-it fashions at low (for Britain) prices, with plenty of designer knockoffs and in-step accessories. Many of the stores look—from the outside—like NEXT; don't be confused, because the looks inside are definitely different.

PRINCIPLES

The Plaza, Oxford Street, W1 (Tube: Oxford Circus)

THE SOCK SHOP

There is not a train station, underground station, or high street in the U.K. that does not have a branch of The Sock Shop. Despite the popularity of these stores (selling socks and pantyhose, and sometimes underwear and umbrellas), we remain baffled. Yes, the styles are incredibly cute, but there are no bargains.

THE SOCK SHOP

Charing Cross Station, WC2 (Tube: Charing Cross)

THE TIE RACK

The Tie Rack is to necks what the Sock Shop is to feet.

THE TIE RACK

Charing Cross Station, WC2 (Tube: Charing Cross)

WHISTLES

A super, on-the-edge chain with high-fashion looks that have prices too high for the young people who can wear these clothes and prices too high for me, even though I may be a little old for some of this stuff. When droopy is in, they do droopy. When wrinkled is in, they do wrinkled. Very L.A. clothes that actually work in fashion circles in London. I once saw a pink plush chubbie with black stencils of Minnie Mouse. That's the kind of place it is.

WHISTLES

Covent Garden, WC2 (Tube: Covent Garden)

SUSAN WOOLF

I'm not sure if this is a multiple-in-the-making or just a designer store with several branches like

NICOLE FARHI, but Susan Woolf is a great company for fashions for a career woman, or someone who likes a casual, clean line and simple elegance that's not overblown, overly young, or matronly either. The clothes are not inexpensive but they aren't unaffordable—maybe £200 or so for a blazer. Dressier than Ann Taylor but not quite Calvin Klein. A fine choice if you need to fit into British style but still want to be comfortable and chic.

SUSAN WOOLF
9-13 Brompton Road, SW3 (Tube: Knightsbridge)
70 New Bond Street, W1 (Tube: Bond Street)

Shoes and Leathergoods

CHURCH'S SHOES
What did you come to London for, if not to buy Church's shoes for him? These are traditional wingtips and slip-ons at high prices; otherwise enjoy this tiny shop with the typical "well-worn" English interior. Actually, there are branches in the U.S.; prices are usually equal—but, get this, the U.S. has some outlet stores.

CHURCH'S SHOES
163 New Bond Street, W1 (Tube: Bond Street)

RUSSELL & BROMELY
If you are looking for your favorite European designer shoe, such as Bruno Magli, Walter Steiger, or Charles Jourdan, stop by this very fashionable shop. There are several locations throughout London, but this elegant store serves social London, for those who want one-stop shopping with lots of brand choice; for men and women.

RUSSELL & BROMELY
24–25 New Bond Street, W1 (Tube: Bond Street)

GINA

OK, let's get a little more hip with these shoe listings. Every single British fashion magazine I read has been raving about Gina, as a source for the well-heeled. It's got a cute little purple storefront and a fancy address, but frankly I have no idea what all the fuss is about.

The designer is named Emma Hope and she is considered the last word in vamps. The shoes are high-fashion, expensive, and sometimes innovative. I think this is a good store, but not the last word. Let me know what you think, or what I'm missing here. Yes, the Princess of Wales does shop here.

GINA

42 Sloane Street, SW1 (Tube: Knightsbridge)

CHARLES JOURDAN

Located conveniently near HARRODS, the Jourdan shop sports a good selection of both clothing and shoes. Prices are great only if the dollar is in your favor. The January sale is spectacular.

CHARLES JOURDAN

39 Brompton Road, SW3 (Tube: Knightsbridge)

BERTIES

A famous London shoe resource at the moderate-price level, Berties has shops all over London as well as branches and department-store distribution in the U.S. They are famous for high style at moderate prices.

BERTIES

Covent Garden, WC2 (Tube: Covent Garden)

PIED À TERRE

Another chain, far more upscale than BERTIES, but not so out of line price-wise that you'll wince. Various designer names, some of them more famous in Europe and Britain (like Michel Perry); many inventive styles as well as staples. Shops are located everywhere; this is almost a high-street multiple.

PIED À TERRE

19 South Molton Street, W1 (Tube: Bond Street)

SHELLY'S

Shelly's seems to have taken over London—their presence off Carnaby Street has been a longtime accepted part of the scene, but now—hold onto your high tops—they have a huge store on Regent Street right at Oxford Circus, in a space formerly occupied by WEDGWOOD, no less. Well, if the shoe fits. . . .

Shelly's has been the purveyor of the hot London foot for years; Doc Martens were probably born here. They carry many other brands as well. Truth is, I kind of liked the platform, granny lace-up in pale turquoise (£40). The chartreuse clogs were £43. They simply sell a high-fashion shoe for a very reasonable price. Bring your teens and 'tweens; otherwise stop by just to convince yourself you've seen it all.

Oh yes, if your kids are younger, not to panic: Shelly's also sells the BUCKLE MY SHOE line, which has some free-standing stores. This is the same look, but for tots.

SHELLY'S

270-66 Regent Street, W1 (Tube: Oxford Circus)

159 Oxford Street, W1 (Tube: Bond Street)

14 Neal Street (Tube: Covent Garden)

21 Fouberts Place, W1 (Tube: Piccadilly Circus)

MULBERRY

Mulberry is an English chain that sells men's and women's ready-to-wear of the traditional English variety, not unlike Ralph Lauren. In fact, the shops look very similar to Ralph's. (See page 114.)

While everything in these stores is super and

you will enjoy browsing, the real standout is the selection of totes and leathergoods. These are traditionally styled, yet so unlike everyone else's initialed luggage that you will feel at once new-fashioned and old-fashioned—not an easy trick. Prices begin at $100 and get steeper, but this is far more quietly handsome than anything with little LVs on it.

Some of the London department stores have their own Mulberry boutiques. The free-standing store is right off Oxford Street, a sneeze from SELFRIDGES.

Please note that I sat next to an English gentleman on the airplane the last trip over, and he was everything you want an English gentleman to be. His carry-on luggage—Mulberry. It was better than Hermès, honest.

MULBERRY
12 Gee's Court (off St. Christopher's Place), W1 (Tube: Bond Street)

Children

HAMLEYS
Pussycat, pussycat, where have you been? To Hamleys, of course; then later, the Queen. Whether you have children or not, Hamleys deserves attention.

If you are beginning to find yourself feeling dizzy, you will be relieved to find a snack bar in the basement. Prices will not make you dizzy—although American toys are more expensive here—but Corgi toys are a bargain. If you're looking for that unusual toy not readily available in the U.S., Hamleys is a must. The gift shop on the street level is the best (and easiest) place we know of to buy gifts for all your friends and neighbors.

If your child collects dolls, you will have a

tough time making a final decision. There's also a huge array of Britains, the small metal British Regiment Guard soldiers for all the collectors in your family.

If you are wondering how you will get your packages home, Hamleys will ship them to your door. The paperwork takes about twenty minutes but is well worth the time. Make sure, of course, that you are sending home an unsolicited gift valued at less than $50. Otherwise, you will pay duty.

HAMLEYS
200 Regent Street, W1 (Tube: Oxford Circus)

THE DISNEY STORE
Give me a break.

THE DISNEY STORE
140 Regent Street, W1 (Tube: Oxford Circus or Piccadilly Circus)

HARRODS
Fabulous toy department; possibly as good as HAMLEYS. There's a sample of every toy imaginable and the kids can play, ride, climb, bite, or torture the toys and each other. Fourth floor.

HARRODS
Knightsbridge, SW1 (Tube: Knightsbridge)

LA CIGOGNA
I am utterly amazed that La Cigogna has survived the recession: the store stands for everything the 1980s stood for—overdressed kids in expensive togs. This shop is loaded with all those wonderful Italian designer clothes and shoes that no one real can possibly afford. But if you have a special occasion or are able to splurge, this is the place. If you have a daughter, the gorgeous array of party dresses next to the entrance seems endless. Also available for your princess are lovely skirts, pants, and sweaters (some hand-knits). There is a small area for infants and toddlers, and the back of the shop is devoted just to boys.

Don't miss the basement for dazzling Italian shoes. And dazzling prices.

LA CIGOGNA
   6A Sloane Street, SW1 (Tube: Knightsbridge)

TROTTERS

Buy your franchise now and open up in an American mall—get rich quick! Trotters is a formula kiddie shop with a great formula and a lot of energy. They have toys, clothes, and a play area—all of it so cute you'll find it impossible to resist. The shopping bag, with the big fat pig, is one of the best bags in London. There's another pig outside, to mark the store.

TROTTERS
   34 King's Road, SW3 (Tube: Sloane Square)

Fun Jewelry

BUTLER & WILSON

If you are a fan of authentic or reproduction Art Deco or Chanel-style jewelry, or just love the chunky costume "glitz," these shops are a must. In fact, Butler & Wilson should really qualify as a British Big Name. Princess Diana wears it; so do most movie queens. There's a desk shop in HARRODS (and in SELFRIDGES) on the street floor— but go to one of the boutiques for more selection and a better deal with VAT refunds. Chic and hot and dynamite.

Expect to pay £25 for earrings or a simple pin; the bejeweled cross on a cord (not a chain) that I was in love with cost £99. They also sell sunglasses, hair clips and other hair doodads, and T-shirts.

There are shops in London Heathrow at Terminal 1 and Terminal 3. By the time you read this, I bet they will have opened in Terminal 4 as well. If they don't open officially there, perhaps I'll set up my own little display in the BA Executive Lounge. Remember that the Harrods'

VAT minimum is £150, so buy your Butler & Wilson elsewhere to get back 17.5%.

BUTLER & WILSON
189 Fulham Road, SW3 (Tube: South Kensington)

20 South Molton Street, W1 (Tube: Bond Street)

ARABESK
Inventive, creative, somewhat outrageous, very dynamic, and more. I actually felt like a fool for having little Cs on my earrings when everything here had so much class and true style. Earrings begin at £25.

ARABESK
156 Walton Street, SW3 (Tube: South Kensington)

VAN PETERSON
Attention trendies! Here's a new source for you, where new work is inspired by the 1920s and is to die for. Jewelry, accessories, and watches. Vintage and repro. Fab, fab, fab.

VAN PETERSON
117 Walton Street, SW3 (Tube: South Kensington)

KEN LANE
If you love fake, then fake it is, and it has to be Kenny Lane—for big-time glitz, anyway. His faux jewelry is a delight to look at and wear. The shop is filled with designs of every style. Cheaper at home.

KEN LANE
66 South Molton Street, W1 (Tube: Bond Street)

Burlington Arcade, W1 (Tube: Piccadilly Circus)

Important Fun Jewelry

Who would even know the British were good at important fun jewelry? I thought that's what they had Tiffany & Co. for. Oh well.

ELIZABETH GAGE

A big-time society jeweler with a salon filled with banquettes, ruffled pillows, and necklaces that are a cross between the elegant hippie look and Bulgari. Each piece is made of the finest metals and gemstones, but is unique in a way that jewelry should be; this is expensive and important stuff, not silly glitz.

ELIZABETH GAGE

20 Albemarle Street, W1 (Tube: Green Park)

KIKI MCDONOUGH

Next time I open my wallet and find a spare £595, I'm rushing out to buy Kiki's 18K, gold-link bracelet with colored stones set here and there. You may think I'm kidding—I'm not! Set into the street that already has numerous jewelers, this one not only has inventive things, but also some traditional-looking designs that, on second glance, turn out to be witty or special. Clients include Princess you-know-who and the former Duchess of York.

KIKI MCDONOUGH

77c Walton Street, SW3 (Tube: South Kensington)

Papergoods and Filo Facts

FILOFAX

This is a free-standing Filofax boutique, not a stationery store that sells the stuff. It's rather fancy, considering the neighborhood and the clientele, and is replete with pages, inserts, and various notebooks in the many sizes. Prices are still half of what they are in the U.S., and they have sales and close-outs.

FILOFAX

21 Conduit Street, W1 (Tube: Bond Street)

PAPERCHASE

The "in" place for papergoods, Paperchase offers a wide range of products—everything from greeting cards, stationery, Filofax pages, and party items to a variety of materials for the serious artist. This is a major multiple now.

PAPERCHASE

213 Tottenham Court Road, W1 (Tube: Goodge Street)

167 Fulham Road, SW3 (Tube: Fulham Broadway)

SMYTHSON

If you're looking for stationery fit for a queen, stop by this very elegant shop, which has been producing top-quality paper since the turn of the century. If you buy your writing papers at Cartier in New York, or any of America's finest paper shops, you'll see some old friends here in London. Aside from the selection of writing papers, there's a wide variety of leather-bound goods, including address books and notebooks, diaries, and lovely desktop accessories. This is an old-fashioned, blue-blooded, blue-haired, very regal kind of place, a bit expensive, but cheaper than in the U.S. for the same goods.

They do not make Jewish New Year's cards. You should have seen the salesman's face when I asked.

SMYTHSON

44 New Bond Street, W1 (Tube: Bond Street)

ITALIAN PAPER SHOP

If you love that swirly, marbleized, antique-Italian-paper look, you may want to poke into the Italian Paper Shop, which is an arcade right between HARRODS and HARVEY NICHOLS. Prices are higher than in Italy and lower than in the U.S. The store lacks the charm of similar shops in Venice or Florence, but the goods are the same. The pencils, at about $1 each, make smashing gift items.

ITALIAN PAPER SHOP
   Brompton Arcade, SW3 (Tube: Knightsbridge)

MORGAN'S

This is a stationery shop with several branches to serve locals, but they have a stupendous selection of Filofax materials. Even their business card is printed as an insert.

MORGAN'S
   22 Goodge Street, W1 (Tube: Goodge Street)

AMERICAN RETRO

A fabulous store for all kinds of neat used clothes, and a fine introduction to what's happening in Soho; but we're sending you here for the latest in Filofax inserts. You may buy the SafeFax here—a leather page with specially sized slots that store condoms. It costs almost $40, but what price safe sex? Or write the manufacturer: SafeFax Ltd., Suite C, 52/53 Dean Street, London W1.

AMERICAN RETRO
   35 Old Compton Street, W1 (Tube: Leicester Square)

BRATS

If you're looking for what's hot and with-it on King's Road, this paper and gift shop appears to have all that is trendy and new in the world of gifts. They have a wide range of organizational systems, including knockoffs of the famous Filofax, as well as everything else from Swatch watches to plastic suitcases.

BRATS
   281 King's Road, SW3 (Tube: Sloane Square)

Florists

MOYSES STEVENS

Stevens has been my regular florist in London ever since the day I had a business need to send hoity-toity flowers to a contact. The recession has forced Mr. Stevens from Berkeley Square into less flashy digs, but the rep is still big. The look is the extravagant English arrangement of formal flowers arranged casually in bouquet or basket.

You may also want to look at the specially made tulip-shaped vases (£15), which I think are super gifts.

You can phone your order from the U.S. and charge it to your credit card: 71-493-8171.

MOYSES STEVENS
157 Sloane Street, SW1 (Tube: Sloane Square)

KENNETH TURNER

For dried flowers, candles, home scents, or live bouquets and arrangements, this name is known throughout the world—he's even done some big jobs in the U.S. and published a book on his arrangements. The gold foil tags are to die for; the flowers will make you faint away.

For delivery in London, call 71-629-7837. You may charge your credit card.

KENNETH TURNER
35 Brook Street, W1 (Tube: Bond Street)

Hairdressers

I've always thought that having my hair done in London was not only a convenience, but a chance to feel smart, with-it, and plugged into British style. Being in London is celebration enough to splurge on an experience you won't quickly forget. Unless it rains.

MICHAELJOHN

I guess it's no secret that I've been going to Michaeljohn for more years than I have been writing the *Born to Shop* books. It's especially great for me to now have John's daughter Kate do my hair whenever I am in London. Not only does she do a great job, but I have the pleasure of feeling as proud as a mother whenever I see her.

Since you might not feel the family connection at Michaeljohn that I enjoy, you may wonder why I chose this salon over the other well-known shops, why you should plunk down what is a pretty price to have your hair done.

I have one simple answer:

Royals.

Michaeljohn is at once chic and casual; it's the kind of place where old friends meet and everyone gets to know you. And everyone looks over at the mirrors to catch the passing of a royal personage on an almost daily basis—there is a small private room in the center of the salon where you may see Princess Anne, the Duchess of Kent, or just the Julie Andrews kind of royalty. Americans please note, you need not bow or curtsy to British royalty. Only British subjects do this. You may not offer your hand, introduce yourself, or talk to them, however. You must wait for a royal to address you.

Now then, the price here is steep, but you get top talent, you get royals, and, in actuality, the prices are the same as in New York. Other big-name London salons actually charge more.

For the basics:

- It's best to call or fax ahead for an appointment. I always book with Kate, whom you can ask for directly, or you can choose your stylist by price range. A cut, shampoo, and dry with the heads of the house (Michael, Frank, or John) comes to about $100 for a woman (less for a man), which is decidedly less than many big-name salons in New York. Kate is about $50. Call 71-491-4401 or fax 71-495-0152 (direct calls or faxes to the attention of John Prothero); the salon will confirm your appointment with a return fax. First appointment of the day is at 8:30 A.M.; last appointment is 5:30 P.M.

- If you order tea or coffee, you will pay for it on the spot or it will be added to your bill. Refreshments are not free as they are in the U.S. Coffee costs £1.

- Men and women co-mingle in the salon. Men are big on treatments in London, so don't be surprised to find men customers on the floor or downstairs in the men's treatment area. Ian comes here for a haircut every now and then, but dotes on the skin treatments, the aromatherapy, and whatever it is that they do to his feet that he can't stop talking about. He usually books in after a big trip to help combat jet lag.

- Tip is at your discretion. Kate gave me the inside poop: on a wash and blow-dry I tip the shampoo guy £1.50, and then the change from £5 (3.50) goes to the stylist.

- If you think the haircuts are expensive, don't give up—price various other services which seem to offer more value. Ian thought his haircut at £50 was expensive, but thought the therapy session at £45 was well-priced. Ian regularly pays £30 for a great cut at SMILE (see page 147), so you can see his point. My wash and blow-dry with Kate is about £30; the exact same price for a wash and blow-dry at Elizabeth Arden in New York ($50).

MICHAELJOHN

23a Albemarle St., W1 (Tube: Green Street)

NICKY CLARKE

Clarke is famous as a hot talent who made his mark by cutting the Duchess of York's hair from long to short when she was still the Duchess of York. Or actively the Duchess of York. Or something. Other clients are big-name models, movie stars, and rock and rollers—men and women.

The salon is low-key, with magazine covers

framed on the walls of the Berkeley Square salon. The prices are not particularly low-key: Clarke himself charges £85 for a cut and blow-dry. There is a five- to six-week waiting list. Phone 71-491-4700 for an appointment.

NICKY CLARKE

130 Mount Street, W1 (Tube: Green Park)

SMILE

Ian has been having his hair cut by Keith, who owns Smile, for a million years, and he gets great cuts. And that's my personal opinion since I've known Ian for eight years and am constantly impressed by Keith's handiwork.

Every now and then Ian splurges with a trip to MICHAELJOHN (see page 144) when he's getting his skin treatment there, but Smile is his regular haunt. Because Keith owns the shop, you don't tip him; price is £30.

The shop is very different from Michaeljohn and the other Mayfair shops; it's sort of a leftover hippie place where the word "unisex" has gone out of use but still applies. Keith has been written up in British *Vogue* for his women's cuts as well, so the man is versatile. Many local TV stars are regulars. If the man's work was not sensational, I would not send you out of your way to get here.

As Ian says, "It looks like an ordinary place, but it isn't."

Take the bus along King's Road; there's no convenient tube stop.

SMILE

434 King's Road, SW10 (Tube: take the bus or walk from Sloane Square)

VIDAL SASSOON

If the only name you trust in British hairstylists is Vidal Sassoon, there is a salon convenient to Covent Garden, and it's attached to a gym and spa called The Sanctuary. Prices at Sassoon are slightly higher than at MICHAELJOHN for women, but men's prices are lower and competitive with Keith at SMILE (see page 147). There are several salons dotted around London. To phone the Covent Garden salon for an appointment call 71-240-6635.

VIDAL SASSOON
    11 Floral Street, WC2 (Tube: Covent Garden)

Bargain Basements

MARKS & SPENCER
    Marks & Spencer has built a retailing empire on the notion that you can get high quality in private label (St. Michael) goods at a fair price. I happen to think that not everything in M & S is a bargain, or even a good price, but there are plenty of items with impressive prices. M & S is technically a full-service department store—they will even deliver your groceries to you at home. They have a home furnishings catalog, as well as an international mail-order hamper business. (For food gifts, not laundry.)
    Only the Marble Arch store carries cashmeres—the price for a crew neck two-ply is £79, the same price you'll pay in the factories in the Borders of Scotland. Not bad, huh?
    I've been wearing a lot of twin sets lately; M & S makes them in lamb's wool at a very reasonable price. I think their men's clothing is prohibitively expensive (£40 for a pair of cords is outrageous); even men's socks are expensive compared to American discount sources. The women's underwear is famous for its quality.
    I've bought bath gels and beauty products here, as well as dishes and home design elements. The grocery store in the lower level always commands my attention when I've set up housekeeping in London. Olive got me hooked on

"Curiously Strong Mints," which I buy from the candy counter (they come in a green tin, 99p) and keep in my handbag. I've tried the house brand of toffee, but I like THORNTON'S better.

MARKS & SPENCER
   458 Oxford Street, W1 (Tube: Bond Street)

BROWNS LABELS FOR LESS
   Browns is the best high-fashion specialty store in London. If you've shopped Browns' January sale, you may be disappointed in their separate sale shop—although the sale shop is open all year. It's small, offering two floors of clothes and things, but not much selection; prices are low, but not give-away.

   A good bit of the merchandise is American, which means expensive (even on sale), and some is too wild to wear at any price. A pair of Pucci pull-on pants at £75 didn't strike me as a bargain; I prefer my DKNY from the outlet store in Woodbury Common, near Harriman, New York.

BROWNS LABELS FOR LESS
   45 South Molton Street, W1 (Tube: Bond Street)

THE REJECT SHOP
   Not to be confused with the REJECT CHINA SHOP. The Reject Shop is large, clean, bright, and conveniently located right on Brompton Road. This is really the dumping ground for a lot of junk, but if you work it regularly, you may find something. I don't think a tourist need go out of the way for a look-see.

THE REJECT SHOP
   245 Brompton Road, SW3 (Tube: Knightsbridge)
   234 King's Road, SW3 (Tube: Sloane Square)

PANDORA
   Locals call this a dress agency; I'll call it heaven. I'll also call it the future, especially in

London, where more and more people are buying secondhand and aren't afraid to admit it. I'm talking $50 for a YSL blouse, $38 for an Hermès scarf. Armani jackets go for a mere $200. (Well, it's mere to some people.) Used clothes are no more than six months old. Hours are 10 A.M. to 5 P.M., Monday to Saturday.

PANDORA

16–22 Cheval Place, SW7 (Tube: Knightsbridge)

PAMELA'S

I discovered Pamela's quite by accident; the store is located where JOHN BOYD used to have his hat shop. Not to worry, I bought a John Boyd hat here for £23! When I cooed over the price, the saleswoman said to me, "You do realize this is a secondhand hat, my dear."

My dear, indeed. This is a very classy secondhand shop. I visited at the beginning of The Season, so hats were prominently displayed. There were plenty of designer dresses, handbags, and accessories. And they take plastic. A true gem.

PAMELA'S

93 Walton Street, SW3 (Tube: South Kensington)

NEXT TO NOTHING

If you owned all those Next stores and the economy was slow, what would you do with everything that didn't sell? Open a factory outlet, of course. Conveniently located on the edge of West Soho for the teen crowd, there's plenty for yuppies as well. Open at 10:30 A.M. on weekdays, 10 A.M. on Saturdays. I wish I could tell you it was great here; I've never found it even worth my time. But it's convenient enough for you to take a look.

NEXT TO NOTHING

129–131 Oxford Street, W1 (Tube: Oxford Circus)

DESIGNS

Closed on Sundays when much of the Hampstead retail scene is hopping, so decide early on if you want to get a look at some slightly used designer duds. Prices are basically one-third the original price.

DESIGNS
60 Rosslyn Hill, NW3 (Tube: Hampstead)

CHAPTER FIVE

ENGLISH STYLE

Shabby Chic

There are purveyors of British style, and they swear by Shakespeare's very definition: they claim that clothes make the man. They believe in expensive clothes that are simple, that last a lifetime, that are conservative to a fine point. They buy quality and expect it to last.

There are British stylists who have the ability to mix a plaid skirt, a cashmere sweater, a strand of pearls, and a Barbour weatherproof and still look somewhat chic. There are men and women who can wear something that is frayed, worn, or scruffed up and make you wish you had one too, make you embarrassed that you have new. It is, in essence, the Ralph Lauren look. And you can buy it where it originated, in Britain.

Note that shabby chic also carries over into the home (see page 180).

While British shabby chic has some things in common with the Paris look, the London look is not really a continental European look, nor is it anything like an American look. If you want to blend in, you'd best study the format and adjust accordingly. Remember that English women are expected to look dowdy (unless they are Anouska Hemphill) and British men should have their hair cut with the front longer than the back, so it can be slicked straight back (with a part on the side, of course).

Women who want to catch the look should:

- Carry a waxed leather handbag;
- Have an Hermès scarf, preferably one with a horsy print;
- Have a single strand of graduated pearls (not too big!)—it's essential;
- Own at least one twin set;
- Own at least one Kanga silk dress for tea.

Note that London basics for women include a navy blazer, long pleated skirt, plain pumps or flats with horsy hardware; a silk shirtwaist dress is also safe in stripes or polka dots (for summer).

Men who want to catch the look should:

- Wear suits that fit;
- Wear simple ties, but not British school ties (unless you actually attended that school);
- Carry a Burberrys;
- Affect shirts with contrast collar and cuffs, no monogram; stripes are OK.

London business basics for men include a dark blue or a gray pin-stripe suit that is *never* double-breasted. A well-cut navy blazer is good for casual business, but not for The City. Good cuff links (preferably antique and witty) are essential.

Veddy, Veddy British

HACKETT

Hackett made its name as the "in" store to buy high-quality used clothes years ago, but now they sell their own very new, very proper preppie, quite "U" clothing. Ian tells me that the reference to anything being "U" or "Non-U" is from the 1970s and really dates me. So *excusez-moi*, but to me the differentiation is very British and says it all.

Now then, years ago, Sloane Rangers flocked here in droves to buy the discarded remnants of nobility and the kind of slightly frayed look that the British find so endearing. Hackett became hot. Nowadays Hackett has gone upscale and has opened a few shops that sell new clothes with the same kind of retro look. *De rigueur* if you plan to fit in; owned by ALFRED DUNHILL.

You can buy everything from the country look to the Witty Britty look to the more staid, trad togs. Much unisex clothing. But then, they also sell bespoke suits at a bargain price—about £900.

The new shop on Sloane Street is an attempt to make Brooks Brothers work in London in the Hackett frame of mind. They plan to open in the U.S. as well. Mail order available.

HACKETT

137 Sloane Street, SW1 (Tube: Knightsbridge)

SIMPSON

A specialty store for men, with some women's things, known for its traditional look and its dedication to the Daks line, a veddy, veddy British traditional line on which Brooks Brothers is based. Prices are high, but this is the place for the solid British look, and the six floors of almost department-store nature make this a one-stop-for-the-works kind of place.

If you are invited to do The Season, this is a solid choice (boring but safe) for him and for her. The ladies' floor is now advertised as "a debutante's delight"—try that on an American audience. They also claim that this store is a great place to meet the right kind of men. Let me know how it goes.

SIMPSON

203 Piccadilly, W1 (Tube: Piccadilly Circus)

GALLERY OF LONDON

A small shop tucked right off Jermyn Street,

this is the place to buy blazer buttons and embroidered patches. That is, if you don't buy yours at street markets.

Buy your regiment's patch, your school's, or one of the Queen's—I bought from the Merchant Navy. Very chic to sew on your sweaters or sweats; prices are about £12 each. All that gold braid just makes you want to stand up straight and salute. Please note that there is a store in Manhattan which sells these patches, beginning at $45 each!

When they have a sale, there are goodies to be had for £2 each. I sewed some on velvet slippers for my friend Michele for Christmas last year.

GALLERY OF LONDON
1 Duke of York Street, SW1 (Tube: Green Park)

BROWNS

Any time you get the urge to pooh-pooh British fashion as dowdy, walk yourself right into Browns—the store, not the hotel—for a look-see at what has been London's temple of high fashion for decades. OK, so it's not so shabby after all.

It's filled with a ready-to-wear selection from the top designers in Europe. SONIA RYKIEL, JILL SANDER, JEAN MUIR, and MISSONI are all represented. The store is a string of connecting town houses; see the upstairs and downstairs levels in each. This can be confusing, but it's worth the trouble. This very chic and with-it shop is patronized by a very prestigious clientele, and that includes celebs and movie stars. Prices are high because these are expensive clothes—but you'll find the velour and cotton groups in the Sonia collection, the cheap line by Jean Muir with her expensive line, and many well-priced unisex items in the men's shop.

In January, everything goes on sale; otherwise the real markdowns are across the street in a special sale shop. Sale merchandise is put in specially made shopping bags that say "Browns Sale," which labels you to the whole world as a piker with good taste. American designers are sold at Browns; there are no bargains, even on markdowns.

BROWNS
23 South Molton Street, W1 (Tube: Bond Street)

Proper Toppers

Hats are more than Ascot to the British; they are a tradition. Women—in London especially—really do wear hats. You need a hat each spring at the beginning of The Season. You need a hat each fall/winter, when hats keep the head warm. How *many* hats you have tells the world how well-off you are.

Few pleasures are greater than a half hour spent on the street floor of HARVEY NICHOLS trying on hat after hat. If you get more serious than that, try some of these resources. Don't ignore markets as a resource for less expensive hats—there are some talented hatmakers in both Covent Garden's APPLE MARKET and at several markets in Greenwich.

Also remember that the best way to wear a real hat is with as little hair showing around the face as possible. If you have long hair, keep an elastic in your handbag for trying on hats. Hat prices begin around £20 for a straw nothing; you'll pay £80 for a nice designer hat; it's going to cost £200–£500 for one of those extravagant things you see in fashion magazines.

JOHN BOYD
My goal in life has been fulfilled; I now own a John Boyd hat. I bought it secondhand, but these days, that's OK. It's still a John Boyd hat. And I

feel rich and famous in it. I feel like a princess in it. I probably look like a fool, but I *feel* more chic than Princess Anne.

Mr. Boyd has been making hats for the Royal Family for many, many, many years. What is wonderful about John Boyd is that he doesn't just produce one look. Princess Anne and Margaret Thatcher are obviously different looks. Can you imagine them in each other's hats? Mr. Boyd will add or subtract bows, veils, and feathers depending on your taste and needs.

The newish Beauchamp Place shop is not forbiddingly *haute*, so don't be frightened—saunter in and sit in front of a mirror for a spell. Prices get real at £100.

JOHN BOYD
16 Beauchamp Place, SW3 (Tube: Knightsbridge)

THE HAT SHOP

This shop gets so crowded on weekends that people have to wait in line to get in. It's also worth it.

Prices are in the moderate range, although little is under £25. Styles range from high fashion to somewhat funky. I went absolutely bonkers for a straw version of the Mad Hatter's Hat from Alice in Wonderland, a mere £25. I wanted to wear it for the next *Born to Shop London* cover, but Ian reminded me that this isn't a costume party. Something tells me I'll find a replacement hat.

This shop is right down the street from Covent Garden; open on Sundays!

THE HAT SHOP
58 Neal Street, WC2 (Tube: Leicester Square)

JAMES LOCK & CO.

One of the most famous hatmakers in London, Lock has an old-fashioned shop amid a street of old-fashioned shops that makes shopping here like being in a history book. Prices here begin quite moderately and go right up to expensive, but you might find what you want for $50. Hats for both men and women are sold here; the color of the hat box differs for each gender.

JAMES LOCK & CO.

6 St. James's Street, SW1 (Tube: Green Park)

RACHEL TREVOR-MORGAN

Her tiny shop is right behind JAMES LOCK & CO.; she does their made-to-measure for ladies and will dye straw or fabric to match your suit.

RACHEL TREVOR-MORGAN

18 Crown Passage, SW1 (Tube: Green Park)

STEPHEN JONES

By appointment only; call 71-734-9666. Be prepared to spend £100–£200; it's three weeks till your creation is ready. Stand by for two fittings and you'll feel ready for a trip to Ascot. Witty and brazen hats are the specialty. Frequented by royal clients and Sloane Rangers, Jones is one of the "in" talents at the top of the heap. Men and women are welcome clients.

STEPHEN JONES

29 Heddon Street, W1 (Tube: Oxford Circus)

PHILIP TREACY

Perhaps the biggest of the "name" mad hatters, Treacy makes those fabulous toppers you see in all the fashion layouts right before the beginning of The Season. Now that I've got my John Boyd, this could be my next goal. Prices begin at £120. Treacy supplies most of the hot London designers with the hats for their collections. You need a strong sense of yourself to wear one of his creations, but you'll never be forgotten if you carry it off.

PHILIP TREACY

67 Elizabeth Street, SW1 (Tube: Sloane Square)

HERBERT JOHNSON

Men's and women's hats in a vein so traditional you may think you are the Queen Mum; several royal warrants.

HERBERT JOHNSON
30 New Bond Street, W1 (Tube: Bond Street)

THE HATMAKERS

If price is an issue, but you still have £15–£25 to spend on a fun, fashionable, and slightly funky hat, this is a great choice—among the vendors at Covent Garden Market.

THE HATMAKERS
Apple Market, Covent Garden, WC2 (Tube: Covent Garden)

Shirts

HILDITCH & KEY

One of several very proper men's shirtmakers on Jermyn Street, Hilditch & Key has two different shops selling the famous men's shirt as well as women's ready-to-wear—in keeping with the look. All the shops look like Old World gems. Please note that there is a full inch of shirt fabric under the cuff, so should the sleeve need to be lengthened, the fabric is readily available. Shirts can be fixed in a day or two if the standard size does not fit you.

Pick from made-to-measure (six-shirt minimum) or a special stock shirt, which is not quite as expensive and means the sleeves are made to measure, but the body is not. If you want a private visit to your hotel room, call 71-930-5336 to make an appointment, or fax: 71-321-0216.

HILDITCH & KEY
37 Jermyn Street, SW1
73 Jermyn Street, SW1 (Tube: Both locations—Piccadilly Circus)

TURNBULL & ASSER

Known basically as a shirtmaker, Turnbull & Asser has become one of the most famous names in British menswear. Prince Charles buys his pj's here. He also buys his shirts, as do many other famous and not-so-famous men who just love the finest cotton and tailoring money can buy. Although—let's get small here—the word on the street is that when times are tough, there are cutbacks even at places like Turnbull & Asser. Many a man is complaining that his old shirt stays don't fit into the new, narrower gussets, that the buttons aren't of the same quality.

Still, for the thrill of it all, a stop by Turnbull & Asser is quite an experience. The main store is on two levels, with the ready-to-wear shirts, bathrobes, and underwear downstairs, and ties, sweaters, and accessories upstairs. One door down Jermyn Street is the Churchill Room, which houses the bespoke department for shirts and the ready-to-wear suits. Entering the shop is like going back in time to the days (1885) when Reginald Turnbull and Ernest Asser first began making hunting gear for the nobility. The walls are wood-paneled and the atmosphere is hushed. However, the sales help is quite helpful and will tell you that if you have time to be fitted, a bespoke shirt will not cost you much more than a ready-to-wear one.

The Turnbull & Asser staff travels to New York and Los Angeles twice a year to see their clients. They take up residence in a hotel suite and make appointments with their longtime customers. When you are in the London shop, ask to be put on their list.

Turnbull & Asser is carried in the U.S. through Bergdorf Goodman in New York and Neiman Marcus in other cities. The popularity of the Turnbull & Asser shirts is so great that when Bergdorf has its once-a-year sale before Christmas, the lines begin to form at 7 A.M.

Turnbull & Asser makes their ready-made shirts with only one sleeve length; if you are tall, have long arms, or are a chimpanzee, you may be out of luck. But don't panic; my friend Barry, who is easily 6'3" and therefore not what you'd call tiny, fits perfectly into a Turnbull ready-made. If your arm is shorter than their shirts, you will be fitted accordingly at the store and the sleeve will be shortened to your measurements. But if you're going to this much trouble to begin with, why not get a custom-made shirt? It is actually cheaper to buy a custom-made shirt in a hotel in the U.S. from the Turnbull & Asser representative than it is to walk into Bergdorf or Neiman and buy a shirt that will have to be altered.

TURNBULL & ASSER

71–72 Jermyn Street, SW1 (Tube: Green Park)

Women's: 69 Jermyn Street, SW1 (Tube: Green Park)

THOMAS PINK

If he wants to try something a little more exciting than a TURNBULL & ASSER shirt but still be in the pink, he may want to ring up Thomas Pink—a guy who became famous by offering more for the money to the very "U" students who were (and always are) broke, but needed bespoke (or almost bespoke). Mr. Pink's shirts have their own logo, a pink square of fabric, sewn into the shirttail.

THOMAS PINK

85 Jermyn Street, SW1 (Tube: Green Park)

HARVIE & HUDSON

This is one of my favorites, just because I never hear anyone talk about them—but they strike me as just as much fun, if not more so, than the bigger names. Little shops; very old-fashioned. I love it here. Same old stripes but great British charm.

HARVIE & HUDSON
97 and 77 Jermyn Street, SW1 (Tube: Green
Park or Piccadilly Circus)

Tartans and Tweeds

Americans have so mangled British English
over the centuries that there is now some confu-
sion as to the difference between a tartan and a
plaid—a difference that will get you into deep
water when you come to buy one or the other. A
tartan is a pattern of fabric, with alternate colors in
the warp and the weft in which the colors repeat
themselves in a set order. A *plaid* is a piece of
clothing worn as part of a Scottish dress uniform.
In the U.S., the term *plaid* does refer to a pattern of
alternating colors set in a sequence, but in
England a plaid is not a tartan. Or vice versa.

Tartans signify the great families of the
Highlands, each family having its own special
way of weaving its colors and stripes into a particular sequence which no one else can copy.
There is usually a battle tartan and a dress tartan
for each family or clan. The men who fought for a
certain clan all wore the same pattern, and certain areas of the Highlands became known for
these patterns.

Now then, if you want to get all gussied up in
proper Highland attire, you will probably want to
wear the right tartan. You may easily discover the
right one for you either by using a chart for your
last name or by using a map and finding the village your family came from. In London and
Edinburgh, retailers have these lists right on
hand, and will gladly help you. Of course, a lot of
people just pick what they like best. I buy
"Graham" because every English hotel that has
ever mangled my last name has made me a
Graham or a Gresham. . . and there's no tartan
for Gresham.

SCOTCH HOUSE in London (2 Brompton Road and 191 Regent Street) has the best charts of the clans; all the shops in Edinburgh (except maybe KINLOCH ANDERSON, where your bloodline must be worn on your sleeve) have brochures and charts to lend you or sell you.

A *tweed* has nothing to do with a tartan, and the two are rarely worn together. Tweed fabric is named for the River Tweed, and is a blend of various colors of wool so that a pattern emerges. Many tweeds are named for the places that created them, such as the Harris tweed. Tweeds are often nubby with a rough hand. They are 100% wool and can be bought by the meter or as ready-made garments. Men's tweed jackets can sometimes be much less expensive in the U.K. than in the U.S. However, I just bought Ian a lovely secondhand Harris tweed sports jacket at my local Goodwill for $10; you'll pay £130 or more in London.

Tweed fabric bought off the bolt will be considerably cheaper—expect a 50% savings. If you're really into saving money, you'll buy the fabric in Scotland and then take it to Hong Kong to have the tailoring done there. Even if you're not Hong Kong-bound this year, you may think about the plan. The best thing about tweeds is that they never go out of style. Hang on to the fabric, get a classic suit made, and it will last twenty years—or longer.

Sweater Facts

The perfect sweater requires three ingredients: chilly weather, home-grown wool, and long winter nights. Ohhhhh, wait a minute—dampness helps too. You have need, you have supply, you have time to knit: Behold, the sweater.

Actually, sweaters date back about 2,000 years and are found in Egyptian tombs. Sweaters as we know them grew up in medieval times, when men were the knitters and guilds specified that this was not women's work. Their business went the way of the Industrial Revolution and became the knitting industry we know and love. Women adapted to the cottage side of the industry and began to knit at home, by the fire, when it was too dark to do much else.

Today's sweater's value is based on who made it and how. A hand-knit sweater is more valuable and will always cost more than a machine-knit sweater; sweaters made with synthetics have the least value, while those made with wool or cashmere (or any other natural fiber, such as cotton, silk, or linen) have far more value.

Cashmere sweaters are valued by the number of plies or strands in the yarn—from one to four is common. The higher the number of plies, the heavier the sweater, and the more expensive it is. Cashmere sweaters are sold all year-round in the many cashmere shops London is famous for; they are only a seasonal item at MARKS & SPENCER and are only sold at the Marble Arch store.

TRADITIONAL SWEATERS

Traditional sweaters are in solid colors and come in crew-neck or V-neck styles, in either pullover or cardigan—men's and women's versions. They are sized for the small European body and have not changed in style in decades; if you are looking for a big, sweatshirt look or extra fullness, you will not find it in a traditional sweater (although women can buy men's sweaters and add shoulder pads). For best selection of these types of sweaters in London, try WESTAWAY & WESTAWAY (see page 170).

TRADITIONAL SWEATERS IN FASHION STYLE

A solid-color sweater, especially in cashmere, that fits into today's fashion styles—such as a sweatshirt cut, a tunic, a double pocket at the hip, or whatever—is extremely difficult to find in England, and will cost a lot of money. N. PEAL (page 168) specializes in this look.

SHETLAND SWEATERS

Shetland is a type of wool that has a slight nap to it; when woven into a garment, the nap is apparent. Shetlands are mostly seen in crew-neck styles, in stripes or solids. While most Shetlands are in standard colors, a few shops sell them in brights and fashion shades.

ARGYLE SWEATERS

Argyles are diamond patterns that are knitted into sweaters (or socks) in contrasting colors. W. BILL and SCOTCH HOUSE stock them.

FAIR ISLE SWEATERS

Fair Isle patterns are lines of zigzag colors that are laid in either at the yoke of a sweater or across the central body, in contrasting colors. Because of the intricacy of these designs, look for higher price tags—especially if the sweater is hand-knit. Try WESTAWAY & WESTAWAY.

ENGINEERED PRINTS

Fairly new to the world of sweaters, engineered prints are designs created by computers or creators on small knitting machines; they produce rows of identical designs—most often animals. The Princess Di sweater with the rows of white sheep and the one black sheep is an engineered design. You'll see these with rows of rabbits, frogs, bears, etc. This is the look Warm and Wonderful made famous; or try SALLY'S OWN at the Covent Garden market.

ARAN SWEATERS

The Aran Islands, on Ireland's western coast, were the home of an isolated group of fishermen.

The women knit sweaters in a certain pattern so men lost at sea could be identified and brought home to rest. Today that pattern is so well-known it is called a "fisherman's sweater," and comes in cream or "natural" wool.

TWIN SETS

Twin sets have come back into style; to British women they never went out of style. I'm fond of them because the under-sweater has short sleeves, so if you feel faint from the warmth generated by two layers of cashmere, you can take off the cardigan and still be wearing a sweater. To maintain the definition, both sweaters must match. Someone told me they thought the height of chic was a mismatched twin set; I leave that up to you.

Twin sets come in cashmere and lamb's wool; I've seen great lamb's wool sets at MARKS & SPENCER. My single best source for cashmere twin sets is a factory in the Borders of Scotland (see *Born to Shop Great Britain*), but you can find them in London in traditional places like N. PEAL, etc. They cost more than in the Borders—a lot more.

ART SWEATERS

Some of these are works of art; some of them cost as much as works of art. London is in the middle of a crafts revival led by a small group of big-name knitting superstars. Look for work by Kaffe Fassett, Jessi & Jamie Seaton, and Susan Duckworth. I think ANNE HIGGINS' work, while in a different category, is also art (see page 108).

The Cashmere Crisis

If the sole purpose for your trip to London was to load up on cashmere sweaters and save a fortune, you are about to get a shocking piece of news: There are very few cashmere bargains these days. In fact, the world of sweaters has been in a cashmere crisis for years and most of the cashmere that comes to market these days is from the Orient.

While English cashmere sweaters are traditionally from Scotland, China also got into the cashmere sweater business in a big way as they gathered steam and faced capitalism and the *garmentos* of New York. Cashmere goods coming out of China could be had at bargain prices, and the demand for cashmere soared. Scotland, although pressured by the Chinese, refused to lower prices and slogged along—often losing the sale to private-label brands sold in giant lots through U.S. department stores. Then the Chinese realized the value of cashmere and raised the prices. The rest is history. The Scottish also raised their prices; both makers lowered production. You might consider buying a sweater made of platinum.

The best way to capitalize on the cashmere crisis is to plan ahead. Watch prices in the U.S., read the fine print in ads, and pay attention to where goods have been manufactured. Cashmere is in high demand, not only for sweaters, but for other items of clothing, and prices are sky-high. Yet there are still big promotional sales.

Price everything in the U.S. before you get to London, then spend some time pricing in regular London sweater stores. After you know the going prices—if you are still standing despite the shock of it—head for the few discounters in London (PORTOBELLO CHINA AND WOOLLENS, WESTAWAY & WESTAWAY) who have factory overruns, seconds, and discontinued colors. These stores don't usually have a large selection, but they do have the best prices you'll find these days.

While it is still possible to buy discounted cashmere sweaters in Scotland, the prices there may not be any less expensive than at the discount sources in London. The selection in the

Borders' towns (especially Hawick) will be far superior to what you can find in London, but there will not be a price break—unless you hit some kind of lucky deal. If you're heading for Scotland, take a peek at *Born to Shop Great Britain* for a full tour of all the sweater factories in the Borders.

Cashmere is at a premium these days. You do not need to pay $500 for a simple V-neck sweater, but you may be asked to pay that by some stores. Just smile politely and then run. You might want to run to a discounter, or you might just want to run home.

Do note the difference in quality between Scottish cashmere and Chinese. Scottish is better. The best you'll do in London on sale or at a discounter is about £99 for a good-quality 2-ply sweater.

Sweaters and Knitted Goods

Since sweaters are so expensive, look to street markets and fairs—especially in Covent Garden —both APPLE and JUBILEE MARKETS always have good buys. SALLY'S OWN and COLINETTE are two famous dealers in the Apple Market; you'll find your own faves as well.

N. PEAL

For the quality- and convenience-conscious, N. Peal offers quite a variety of wools and cashmeres in a multitude of colors and styles. They are top-of-the-line in the business, but frankly, I could faint from the prices. Holy hot flash (or flush, as the British say)—who needs cashmere at prices like this? N. Peal is in the Burlington Arcade, where you'll be anyway—the women's shop is at 37 and the men's shop is at 54 Burlington Arcade. Both shops look small, but they have underground levels. As other merchants in the arcade go out of business, Peal moves into their space as well, so don't worry about lack of stock. Then there's a whole other medium-sized shop on Piccadilly, near HATCHARDS.

Peal is the kind of shop you swear you won't patronize because of the high prices, but then you go back after you've been to every discount resource in London. While you can get traditional sweaters in any number of places and at a variety of prices, Peal is one of the few outlets that sells fashion merchandise made out of cashmere. Notice that their sweaters are entirely different from the look-alikes you'll see everywhere else. They do have twin sets, they have bodysuits (called a "body" in British) and they have blends of cashmere and silk or even just plain old-fashioned wool. Their color palette will leave you drooling. The quality puts cheap cashmere to shame. And look at that shawl with the little ruffle.

N. PEAL

37, 54, and 71 Burlington Arcade, W1 (Tube: Piccadilly Circus)

94 Brompton Road, SW3 (Tube: Knightsbridge)

192 Piccadilly, W1 (Tube: Piccadilly Circus)

SCOTCH HOUSE

A must-stop for the lover of those classic Scottish tartans and kilts, for sweater lovers, for lovers of grand wooden staircases and stores that look like stores should look. The store on Brompton Road in Knightsbridge is the nicer, but Regent Street is very convenient.

They carry all the major brands and have matching sweaters and jackets for many styles. This also is a wonderful place to purchase scarves in the traditional tartans or in more subtle colors to take home as gifts for your family. Remember when you were six and Mommy brought you back a kilt of your own? (You always lost the pin, too, didn't you?) This is where you can return the favor for someone on your gift list. The kids' department is excellent; don't miss their chart of tartans and clans.

SCOTCH HOUSE

84 Regent Street, W1 (Tube: Piccadilly Circus)
191 Regent Street, W1 (Tube: Oxford Circus)
2 Brompton Road, SW1 (Tube: Knightsbridge)
7 Marble Arch, W1 (Tube: Marble Arch)
187 Oxford Street, W1 (Tube: Bond Street)

SHIRIN CASHMERE

You've got the money, you're ready to pay, but you're desperate to escape shabby-chic classics and find something wild and wacky or just lush and plush? Step this way. Shirin sells high-fashion looks in cashmere. Very chic, very now, very expensive.

SHIRIN CASHMERE

11 Beauchamp Place, SW3 (Tube: Knightsbridge)

WESTAWAY & WESTAWAY

If you can't stand wondering who has the cheapest sweaters and the best selection, take my word for it and head to Westaway & Westaway. It's located across the street from the British Museum, and you are guaranteed to find any sweater in any color and style that might be desired.

There are two shops, which carry a large selection of knitted garments from Scotland and Ireland, as well as the classic cashmere and lamb's wool favorites. They have slightly discounted Burberrys and Aquascutum items, kilts, shawls, and yardgoods in one shop, and then sweaters, sweaters, sweaters in the other shop. In both shops notice there are rooms upstairs and downstairs as well as a back, back room that you might have trouble finding if you don't know it's there. We buy men's cashmere sweaters and sew in some shoulder pads. (Men's sweaters cost less than women's.) Don't forget to look at the sale merchandise on the lower shelves in the downstairs rooms. There also is a more fashion-oriented shop one block away. To order, call toll-free in the U.S.: (800) 345-3219.

WESTAWAY & WESTAWAY

62–65 Great Russell Street, WC1 (Tube: Holborn)

92–93 Great Russell Street, WC1 (Tube: Holborn)

PORTOBELLO CHINA & WOOLLENS

If you love crazy fun, this one's for you. This is Bargain Sweater City. Sweaters that elsewhere cost $100 are $75 here. There are seconds; some of the merchandise is big-name without labels, but the help will tell you what it is. It is worse than mobbed on Saturday, and you have to be the kind who likes this kind of stuff to endure it.

I happen to think it's funny. Last time I was there, they pulled out zillions of sweaters for me; searched for cashmere twin sets for me, and were most helpful and polite considering I didn't buy a thing and the shop was jam-packed. Prices here are among the best in London—probably in all England.

There is not a big selection. But if you give up on a sweater, you can always buy a teapot.

PORTOBELLO CHINA & WOOLLENS

89 Portobello Road, W11 (Tube: Notting Hill Gate)

Local Heroes

FREED OF LONDON LTD.

If you are a ballet freak, you have long known of Freed of London, one of the most famous names in slippers and stuff. Freed has not stayed back in the Dark Ages of the Ballet Russe. In fact, they have jetéd right into the future with a dance and exercise line.

FREED OF LONDON LTD.

94 St. Martin's Lane, WC2 (Tube: Leicester Square)

BUTTON QUEEN

You have to go back a little farther than the tourist mainstream to find this shop, but it's convenient enough for you to go for it—especially if you sew, knit, or collect. The small shop has everything from old to new, to hand-painted to WEDGWOOD buttons. The Wedgwood set is rather pricey, but other prices do begin at about a quarter per button. If you are considering making a sweater or having one made from a designer kit, come by here to get the buttons.

The store is only two blocks from Oxford Street, so don't let the address throw you. Get there through Cecil Court and you won't mind the walk.

BUTTON QUEEN

19 Marylebone Lane, W1 (Tube: Bond Street)

THE IRISH LINEN COMPANY

In business in London since 1875, this is the perfect little shop for those in search of visual traditions. It's in the Burlington Arcade, and the windows are draped with tablecloths and place mats. Everything reeks of tradition, high tea, and *grand-mère*. While they aren't giving away the stuff, the prices are rather moderate.

THE IRISH LINEN COMPANY

35–36 Burlington Arcade, W1 (Tube: Piccadilly Circus)

SWAINE, ADENEY, BRIGG & SONS

If you are looking for one shop in all of England that represents the upper crust, then this has to be it. It's more of a museum than a shop—you come here for your hunting, riding,

and fishing supplies as well as the perfectly craft-
ed brolly (umbrella), your tweeds, sweaters,
Shetlands, and other day-to-day needs. There are
business clothes, leathergoods, and women's
things as well.

A virtual mini-department store for a way of
life that only a small percentage of the world can
still afford to subscribe to. The firm holds several
royal warrants, has a branch store in San
Francisco, and has been in business since the
1700s. This is the real thing, folks.

SWAINE, ADENEY, BRIGG & SONS
185 Piccadilly, W1 (Tube: Piccadilly Circus)

Anglo Addictions

CHARBONNEL ET WALKER

If you can't get through the day without a fix
of chocolate, stop by Charbonnel et Walker,
which happens to hold a royal warrant. Sources
outside of Buckingham Palace say that
Charbonnel et Walker is the best chocolatier in
the world. Prince Philip likes the Mocha Crisp.
The chocolate milk mix makes a great gift. During
The Season they offer "strawberries and cream"
truffles. In winter, they host chocolate tastings.

CHARBONNEL ET WALKER
28 Old Bond Street, W1 (Tube: Bond Street or
Green Park)

THORNTON'S

If you're more the type who needs a candy fix
and not a royal pedigree for your bonbons,
there's a large British chain called Thornton's,
which is popular all over the U.K. At Easter they
will personalize any chocolate egg for free.
(Makes a great gift, but hand-carry yours on the
airplane because the egg is hollow and it will
shatter if packed in your luggage.)

Thornton's has many branch stores and some counters in various department stores, such as SELFRIDGES. I happen to be addicted to their toffee. This is also the home of the Jelly Welly, the best gift you'll ever buy for 50p (see page 8).

THORNTON'S
Covent Garden, WC2 (Tube: Covent Garden)

PRESTAT

Famous for their red candy boxes, their truffles, and their animal shapes in chocolate, this shop holds a royal warrant. This is where I got the chocolate sardines for my friend Carolyn's birthday—£5.

PRESTAT
14 Prince's Arcade, SW1 (Tube: Piccadilly Circus)

H.R. HIGGINS

One of the great gifts to take back home is a tin of tea—which is OK with Customs. Coffee also can be brought back. H.R. Higgins is the "in" coffee provider, and since it's conveniently located for all our West End shopping, we always stop in for a sniff and a bag of beans. This really impresses your friends when they rave about your brew and you tell them it's from London. Ho-hum. (They do mail order.)

H.R. HIGGINS
79 Duke Street, W1 (Tube: Piccadilly Circus)

R. TWINING & CO., LTD.

Sound original enough for you? R. Twining & Co., Ltd., which holds the royal warrant and is famous the world over. There's a tiny museum of tea and a shop; it's really quite out of the way and fun and special.

R. TWINING & CO., LTD.
216 The Strand, WC2 (Tube: Charing Cross)

English Toiletries

France has the big discounts, not London, but local brands are famous and make good gifts. Prices are usually moderate. Also note that the new European fragrances are introduced in France first, then the Continent, then London, and then the U.S., so you may be able to find a new scent that is not yet available in the U.S.

J. FLORIS LTD.

London has two leading local perfumers; Floris is one of them. Special floral perfumes include Roses, Lilies, Lavender, and on and on. Nice for gift items and soaps.

J. FLORIS LTD.
89 Jermyn Street, SW1 (Tube: Piccadilly Circus)

PENHALIGON'S

Especially well-known for their toilet water and soap that men adore, Penhaligon's holds a royal warrant. Their products are produced according to the original formulas of William Penhaligon, who began his business as a barbershop in 1841. It's very olde England in here, and fun to sniff around. Kids seem to like it here, too.

PENHALIGON'S
41 Wellington Street, WC2 (Tube: Covent Garden)
110A New Bond Street, W1 (Tube: Bond Street)
Burlington Arcade, W1 (Piccadilly Circus)

JAMES BODENHAM & CO.

Related to the Floris family by marriage, James Bodenham is a Victoriana kind of shop with gift items as well as potpourri and smell-good items and fragrances. There are many food items (jams and spices, as well as teas) and fragrances, but it's the apothecary nature of the store that makes it so much fun.

JAMES BODENHAM & CO.
    88 Jermyn Street, SW1 (Tube: Green Park)

CZECH & SPEAKE

Trendy Italian and old-fashioned English in the same breath, this bath shop specializes in brushes and bath-time accessories, as well as its own brand of fragrances. The shop is all gray and black and brass; the packaging is very special in a high-tech-traditional manner. One of the most interesting shops in London, with a product that not too many Americans know about. The ideal gift for the person who has everything.

CZECH & SPEAKE
    39C Jermyn Street, SW1 (Tube: Piccadilly Circus)

MOLTON BROWN

Molton Brown is a very chic Mayfair beauty parlor. They sell their own hair products (HARRODS also has the line), which are made from old-fashioned natural recipes. I still use the seaweed setting lotion whenever I set my hair in rollers.

The line comes in amber plastic bottles which look like old-fashioned apothecary bottles with Victorian-style labels. Don't forget the Molton-Browners, big pipe cleaners for rolling your hair. The makeup line is carried in New York at Barneys. I don't happen to use this salon as my local hairdresser (it's famous—you certainly might want to give it a try), but I do love their products—and they make great gifts.

MOLTON BROWN
    58 South Molton Street, W1 (Tube: Bond Street)

Aromatherapy

Aromatherapy has been big in London for years; I'm just now accepting the fact that not only is it here to stay, but it's fun. I dab my pillow with lavender oil every night and float orange oil in my office. I'm not sure that there are any true benefits to do this, but the smells are pleasing.

The essence of aromatherapy is that different smells affect your brain in different ways, therefore you can manipulate your feelings and your health by what fragrance you sniff. Even airlines offer samples of products that fight jet lag. Ian goes to MICHAELJOHN for aromatherapy every time he returns to London from a big trip in which he's had a major time change (see page 144).

You can buy aromatherapy products just about everywhere in London, from department stores to specialty stores such as CULPEPER THE HERBALISTS (my personal source), to chemists such as BOOTS. British Airways gives you essential oils on the plane to help combat jet lag; the LANGHAM HILTON has them waiting for you in your room.

Horse and Rider

My friend Carolyn Blain tells me I can never retire to England to live happily ever after until I learn how to ride. She doesn't mean Western. In fact, she means dressage. Hmmmmmm. Well, I read Jilly Cooper. That's a start, isn't it?

If you're into the horsy set, and won't find your trip to London complete without a sniff of saddle soap, you'll find the horse trail of retailing to be marvelously old-fashioned England, steeped in dark-grained wood and tradition and foxtails. Is your Hermès scarf tied in a knot around your waxed leather handbag?

J.A. ALLEN

If you have a horse-crazy daughter, perhaps she'd like a book from J.A. Allen, the foremost equestrian bookstore and publisher. You name it, and they've got it here. If you just want to soak up horse vibes, this is the place to do it. The sales help is most helpful, and they never say "neigh."

J.A. ALLEN

1 Lower Grosvenor Place, SW1 (Tube: Victoria)

HENRY MAXWELL

Once you've got a leg up on horse lore, you'll need boots. So trot on over to Maxwell (in the basement), where you will be glad you're close to ground zero when you see the prices. We're talking heavy-duty royalty and polo-playing playboys for customers, and well over $1,000 for a pair of polo boots. A Maxwell boot is *le dernier cri* to those in the know, so if you've got it—flaunt it. If you're planning on crashing Virginia fox-hunting society, Maxwell will start you on the right foot. Bespoke shoes and boots.

HENRY MAXWELL

11 Savile Row, W1 (Tube: Piccadilly Circus)

TRICKER'S

If you find HENRY MAXWELL a tad pricey, but don't mind spending $1,000 or more for a pair of riding boots, try Tricker's. Shoes start at £300.

TRICKER'S

67 Jermyn Street, SW1 (Tube: Piccadilly Circus)

JAMES LOCK & CO.

If you need the right hat for the fox hunt, you'll pay about $200 for a very proper bowler at a firm that has been in business since the mid-1700s and knows a lot about crowning glory; silks here, too. Lock sells all sorts of hats, by the way, and they hold a royal warrant.

JAMES LOCK & CO.

6 St. James's Street, SW1 (Tube: Green Park)

J. DEDGE & SONS

For traditional riding garb, try J. Dedge & Sons, which specializes in garments for showmen and hunters; they will fit you in London and then send your order within two months. Dressage heaven.

J. DEDGE & SONS
16 Clifford Street, W1 (Tube: Piccadilly Circus)

GIDDEN
This saddlemaker has recently opened a retail shop in the Burlington Arcade to sell handbags and small luggage pieces, and they are to die for. As chic and properly British as MULBERRY, but a little bit less nouveau. The look is colored leather with natural trim; this is sort of a sophisticated version of Dooney & Burke with even more horse-and-rider country style.

They will also make you a saddle as they have done for the Royal Family for years. And years. Riding habits, boots, and the needed repairs, etc.

GIDDEN
15d Clifford Street, W1 (Tube: Green Park)

Burlington Arcade, W1 (Tube: Piccadilly Circus)

Shooting and Fishing

JAMES PURDEY & SONS LTD.
Gun and rifle makers; three royal warrants. Keep their catalog on your coffee table merely for the fun of it. Take your kids as if you were in a museum. Pretend you are going on safari with Clark Gable. Or going shooting with David (King Edward VIII). Don't miss it. This store is right behind the DORCHESTER.

JAMES PURDEY & SONS LTD.
57 South Audley Street, W1 (Tube: Green Park or Marble Arch)

HARDY BROTHERS
Made Queen Victoria's fishing rod. Need I say more?

HARDY BROTHERS
61 Pall Mall, W1 (Tube: Green Park)

CHAPTER SIX

HOME FURNISHINGS, DECOR, AND DESIGN

English Decor

While a large number of the tourists who go to London are seeking raincoats with zip-out linings and matching kilts for the kids, I'm going to attempt to redirect your thinking. Or some of your thoughts. This is the shopping police: Have you thought about your living room today?

Ralph Lauren has proved quite handsomely (and expensively) that Americans want the olde English, shabby-chic, hounds-and-horses, cabbage-roses-and-faded-fringes look of yesterday. Maybe I can't get it for you wholesale, but I sure know a lot of places to shop for this kind of look in London, places with cheaper prices than in the U.S. Not everything (especially Ralph Lauren) is going to cost less in London, but there are a lot of buys out there and many more choices at prices that are competitive to the U.S.

English Design

The look has taken generations to develop. However, fear not. Thanks to the foresight of a group of designers, antiques dealers, and fabric manufacturers, the English look has been packaged and is for sale in London. You can actually wander throughout certain areas of London and see showroom after showroom, each with a different—but totally acceptable—version of The Look.

Many Americans give Laura Ashley credit for popularizing the use of English patterns and actually sprucing up the colors to appeal to a worldwide audience. Truth is, Laura Ashley popularized a bastardized version of Country Chic with tiny flowers and a dense repeat. Your real English gentry most likely will mock Lady Ashley's look as fake and way too floral.

The popularization of authentic Country English style actually goes back to the beginnings of Colefax & Fowler over fifty years ago; there is no question that John Fowler is the grandfather of The Look as we know it now. And having Colefax & Fowler prints in your home is a status symbol.

It's been said that the British national character is one that resists change, has tremendous respect for tradition, and likes to do things the way they have always been done in generations past. So it is with English decorating: the themes show a slow transition as generation after generation adds only a small mark to the whole look.

While the British have a healthy respect for eccentrics, English style has touches of eccentricism woven into the traditional art forms. Even Vanessa Bell's Charleston House with its 1930's Arts and Crafts revival wackiness is considered a classic British take.

Eccentrics have always been appreciated (try buying a piece of Clarice Cliff pottery these days without flinching), but period continuity is what Americans count on as part of the base of goods available to them. With that comes the essentials of the English lifestyle that Americans seek to absorb, emulate, or simply mimic: dog, horse, garden.

The fact that England has dramatically

embraced some elements of modern design is at first ignored by Americans, who can get that sort of thing at home. But the impact of the Conran/Habitat empire of stores cannot be overlooked, nor can the effects of modern architecture—whether Prince Charles likes it or not. One look at Lloyd's, which either thrills you or chills you, should be enough for you to realize that Lloyd's meets Habitat in the stores and living rooms of the British public. British yuppies, who may live in houses or flats that are hundreds of years old, are no longer falling back to the classics, but instead are looking to affordable post-modern solutions. There are few middle- or upper-middle-class British families that don't have at least some of their table arts from either Habitat or Next. Today shopping in London means taking the modern, as well as the antique, seriously.

Shoppers and design students now crave the likes of stores stocked with designs by Katharine Hamnet, Joseph, Department X, and the like. So it is that today's British design represents this very strong dichotomy between old Wellies and new wisdom. The shoppers who prowl these modern tributes to the new age and the new hope of British design are often wearing less-than-fashionable statements of age and class and are almost always combining what they buy with design elements that have existed for centuries. Making the old stand tall while taking on only a few touches of the new may prove to be the future basic strength of British design.

Shopping the Sources

There are a few rules to be aware of when buying in London:

- Have plenty of business cards on hand—if you are working as a member of the trade, introduce yourself when you enter a shop; ask upfront what trade discount or courtesies are offered.

- It is proper etiquette for dealers to identify themselves; they usually give themselves away by their knowledge anyway, but go ahead, tell 'em who you are. If you've brought along an expert for a second opinion, don't be shy. Introduce.

- British decorating and design houses are not in the business of reducing prices unless you are an established client with an open account. Be prepared to show that you are indeed a professional, that you have a credit rating, etc. It's best to have at least three references from big U.S. firms where you hold open accounts. It's not a bad idea to have U.S. showrooms write, call, or fax ahead to a London showroom, or cohort to give you the OK.

- Very often English design firms will not take personal orders from out-of-towners. This is especially true if the firm has an agency in the country where you wish the goods to be shipped. They will not compete with their own overseas agents. However, they will sell goods directly from their London showrooms to anyone.

- Be prepared to handle your own shipping.

- When shopping in a market such as BERMONDSEY, or on PORTOBELLO ROAD, expect to bargain. If you pay the price as marked, you will be overpaying. In this kind of circumstance, having a knowledgeable local at your side can be beneficial. As a member of "the trade" you are expected to know the proper value and negotiate accordingly. At least know the U.S. price for a similar item.

- Deal with cash when possible. Often a store will offer a discount for cash transactions because they do not have to deal with cred-it-card fees. In the markets, only cash is accepted. Many stalls will not even take travel-er's checks. If the store does not offer a discount for cash, ask to see the owner and make your point.

- English fabrics are sold by the meter or the yard (ask); wallpaper rolls are very often double rolls, not single rolls. Always verify the width of the fabrics (most American fabrics are 54 inches wide) and the size of the repeat, as both will affect the amount you need to purchase. If you are buying for a particular piece of furniture, take the measurements of the piece and a photo with you. Most fabric houses have trained staff who will help you determine how much fabric is necessary for your job. If there is any question, buy extra. Yes, you might be able to find the same fabric at home, but the dye lot will be completely different and your two pieces will never match. You are safer having the extra for pillows, if you don't need it for your job.

- When you are in the fabric house, ask if there are any close-out bins. Quite often fabrics are discontinued or half rolls are sold and the showroom cannot sell the pieces left. There just might be some wonderful leftovers that are perfect for your home or for a piece of furniture you hadn't thought of re-covering. LAURA ASHLEY is famous for its close-out bins.

- When buying wallpaper, ask about the life expectancy of the paper. Once again, printing processes differ, and the wallpaper you are dying for could in fact be printed on a paper that is not as sturdy as your needs. Many of the LAURA ASHLEY papers are wonderful but have a life expectancy of only four to five years. Some are not coated, and they absorb dirt at a rapid rate. These are considerations that every designer worries about when doing a design job. Since you will be doing it yourself, you, too, must be aware! There are Laura Ashley vinyl wallpapers, but there are two types: British vinyl and American-made vinyl from a different company. Not all patterns are made by both houses.

- If you are buying fabrics that need trimmings to match, buy them at the same time and with the fabrics in hand. The English trimmings (fringes, ropes, tassels, etc.) are designed and colored to match the fabrics. Do note that in Britspeak, the word "fringe" refers to the bangs of a hairstyle. Use the word "trim." These trimmings are not cheap, but they can be much, much less in England than in the U.S. Also, the London selection is superior to what you'll find in the U.S.

- If you are planning to buy a lot of furniture, make arrangements with a shipper before you start your spree (see page 193). Very often the fabric houses will ship for you, but the furniture dealers prefer that you make your own arrangements. If you are buying antiques valued at over £2,000, you will need to have an export license from the British Customs offices. A good shipper will also help arrange this for you. It is easier to have all your goods arrive in one container than in dispersed shipments. Ask your shipper if they will pick up from a variety of sources and if there is any charge for this extra service. Be sure to get the best insurance possible on your goods. Don't save money on shipping. Shop the options, but buy the best!

- When buying at auction be aware that you will be bidding against dealers who know their goods and what they are worth. Do a very careful inspection of the auction items the day before and check carefully for repairs and/or replacement of parts. The technology of furniture repair has made it possible to repair and/or replace damaged parts of a piece of furniture without the untrained eye being able to see the work. If you are not buying to collect but only to enjoy, this won't matter. However, if you are collecting Georgian antiques, every repair changes the value of the piece. If the dealers are not bidding, take their clue that something is wrong. If you want a piece badly enough, however, you can very often outbid the dealers. They need to resell the piece to make a profit and therefore need to stop well under the street value for that piece. This is where you will have the advantage. You can save money and get a valuable piece of furniture/art/carpet or collectible while having the fun of beating the dealer.

- When buying period pieces, whether at auction, through a dealer, or at a stall, remember to get papers of authenticity. Any item 100 years old or older is free of U.S. Customs duties. However, you will be asked for proof of age by officials. They are on to tricks in this area, so don't try to pass off a new tea service as antique. However, this is also a gray area in British law. If you buy a chair that is Georgian but has had some parts replaced, this would be considered a reasonable restoration and would be fine. But if more than half of the chair has been restored so that most of the parts are new, the law is not clear, and your chair may not be considered duty-free.

- Don't expect to be able to buy a national treasure. Important pieces must be approved for export by the country of origin before they are granted an export license. If you are bidding against a museum in an auction, it is quite possible that the work will be awarded to the museum even though you can outbid them. All countries are unwilling to let go of their finest works of art and furniture.

- If the work of art or piece of furniture is not wanted by the museum, be sure that the price you are paying is not more expensive (taking shipping, insurance, etc., into account) than it would be to buy a similar piece through a dealer in the U.S. If it is a special, one-of-a-kind find, of course the value is there, regardless of the price. But the average antiques shopper is not a pure collector and possibly could do better by buying at home. Doing your research at home before you go is always the key to a good buy.

Booking English Style/1

If you're interested in English style and decor as much as I am, you'll have a ball with all the magazines your news agent can sell you. Go to several different news agents, because even the biggies in the train stations don't always have the full range.

My favorite (or should I say *favourite*?) decorating magazines in order of preference are:

- *House & Garden Incorporating Wine & Food Magazine*
- *British Homes & Gardens*
- *Country Homes & Interiors*
- *Period Living*

Booking English Style/2

British publishing has far more choices in the subjects of design, architecture, style, crafts, and reference for buying antiques. Alas, British book prices are also outrageously high. Make sure there is no American edition to a book you are planning to buy before you go hog wild at your nearest HATCHARDS or DILLON'S.

Also note that if you buy price guides, prices will be in pounds sterling pegged to local values; many items are more (or less) valuable across the pond.

For an almost staggering selection of books on design—not just British—be sure to visit the DESIGN CENTRE OF LONDON, which has a huge book-selling space divided into many categories of the arts, including architecture.

DESIGN CENTRE OF LONDON
28 Haymarket, SW1 (Tube: Piccadilly Circus)

Design and Decorating Classes

Since DIY (Do-It-Yourself) is such a big notion in Britain, there are scads of design and decorating classes for ladies with a little time and a little talent on their hands. Sometimes the classes are day-long seminars in London studios or shops; sometimes they are weekends out of town.

You may often see events advertised by the various style publications; sometimes they are offered as promotional events. Almost all events cost money and must be booked ahead; check to see if the price includes the materials you need. (It usually does.)

Contact KLC Interior Design Training, KLC House, Springvale Terrace, London W14.

Design on Sale

Not only do showrooms have sales, but there are big social sale events held once or twice a year—usually to raise funds for charity—where designer furnishings are sold off. The Grand Sale is an annual event sponsored by *House & Garden* and held in a huge hall for maximum fun; it's usually in the fall—ask your hotel concierge or watch for ads in the magazine's pages.

Also pick up brochures in design showrooms; frequently they announce sale events.

Chelsea Design Week

This is an event for the trade: it includes complimentary chauffeur-driven cars to whisk you to various participating showrooms, where they lay it on thick. Only the big names play. One day is open to the public. The event is usually in March; write Chelsea Design Week, The Basement, 4 Charlwood Place, London SW1V 2LU.

Auctions

The designer's best secret is the London auction, where more and more people are hoping to get a deal. Because prices are set at auctions and then determined for similar items throughout the art and furniture world, you may not find a bargain at all. Naturally, the London auction scene is the big time, whereas country auctions are easier to deal with and may offer better prices. We must admit, with a warning, that we went to a country auction and found that the furniture was desirable and well-priced, but the cost of shipping it back to the U.S. did not justify buying anything.

Nevertheless, auctions are a tremendous amount of fun and should be considered for pure entertainment's sake. In London, however, there are certain auctions that are quite serious and important and, while fun, are taken without much of a sense of humor. If you attend a big auction at a prestigious house, ask around about proper wardrobe. Ladies should plan on simple suits or silks for day. Evening auctions can be black-tie events—they are seldom white-tie. Viewings are almost always during the day, as are the majority of auctions. Proper business clothes are essential, even if one isn't bidding.

Like all major cities, London has an auction season: October to May. Country auctions are often held in the summer, but fancy auctions are held only at auction houses in the city during the season. Occasionally auctions are closed to the public—like the fur auctions in St. Petersburg, where pelts are sold to furriers in lots—but usually you can be admitted to an auction by catalog or for free. Weekly auction programs are published in *The Times* on Tuesday and in *The Daily Telegraph* on Monday. Some houses sell certain types of works on specific days of the week, like china on Monday and European oil paintings on Friday—or something like that. In season, there will be about a hundred auctions a month in London alone.

It would be a mistake to assume that everything you buy in an auction is a bargain. Various auctions have various functions in their respective fields; often it is to set the prices for the rest of the world. On the other hand, you should not be intimidated. You may indeed get a real "steal," or you may be shopping in a country where the market price for an item you are interested in is considerably less than in the U.S.

Please note that there is no VAT on antiques.

Do be wary of fakes at auctions, particularly from the less famous houses. If you buy an item because you love it, and if it doesn't matter whether it's real or not, that's one thing. But if you are buying for investment, name-dropping, or status-seeking purposes, use a house expert or, better yet, a private expert as a consultant. The better houses will not intentionally sell you a forgery or a fake; small-time auctioneers may not care what's in the lots, as long as they move them out. A house may even admit they don't know if a piece is authentic. SOTHEBY'S uses the full name of an artist in the catalog listing when they know the work is authentic, but only the initials of the artist if they have some doubt as to the provenance of the work.

The experts at the big auction houses are trained to not only know their stuff, but also to be informative and polite. If you want to bone up on a point of curiosity or just pick someone's brain, wander into a good auction house and speak to someone at the front desk. They well may give you information you never knew or turn you on to a free and expert opinion.

The most famous auction houses in London are SOTHEBY'S and CHRISTIE'S, but don't underestimate PHILLIPS SON & NEALE or BONHAM'S, which have been around since 1793— they probably know quite a bit. Some London auction houses are:

BONHAM'S
65–69 Lots Road, SW10 (Tube: Take a taxi!)
Montpelier Street, SW7 (Tube: Knightsbridge)

CHRISTIE'S
8 King Street, St. James's, SW1 (Tube: Piccadilly Circus or Green Park)
South Kensington, 85 Old Brompton Road, SW7 (Tube: Earl's Court)

HARVEY'S AUCTIONS
14–18 Neal Street, WC2 (Tube: Covent Garden)

PHILLIPS SON & NEALE
101 New Bond Street, W1 (Tube: Bond Street)

SOTHEBY'S
34–35 New Bond Street, W1 (Tube: Bond Street)

There are also stamp and coin auctions. HARMER'S (91 New Bond Street, W1; Tube: Bond Street) is the leading stamp auction house.

Don't forget country auctions that you may find on a weekend outing, which usually are charming—but if they had something truly *important* to sell, it would have gone to a big house in a major city to command a big price. So enjoy. At a country auction, expect to pay cash for your purchase. Be prepared to have to make your own shipping arrangements (see page 193).

When you shop at an auction of any kind, remember:

- The house is not responsible for the authenticity of the article.
- There is a house commission (8% to 10%) charged to the seller, but the buyer will have to pay taxes. Some houses also commission the buyer—ask, as this can raise the price of your item by another 10%.
- You are entitled to know the price a similar item went for in previous years and the price the house expects the item to go for at the current auction. Often these prices are posted at the viewing or may be published in the catalog.
- Find out before you bid what currency you must pay in. International houses often accept many currencies, and you may do better with your dollar converting to one rather than another. This can pay off with a large purchase.
- If bidding is not in U.S. dollars, keep a calculator in your hand during the bidding to know what the prices are; remember to do your figure at the current American Express rate of exchange rather than the bank rate. The bank rate will be more favorable than the one you will actually be paying, so don't cheat yourself from an accurate conversion of what you will truly be paying.

- Expect to pay tax on the item when you call for it. Find out the tax ahead of time. VAT is not paid on antiques.
- The auction house may pack and ship your purchase for you, but it may be cheaper to do it yourself, or ask your hotel concierge to handle it for you.
- Make sure that the item you are about to buy may leave the country! Some countries won't let you out with what they consider to be items of their heritage. Conversely, make sure you can get it into the U.S. You will not be reimbursed if the government confiscates any of your property. If the item is an antique, get the papers that verify its age. (According to Customs, an antique is any item 100 years old or more.)

Shipping

The good news: You've just found the most wonderful, gorgeous, fabulous, chic, and inexpensive sideboard. You've longed for one for years, know it will be the envy of all who see it.

The bad news: It certainly won't fit into your suitcase.

Whether the item is as cumbersome as a sideboard, as small as a few bottles of perfume, or as fragile as dinner plates, you can arrange to ship it home. All it takes is a little time and a little more money.

You will want to know enough about shipping costs to be able to make a smart decision about the added cost of your purchase. To make shipping pay, the item—with the additional cost of shipping, duty, and insurance (and Customs agent, etc., if need be)—still should cost *less* than it would at home, or be so totally unavailable at home that any price makes it a worthwhile purchase. If it's truly unavailable (and isn't an antique or a one-of-a-kind art item) at home, ask yourself why. There may be a good reason—such as it's illegal to bring such an item into the country! If you are indeed looking for a certain type of thing, be very familiar with American prices. If it's an item of furniture, even an antique, can a decorator get it for you with a 20% rather than a 40% markup? Have you checked out all the savings angles first?

There are basically two types of shipping: surface and air. Air can be broken down two ways: unaccompanied baggage and regular air freight.

Surface mail is the cheaper of the two. Surface mail may mean through the regular mail channels—i.e., a small package of perfume would be sent through parcel post—or it may require your filling an entire shipping container, or at least paying the price for use of an entire container. Many people make the mistake of assuming that only the weight of an item will matter in the shipping. While weight matters, there may be a 500-pound difference per price bracket!

A piano may weigh more than two Queen Anne chairs, but they may cost the same to ship. Surface mail may take three months, but we've had delivery in three weeks. Allow three months to be safe, longer if so advised by the dealer.

If you are shipping books (antique or otherwise), note that there are special surface rates and no U.S. duties.

Generally speaking, rates are per cubic foot and include:

- picking up the purchase;
- packing the goods (crating may be extra);
- handling export documents;
- sea-freight charges;
- Customs clearance on the U.S. end.

If you want to save money, ask about groupage services. Your goods will be held until a shipping container is filled. The container will then go to the U.S., to only one of four ports of entry (Los Angeles, New York, San Francisco, or New Orleans), where you can meet the container at the dock, be there when your items are unpacked, and then pay the duties due. A full container is 1,100 cubic feet of space (or 8', 6" by 8', 6" by 20' long—or big enough for about one hundred pieces of furniture) and will not be delivered to your door (no matter how much you smile). A container to New York will cost you £3,000, which includes wrapping, shipping, and London paperwork. U.S. collections and bills of lading usually add £100 to the bill. Insurance costs 1-1/2 of the total value of the goods.

Air freight is several times more expensive than surface, but has the assurance of quick delivery. You can air freight small items up to 50 pounds (in weight, not price) through traditional business services such as DHL and Federal Express. Or you can use freight services which will air freight larger-sized packages and even furniture.

If your purchase was so delicate and so important as to need to be flown, it might indeed need an international courier, who is a person who hand-carries the item for you. (This is often done with pieces of art or valuable papers.)

If you're looking for names and contacts, try TRANS EURO, a firm that offers complete packing and shipping services. They will collect your purchases from anywhere in the U.K. (or Europe), pack them, and ship them to you by sea or air. They have brokers who will land the package and bring it right to your door; all paperwork is handled by them. They have insurance from Lloyd's of London and do a huge business with England's antiques fairs.

TRANS EURO

Drury Way, Brent Park, London NW10 (Telephone: 81-459-8080; Fax: 81-451-0061)

I found another complete service through the people who organize the Saturday part of Portobello Road: LOCKSON SERVICES LTD. They will do full loads, part loads, and single items; they pack fine art and antiques as well and serve worldwide destinations.

LOCKSON SERVICES LTD.
29 Broomfield Street, London E14 6BX (Telephone: 71-515-8600; Fax: 71-515-4043)

Other shippers and packers approved by the LAPADA (London and Provincial Antique Dealers Association) include FENTONS, Beachy Road, Old Ford, London E3 (Telephone: 81-533-2711; Fax: 81-985-6032); and FEATHERSTON SHIPPING, 24 Hampton House, 15–17 Ingate Place, London SW8 (Telephone: 71-720-0422; Fax: 71-720-6330).

When you choose a shipper, ask for a buying kit.

Insurance

Insurance usually is sold by the package by your shipper. Do not assume that it is included in the price of delivery, because it isn't. There are several different types of insurance, with deductibles or all-risk (with no deductible), so you'll have to make a personal choice based on the value of what you are shipping. Remember when figuring the value of the item for insurance purposes to include the price of the shipping.

If you bought a desk for $1,000 and it costs $500 to ship it home, the value for insurance purposes is $1,500. If you have the replacement-cost type of insurance, you should probably double the price, since that is approximately what it would cost you to replace the item in the U.S.

China, Crystal, and Silver

The British are blessed with a crazy location in the sea of geography: they've got coal and they've got clay. As a result, they have a centuries-old tradition of producing bone china. You can visit the china factories in the countryside (see *Born to Shop Great Britain*), or you can visit all the china stores in London.

- Most china stores in London sell only first-quality. The prices are usually 30% less than in the U.S., but if the dollar is bad, that saving may shrink. During sales, especially in January, you may discover a 50% savings. During sales, some of the biggies (like HAR-RODS and LAWLEY'S, for example) do truck in seconds, which are so marked.
- The problem with really saving big on china comes with the shipping. China must be packed, crated, insured, and—in some cases —you must pay duty on it (not if it comes home in parcels worth under $50 and marked "unsolicited gift"). Even with VAT refunds, you will still raise the cost of your purchase appreciably. But that doesn't mean you shouldn't consider a big haul. It just means you need to mentally register the landed price, not the asking price.
- Prices on the same items are supposed to be the same in each retail outlet, but may vary by as much as £2 per place setting. If a retailer is overstocked with a certain pattern, he may deal on the price of a large order.
- If you want to buy seconds, consider a trip to Stoke-on-Trent; if not, come to London for the January and June/July sales, or even order by telephone during a sale period. HAR-RODS has a toll-free phone number during the January sale, to make it even easier.
- Silver, even silver plate, is getting more and more expensive each year, but is still a good bet when bought secondhand. Avoid the fancy stores and stick to street markets, such as BERMONDSEY or the famous THE LON-

DON SILVER VAULTS (page 203). By law, silver must be marked—look for marks, or ask. To bring silver (or plate) into the U.S. tax-free, it must be over 100 years old. Get a receipt that says so from the dealer at the time of purchase.

- England is also famous for its lead crystal, although the most famous brands come from Ireland or Scotland. You can buy crystal during the big sale periods when you buy china, or head for the factory-outlet stores, which usually feature the best prices on discontinued patterns. If you are filling in an existing pattern, you may want to buy at the airport either in London or Shannon.

CHINACRAFT

Chinacraft is the leading dressy mass merchant for china and crystal, which is indeed a special niche to fill. There are several stores in London; you'll find them easily in major tourist and trading areas. They offer stock on all the biggies—Spode, Minton, Royal Crown Derby, Wedgwood, Aynsley, Coalport, and Royal Worcester. Quite a selection of crystal is also available, including patterns from Waterford and Baccarat.

Oh, yes, and here's a little secret or two for you about Chinacraft: If you buy a lot (over $500), see if you can politely negotiate a discount. The salespeople are used to big spenders who will come in and order half a million pounds' worth of delectables, but you can buy less and still get a discount—if you are nice. Discounts vary on stock—if they have a lot of something they want to move out, they will discount it up front. Anyone walking in may ask about a pattern, and they may tell you that they'll take 15% off on that pattern. On another pattern—perhaps one that is out of stock and has to be ordered for you—a discount would be impossible. It's all very flexible.

A catalog with prices in dollars costs $5, but

best news of all, Chinacraft comes to the U.S. and takes hotel space to show their goodies in major U.S. cities. You may go for tea and order your goods at London prices. You also may phone. You are guaranteed safe delivery.

People often wonder why one would shop here rather than at REJECT CHINA SHOP (see page 201). So here goes: The two offer entirely different attitudes and shopping experiences. Please note that prices may not vary significantly! Chinacraft is a somewhat elegant store selling masses of fancy merchandise; Reject China is a mass store selling fancy merchandise as if it was discounted, which it often is not. Chinacraft gives you the personal attention of a specialty shop. Furthermore, the prices are usually identical.

CHINACRAFT

71 Regent Street, W1 (Tube: Piccadilly Circus)
198 Regent Street, W1 (Tube: Oxford Circus)
98 The Strand, WC2 (Tube: Charing Cross)

THOMAS GOODE
If you're looking for the ultimate shopping experience for your selection of china, glassware, silver, or exquisite accessory pieces, this elegant shop is a must. In fact, if you were looking to pick one simple, very London, very elegant shopping experience that epitomizes why you travel, why you *have* to shop in foreign cities, and what can be gained by educating your eye in the world's best cities, well, Thomas Goode just might be your best choice.

The store is almost the size of a city block and rambles through a variety of salons; don't miss any of them—including the far back where the antique knickknacks are sold, or the far side where KENNETH TURNER (see page 144), the florist, is located.

Don't bring your children. Do bring your credit cards. And possibly your camera. I took snapshots of the garbage at Kenneth Turner. It was the most gorgeous garbage I'd ever seen (flowers, flowers, flowers, and they weren't even dead).

Goode carries all the top European brands of china and crystal and has monogram services available on the premises. They have a number of innovative designs for tabletop and a lot of expensive doodads that you can also find at a plebeian place such as HARRODS, but which are much more pleasing to the eye in the surroundings of Thomas Goode. The sales help is incredibly well-bred and nice.

No bargains here. Well, maybe that's not totally true. I bought a Kenneth Turner candle for £8.50, which I did think was a bargain, in the fabulous gift department. They sell them at Harrods, but there's no reason to think you can't afford *anything* at Goode.

THOMAS GOODE
19 South Audley Street, W1 (Tube: Green Park)

WEDGWOOD/GERED

Gered is connected to WEDGWOOD and Wedgwood-owned factory-made items only. Because of their connection to Wedgwood, go here if you want Wedgwood and if REJECT CHINA SHOP didn't have what you wanted. Gered is well-equipped to send you a price quotation in U.S. dollars and to ship; you may pay with a personal check on mail order. . . and still save money. This is the uptown shopping situation for those with no time to waste, who know ahead of time that they want Wedgwood.

Note that Wedgwood is very anti-discounting; they have a seconds shop at their factory, but it's not very well-stocked and your chances of finding what you want there are very small. So if you know you want Wedgwood, this may be your best bet.

WEDGWOOD/GERED
173–174 Piccadilly, W1 (Tube: Piccadilly Circus)

LAWLEY'S

I love Lawley's because of the contrast in styles: its blue carpets and velvet cases and department-store elegance during the year, and its plank tables of bins of seconds during the sale periods. The selection is vast; the prices are fixed—as are everyone else's.

The sales are advertised in the regular newspapers (such as *The Times*, not *The Sun*) and are called midwinter and midsummer sales. That means the January sale is in the second to third week in January; ditto the summer sale—it's in the middle of June. Don't assume that all London summer sales are in July.

During the sale period, you will get factory prices right there in downtown London, on Regent Street, no less.

Plate collectors please note that Lawley's caters to the collector's set for all categories of china.

LAWLEY'S
154 Regent Street, W1 (Tube: Piccadilly Circus)

ROYAL DOULTON/LEATHER & SNOOK

Another traditional shop with a large selection, Leather & Snook has the Doulton collectors' club on its lower level. They seem to specialize more in figurines and gift china, but they certainly have the patterns and choices that other shops have.

ROYAL DOULTON/LEATHER & SNOOK
167 Piccadilly, W1 (Tube: Piccadilly Circus)

REJECT CHINA SHOP

After many years of shopping Regent Street and the wonders of London, I've about given up the thrill of this branch store. I just can't figure out where the bargains are, and I get overwhelmed by the stock and the tiny print on the price lists and the feeling that I can't find the bargain.

On Beauchamp Place, there are three small stores with differing stock, which I actually find more fun to browse, although frankly I haven't bought from this store in many years, because I think they infer a bargain without really delivering one.

The Covent Garden store is tiny and specializes in mass-market teapots with a few pieces of Portmerion and some blue-and-white; all at the going bargain price you can find around town. No bargains, but the store is tiny and crowded and cute and definitely part of the fun of shopping Covent Garden.

The Beauchamp Place shops in Knightsbridge are divided up and therefore harder to shop on an overall basis, but each one is fun for a browse; the store closest to Brompton Road has both the Blue Italian and the Portmerion, my two patterns.

They are used to tourists and will ship for you with ease. Catalogs/mail-order/telephone orders with credit cards. Prices on some items are 20% less than the fixed prices; you can deal on big orders. Discuss the VAT refund and shipping prices carefully and make sure everything is clear to you. It helps to come with a price list of your pattern from the U.S. if you are after real savings. Firsts are often priced exactly the same as in non-discount stores; "bargains" may or may not be better than anyone else's bargains.

This is a good place to shop, but don't fool yourself into thinking it's the best place in town.

REJECT CHINA SHOP

134 Regent Street, W1 (Tube: Piccadilly Circus)

33–35 Beauchamp Place, SW3 (Tube: Knightsbridge)

56–57 Beauchamp Place, SW3 (Tube: Knightsbridge)

Covent Garden, WC2 (Tube: Covent Garden)

THE LONDON SILVER VAULTS

Originally founded in 1882 as a large safety-deposit box and now in the Holborn section of London, the Silver Vaults comprise thirty-five shops selling a variety of large and small items at all prices. Only one shop is at street level; the rest are underground. Expect to find everything from silver buckets to Fabergé jewelry.

THE LONDON SILVER VAULTS

53–64 Chancery Lane, WC2 (Tube: Chancery Lane)

English Moderne

Contemporary looks are frequently combined with old-fashioned architectural styles in London; the look has moved through the 1960s and come out the other end with clean lines and moderate prices.

HABITAT

Habitat made British home-furnishings history, although not in the same way as Mr. Chippendale. After the spare Scandinavian look came the modern British look—an update of Scandinavian chic with a touch of high tech. It was all begun by Terence Conran, who was later knighted for his contribution to the world. Habitat, although no longer owned by Sir Terence, is still a glorious place to shop, even if the look isn't the newest look and you can see a lot of this stuff at home in the U.S.

Habitat is pretty much a high-street multiple; Bumble even recommends the catalog. If you shop Pottery Barn or Conran's Habitat in the U.S., you'll love Habitat.

Note that there is a difference between Habitat shops and THE CONRAN SHOP in Michelin House in London.

HABITAT

196 Tottenham Court Road, W1 (Tube: Goodge Street)

206 King's Road, SW3 (Tube: Sloane Square)

THE CONRAN SHOP

The Conran Shop should not be confused with the now defunct Conran's in the U.S. The rehabbed Michelin House with its Deco tiles and hoopla welcomes you first into a cafe, and then a store of mini-showrooms with modern yuppie furniture. Go downstairs for a less stark and more moderately priced version of the first floor—here's where you'll find the fun: baskets, gifts, dried flowers, china, toys, books, foodstuffs, coffees, luggage, umbrellas. . . everything. The shop opens at 9:30 A.M. every day except Sunday and Tuesday. On Tuesday it opens at 10 A.M. There are no Sunday hours.

THE CONRAN SHOP

81 Fulham Road, SW3 (Tube: South Kensington)

NEXT

The bigger Next shops have small decorating/home-furnishing areas where you can buy table arts, gifts, and usually fabrics, sheets, etc. The style is another version of what you're probably already familiar with from Conran's Habitat or the Pottery Barn, but prices are modern and the look is competitive with whatever else is hot in the design trends.

NEXT

160 Regent Street, W1 (Tube: Piccadilly Circus or Oxford Circus)

Dealers: Fabrics/Furniture/ Objets D'Art

It is hard to separate the fabrics, furniture, and collectibles sources from each other. Most often a fabric showroom will also carry a line of furniture, and a furniture dealer will have an exclusive line of fabrics. Many of the showrooms make individual items out of their fabrics—cosmetics bags, novelty gifts, etc.

DESIGNER'S GUILD

Tricia Guild has been going for a long time with her Designer's Guild, one of the best-known sources in town for all the pieces you need to put together a look. She has prospered because she has been able to change that look and not grow stale. She is currently into hot colors, voluptuous prints, texture, color, and handicrafts—all mixed together with a giant splash. Kaffe Fasset does a line for her; many other designers contribute. The effect is stupendous. If you're tired of the old Country English look, you'll revel in all this color and excitement. There are two shops, a few doors apart. Don't miss either. Even if you aren't going to buy so much as a meter of fabric, come in and absorb all the trends. This is hot. Warehouse sales are advertised annually. Open to the public.

DESIGNER'S GUILD
271 and 277 King's Road, SW3 (Tube: Sloane Square)

JOHN STEFANIDIS

One of the big-time hotshots of British interiors with his own books and his own following, Stefanidis offers a more modern version of John Colefax, without a look over the shoulder to the English manor house: no big cabbage roses to blind you. The small showroom offers two floors of things to look at, including wallpaper, fabric, furniture, and some gift items. We're talking about $50 for a roll of wallpaper—but an English roll of wallpaper is double the size of an American one. The shop is in a wonderful location near a string of other design showrooms and antiques shops; anyone may browse and buy.

JOHN STEFANIDIS
253 Fulham Road, SW3 (Tube: Fulham Broadway)

ANNA FRENCH

Although Anna French features a lot of lace and lacy looks, her design showroom offers a complete range of all the items necessary to the Country English post-modern look: marbleized wallpapers, faux finishes, swags of lace, fabrics printed with big flowers that aren't cabbage roses. The look would coordinate well with many JANE CHURCHILL or DESIGNER'S GUILD choices; there's a lot of Arts and Crafts inspiration in current works. But more classical possibilities are also available. Open to the public.

ANNA FRENCH
343 King's Road, SW3 (Tube: Sloane Square)

JANE CHURCHILL

The line designed by Jane Churchill is English in feeling (it goes with her last name), but international in scope. It's higher in cost than LAURA ASHLEY, but with a younger look than COLEFAX & FOWLER. The look is very packaged and is positioned a few rungs up from Laura Ashley. There are sheets and prints downstairs. Quite affordable and worth looking at.

Trade operates a separate business; the shops provide regular retail for the general public.

JANE CHURCHILL
81 Pimlico Road, SW1 (Tube: Sloane Square)
135 Sloane Street, SW1 (Tube: Sloane Square)

NICHOLAS HASLAM

To show you are "in," please refer to this man as "Nicky" and act like you know him and his famous touch: his handmade kilim shoes. The shop is on a small street that intersects Pimlico Road and Sloane Square. His showroom is a wonderful collection of every period and style, with preference to none. The truth is that Nicky

Haslam is one of London's more sought-after designers, with a very versatile design ability. He will do both small and large jobs, but you must have an appointment to meet with him in person.

NICHOLAS HASLAM
    12 Holbein Place, SW1 (Tube: Sloane Square)

NINA CAMPBELL

One of the most famous names in London design, Ms. Campbell became well-known to Americans when she stepped in to rescue the Duke and Duchess of York from their American design team. Turns out her career lasted longer than the Duchess of York's.

Obviously you work with her personally to design your estate, but her small shop does have some gifts and things to drool over; there is also a boutique in HARVEY NICHOLS with more of the same merchandise. I bought a fabric-covered "bulletin board" (the chicest bulletin board ever created, I might add) for a wedding present—it was £35, but so sophisticated you could die for it.

NINA CAMPBELL
    9 Walton Street, SW3 (Tube: South Kensington)

English Fabrics

OSBORNE & LITTLE

Along with COLEFAX & FOWLER, Osborne & Little reigns as top of the line for The Look. The firm began as antiquarian booksellers, with a sideline of hand-printed wallpapers. However, when Sir Peter Osborne and his brother-in-law Anthony Little won the Council of Industrial Design Award for their first wallpaper collection in 1968, they began a revolution in the interior design and manufacturing business. Shortly after, the firm gave up the interior-design aspect of the business to concentrate on the design and production of fine English wallpapers and fabrics.

Osborne & Little designs are wonderful because they are always based in history but not limited by it. A charming English botanical print might be reinterpreted in bolder colors. A whole line of wallpapers reflects the paint effects of marbleizing and stippling found in old Italian villas. Because they are now machine-produced, the fabrics and wallpapers are even affordable. The showroom is quiet and dignified, just the kind of place where you might like to have high tea.

Anyone may browse and buy.

OSBORNE & LITTLE
304 King's Road, SW3 (Tube: Sloane Square)

COLEFAX & FOWLER

The king of English chic is located, appropriately, near South Molton Street and Old Bond Street, home to all the best designers. Entering the Colefax & Fowler showrooms is like taking a step into an English country home. The building was built in 1766 by Sir Jeffrey Wyattville and is clearly being held together with chintz. Inside, the rooms are the size of small sitting rooms, the carpet is worn, and the furnishings are old. However, this is all part of the mystique. Upstairs houses the most magnificent collection of English chintzes ever to be desired by an Anglophile. Every year their designers bring out a new collection of fabrics and wallpapers more beautiful than the previous year's—assuming you like the look, of course.

Anyone may browse and buy.

COLEFAX & FOWLER
39 Brook Street, W1 (Tube: Bond Street)
110 Fulham Road, SW3 (Tube: South Kensington)
151 Sloane Street, SW3 (Tube: Sloane Square)

TISSUNIQUE LTD.

Formal fabrics are the speciality of this house, located on a side street that intersects Regent Street before you reach Oxford Street. It is an unusual location for a fabric firm, but when you have a royal warrant and a fabric line as unique as Tissunique's, who cares where you are located? Since its founding in 1967, the firm has grown and expanded from a French importing firm to one that also prints its own line of English antique-style fabrics.

Trade only.

TISSUNIQUE LTD.
58 Berners Street, W1 (Tube: Oxford Circus)

WARNER & SONS LTD.

I keep a swatch of Warner fabric on my bulletin board, awaiting the day I can reupholster the living-room furniture. I'm not the only Warner fan—they hold a royal warrant.

Benjamin Warner began the firm in 1870 as a silk-weaving company. As a matter of fact, Warner & Sons still uses the original silk-weaving Jacquard hand looms for some of its work. The archives document over 30,000 fabrics by name of designer, year designed, and a sample of the fabric whenever possible. Warner will reproduce any of the designs in their archives for a minimum order of 120 meters per colorway. They will also custom-design a fabric for your job if a reproduction is not to your liking.

Trade preferred.

WARNER & SONS LTD.
7-11 Noel Street, W1 (Tube: Oxford Circus)

ARTHUR SANDERSON & SONS LTD.

OK, OK, truth first. I know where one of the Sanderson factory-outlet stores is (it's in Manchester; see *Born to Shop Great Britain*) and I buy my Sanderson glazed chintzes for £5 a yard and brocades for £3! Indeed, Sanderson is one of

Britain's most famous fabric houses; they celebrated their 125th anniversary in 1985.

Back in 1860, Arthur Sanderson decided that what the English needed was a little of what the French already had—and we are not talking pâté! He began his firm to import French wall-hangings to the Brits. As this did not satisfy the demand, he opened his own hand-block printing factory in 1897. Shortly after his death, his sons decided to expand again and took over the printing presses of Jeffrey & Co., which was also printing the work of William Morris. In 1940 they bought the original designs of William Morris and to this day are still reprinting these hand-block prints.

Sanderson is now owned by a much larger company (Reed International), but still retains the original quality that made them famous and for which they received a royal warrant. They have a line of sheets and bed linen in their fabric patterns.

Anyone may browse.

ARTHUR SANDERSON & SONS LTD.
53 Berners Street, W1 (Tube: Oxford Circus)

COLE & SON LIMITED

This house still hand-prints many of their wall-coverings from an extensive (over 3,000) collection of wood blocks dating back as far as the 18th century. If you have or are building your own palace, Cole has the original blocks used to print the wallpaper for Kensington Palace, the Brighton Pavilion, Hampton Court, and the Houses of Parliament. They even welcome mail orders if you can't make it to London during your construction.

COLE & SON LIMITED
18 Mortimer Street, W1 (Tube: Oxford Circus)

French Provençal Fabrics

SOULEIADO

With PIERRE DEUX getting harder and harder to find in the U.S., I thought you might like this resource at hand—Souleiado is the mother house of this French fabric concern. As much as I've been talking about English looks, I have seen several traditional English homes that use Souleiado fabrics—especially in table linens that mix so beautifully with blue-and-white dishes.

Souleiado sells fabric as well as already made-up accessories for home and fashion.

SOULEIADO
171 Fulham Road, SW3 (Tube: South Kensington)

LES OLIVADES

This is simply the competition to SOULEIADO; they are in a new location, so don't go to the old one. Located at the beginning of the Walton Street fun (or the end of it, depending on which direction you are walking), this house sells the same French Provençal fabrics with a similar look to Souleiado.

LES OLIVADES
7 Walton Street, SW3 (Tube: South Kensington)

CHAPTER SEVEN

ANTIQUES, BOOKS, AND COLLECTIBLES

London, Queen of It All

It's not possible to write a chapter (or even a book) that completely covers the antiques scene in London: the specialty dealers, the collectibles, the books (old and new), or the tons of fun that you can have every minute of every day—even Sunday—when you shop for these things in and around London.

My husband Mike has taken to the streets to help me with this, but please note that with the recession, there are constant changes in the antiques and secondhand scene.

We've listed what we consider to be the best and brightest in all these categories. We offer you some of the best shops in the most convenient locations; you'll be emotionally and visually satisfied, even if you come away with just some ideas to tease your creative talents.

The best thing for an American to remember about shopping for used items in London is that all prices are possible. While a lot of people pooh-pooh Portobello Road and say the bargains are gone, I disagree strongly. In fact, I have two things to say about Portobello, but they offer an entire overview of the antiques and collectible scene in London:

- It ain't 1969 anymore.

- There's still plenty to buy.

The 1990s have their own language of value. There are plenty of bargains to be found on Portobello Road—if you know what you are doing. In fact, if you have only one day for antiques shopping in London and your budget is limited, I'd happily send you to Portobello Road. It's more fun on a Saturday, but during the week you'll find it calmer and more open to serious business.

As I mentioned in the previous chapter, I do not have museum-quality belongings; I am not particularly interested in what the trade calls "important" pieces—those that cost thousands of pounds and are collected by the rich and richer-still set.

We have a limited budget and want to have some fun with what we buy. I like to look in the showrooms and get ideas (Mike doesn't); I buy a lot of junk and rehab it.

When you shop London, try to get a mix of everything when you shop, and remember: You cannot get a good price until you know what the going price is; you cannot get a "bargain" until you know exactly what you are buying. Only by studying the finest examples can you decide if an item is a fake, a copy, a handsome repro, or a deal.

You can easily spend all your time in London seeing and learning. Ask a lot of questions; take a lot of time. After all, most of this stuff has been around for a hundred years or more. It'll keep.

Booking Antiques

The London and Provincial Antique Dealers Association (LAPADA) publishes a paperback book called *Buying Antiques in Britain*, which is filled with advice, tips, resources, and advertising. Most of the ads have pictures. This is an invaluable little guide for those just getting started. You can buy it at antiques markets or through the association at 535 King's Road, London SW10.

There are also several collectors' magazines sold on newsstands; they have information on fairs and auctions and editorials about collecting. They usually cost about £2–£3 an issue, but you'll enjoy them heartily. Try the *Antique Dealer and Collector's Guide* (U.S. subscriptions cost $50 a year), *Antique and Collectors' Fayre*, a more low-end collectors' magazine, and *Antique Collector*, published by the National Magazine Company and our favorite of the bunch (U.S. subscriptions cost $30). *The Collector* is a small-sized freebie published by Barrington Publications that is often given away in shops and includes maps of London's antiques areas, as well as the usual advertising and lists. A new consumer magazine called *Miller's Magazine* (£2), published by the famous couple, is the talk of the trade; BBC also has their own antiques magazine, price guide, and editorial based on their Roadshow experiences.

Most important to the trade is a tabloid newspaper called *Antiques Trade Gazette*, published each Wednesday by Metropress Ltd., 17 Whitcomb Street, London WC2. You can buy a single copy at some West End news agents or kiosks, or apply for an American subscription through Joyce Golden & Associates, 551 Fifth Avenue, New York, NY 10176.

Defining Antiques

The U.S. government has been defining an antique as any object that is 100 years old, or older. There is some discussion that this rule will be changed to use the beginning of the 20th century as the new cutoff point. If you are sweating it out, ask before you leave home.

If your purchase does not meet this definition, it is merely "used," and you must pay duty on it at the regular rate.

Antiques Fairs

One of the best ways of learning something about the London antiques market is to attend a few antiques fairs. Antiques fairs come in several categories; most of the London ones are *vetted* (a committee certifies that all goods are genuine) and cost several pounds for admission. They may be associated with a charity or fancy-dress ball on opening night. Some fairs are vetted but less formal, and others are just plain old country fairs where anyone can show. By and large the antiques fair scene in London is serious, and normally the country shows are held in the country. In the city it's strictly the big time.

While goods are sold at these fairs, I certainly don't buy them. In fact, I use these big-name fairs merely as an educational device to learn about quality; I cannot begin to afford to buy at these fairs. To be quite honest about it all, I sometimes find the price of admission to such an event more than I can bear—the thought of actually buying an item is almost obscene.

Learning to establish fair prices on authentic items is imperative if you are going to shop in non-vetted markets or fairs; otherwise you can expect to be cheated. Use museums, auction houses, and high-quality fairs as your educational stomping grounds to bone up on the best of Britain.

To get dates of fairs, check *Miller's Magazine* or the trade periodicals (see page 214), ask your concierge or the British Tourist Authority, or check out our list of the standing events. There are usually four fairs a month, although most of these are not famous. You can also write to the fair organizers for more information (see below).

Also note that each fair has its own rep, its own crowd, and its own fame. Some fairs are fancy-shmancy (the month of June is chockablock with these events, which are almost part of The Season), while some are ragtag affairs. Anything at Alexandra Palace is my kind of fair; anything at the Grosvenor House is not.

Only you know what's inside your wallet and your living room.

OLYMPIA DECORATIVE ARTS AND ANTIQUES FAIR

Earls Court Exhibition Centre, SW5, is an international fair; several hundred dealers participate. Stands are most often arranged as room sets. The date of the event is often piggybacked with another big fair so that people can plan to attend both. Olympia is usually considered a less expensive fair than some of the other high-end ones, but it is not a jumble sale. It is a vetted event. Call 81-385-1200 for more information, or contact Carolone Carfrae, Philbeach Events Ltd., Earls Court Exhibition Centre, London SW5. (Tube: Kensington Olympia)

THE LITTLE CHELSEA ANTIQUES FAIR

Chelsea Old Town Hall, King's Road, SW3, is held twice a year with less than a hundred participating dealers, and should not be confused with the CHELSEA ANTIQUES FAIR, a bigger and fancier show (see page 218). Both are vetted. (Tube: Sloane Square)

WEST LONDON ANTIQUES FAIR

Kensington Town Hall off Kensington High Street, W8, is one of two fairs run by the Penman Antiques Fairs Company, the other one being the CHELSEA ANTIQUES FAIR (see page 218). This fair, like the Chelsea, is held twice yearly (August is the second time) and attracts good-quality dealers. To find out their specific dates, write to Penman Antiques Fairs Company, Cockhaise Mill, Lindfield, Haywards Heath, Sussex, England. (Tube: High Street Kensington)

GROSVENOR HOUSE ANTIQUES FAIR

Grosvenor House Hotel, Park Lane, W1, is one of the best antiques fairs held in London and is timed each year to run after the Derby and before Ascot and Wimbledon. This is The Season, my dears. The top antiques dealers from all over Britain are invited to exhibit their best pieces, and everything except paintings has to be over 100 years old. A committee reviews all items for authenticity. This is also one of the top social events of the season, and watching the crowds is as much fun as examining the antiquities—some are the same vintage. There is a preview night before opening; it's a formal gala at £500 a pop. (Tube: Hyde Park Corner)

INTERNATIONAL CERAMICS FAIR

Dorchester Hotel, Park Lane, W1, has become an annual event with a substantial following. The fair usually coincides with the GROSVENOR HOUSE ANTIQUES FAIR (see above), because they complement each other. Some of the antique glass pieces on exhibit here are so delicate that the technique of getting them from the fair to your home would pose an interesting problem. All forms of ceramic-ware are on exhibit, including those from other countries. (Tube: Marble Arch or Hyde Park)

ANTIQUARIAN BOOK FAIR

Park Lane, Piccadilly, W1, does not have much to do with furnishings; however, no good library would be complete without a rare book or two in its collection. Collectors and dealers swap stories and collection items, including book illustrations and prints. (Tube: Green Park or Hyde Park)

CHELSEA ANTIQUES FAIR

Chelsea Old Town Hall, King's Road, SW3, is held twice yearly, in March and September. Our favorite time to go is September, because the weather usually is wonderful and most of the tourists have left town. However, the March fair is not as crowded, and better deals might be made then. This fair has been going on for over 60 years and probably will continue for another 260. Note that this venue is near several King's Road antiques galleries. (Tube: Sloane Square)

THE BURLINGTON HOUSE FAIR

The Royal Academy of Arts, Piccadilly, W1, is a fair for antiques dealers, but is open to the public. All works of art and antiques are vetted and are of superior quality. The pieces are international and not strictly limited to England. For information, ask your concierge for dates of the next one; write to the Burlington House Fair, 10-16 Elm Street, London WC1X. (Tube: Piccadilly Circus)

THE BRITISH ANTIQUE DEALERS' ASSOCIATION FAIR

The Duke of York's Headquarters, SW3, is another Chelsea fair held in early May. It usually kicks off with a big charity gala. (Tube: Sloane Square)

Street Markets

In London, many market areas are so famous that they have no specific street address. It's usually enough to name the market to a cabbie, but ask your concierge if you need more in the way of directions. Buses usually service market areas, as may the tube. There are markets that have everything from clothing to jewelry to books and art. Some specialize in antiques; see page 227 for more on serious antiques markets, and page 225 for the antiques supermarkets.

APPLE MARKET

The Apple Market is the official name of the marketplace held under the rooftops of Covent Garden in the courtyard space between the brick lanes of stores. This is a rotating affair which usually houses craftspeople, so this is the part where you get out the highlight pen: antiques are sold on Mondays *only*, in order to coordinate with the antiques goings-on across the way at the JUBILEE MARKET.

It's easiest to understand what this market is in contrast to the Jubilee Market. Jubilee is often junky; Apple is always classy. And it offers some of the best prices on British crafts.

The courtyard space is filled with vendors who set up little stalls and pin their wares to backdrops; sometimes boxes of loot are under the tables. The market is vetted, so the participants must apply for permission to sell and be granted an official space and day. If they show up on other days—which many do—they set up in stalls other than their regular one. Thus you can prowl the market on two different days of the week (ignore Mondays for this example) and see the same people in different places, with a few new faces interspersed. Mondays are more formal because this is the sole antiques day. Any day is a good day for the Apple Market.

Many vendors take plastic; some will bargain if you buy a lot. They don't get set up before 10 A.M., and many are still setting up at 11 A.M. They do stay there until dark, which is later in summers than winters.

APPLE MARKET

Covent Garden, WC2 (Tube: Covent Garden or Charing Cross)

JUBILEE MARKET

It's not fair to compare the Jubilee Market to BERMONDSEY or even to GREENWICH, because it's a small-time affair. Hell, it's not even fair to

compare the Jubilee Market to the APPLE MAR-
KET, a few hundred yards away. Jubilee Market is
basically a very touristy, teen-oriented, crass
marketplace at the back of Covent Garden.
However, on Mondays all the dealers (about 25 of
'em) are antiques dealers and the market is much
more fun. It never turns high-end, but it is affordable and is very much worth a look.

Jubilee Market gets going earliest on
Mondays: There are people there at 8 A.M., but
since nothing else is open at that hour, you may
find yourself high and dry and bored. The Apple
Market dealers don't set up until about 10 A.M.,
so consider 9:30 A.M. as a good time to begin
prowling Jubilee Market.

JUBILEE MARKET

Covent Garden, WC2 (Tube: Covent Garden or
Charing Cross)

BERMONDSEY MARKET

Also known as the NEW CALEDONIAN MAR-
KET. Open Friday only from 7 A.M. until 2 P.M. Go
early for the best deals. Take a torch (flashlight)
and elbow the dealers who are there to buy it all.
Many of the deals are done out of the trunks of
cars, or in the indoor cafe across the street. The
dealers who are buying arrive as early as 5 A.M.
and leave early too. The official market opens at 7
A.M., but by this time the good pieces will have
left, only to appear the next day on PORTOBEL-
LO ROAD, or in CAMDEN PASSAGE.

There is also a covered market building across
the street called the BERMONDSEY ANTIQUES
MARKET AND WAREHOUSE, which is run by the
London Borough of Southwark (say "Suthack") as
a commercial retail operation. There are around a
hundred stalls. In this building you will find a
bureaux de change and a cafe (entrance from the
outside of the building).

Now then, this is one of the points on which
Ian and I fight at least once a year: he says you

must be at Bermondsey Market before noon because the dealers start to pack up by then; he says he knows better than I do because he not only lives in London, but lives near Bermondsey Market and passes there frequently in his motor car.

I say that I've been there at 2 P.M. when the dealers start to pack up and that it's not over until 3 P.M.

Either way, go early in the morning and then you won't have to worry about which one of us is right. Should you get there any time after noon, do send us a postcard and let us know your opinion.

BERMONDSEY MARKET
Corner of Long Lane and Bermondsey Street at Bermondsey Square, SE1 (Tube: London Bridge, then cab it)

PORTOBELLO ROAD
Saturday in London means Portobello Road; Sunday means GREENWICH. That's the way I love my London weekends, no matter what time of the year. . . even in slight drizzle.

I buy every time I'm in town. Not only antiques, but new items like hand-knit sweaters and cashmeres, dishes, reproductions of expensive botanicals that look great when framed, old linens, buttons, and more, more, more.

Here's the skinny: the people with the stands and tables and stalls are just there on Saturday. The shops behind them are also open on Saturday but do not sell the stuff you see in the streets, so don't get your vendors mixed up. If you are a more serious antiques shopper, come back during the week and explore the three or four dozen serious shops; see page 230.

The street market is open from 6 A.M. to 4 P.M. on Saturday only. Some businesses open just Friday and Saturday; no one is open at all on Sunday. Don't forget to explore the shops on

Pembridge Road and Westbourne Grove after you've shopped the full range of Portobello Road.

PORTOBELLO ROAD

Portobello Road, W11 (Tube: Notting Hill Gate)

CAMDEN PASSAGE

There are over 200 antiques stores open every day, and on Wednesday and Saturday the area becomes crowded, with hundreds of stalls selling just about everything imaginable. The more permanent shops have a good collection of fine-quality antiques; this is more upscale than PORTOBELLO ROAD. Open Monday, Tuesday, Thursday, and Friday from 10 A.M. to 5 P.M.; Wednesday and Saturday from 8 A.M. to 4 P.M.

CAMDEN PASSAGE

Upper Street, Islington, N1 (Tube: Angel)

CAMDEN LOCK

This is definitely the lower end. Located in the Regents Canal section of Camden, where canals once provided a practical means to transport goods from the docks in the East to the main canal that carried on to Birmingham. However, the area around the Camden Lock has become the home of black-leather fashions and cheap old clothes. This is really a teenage vintage clothing neighborhood more than anything else; this is really a scene that may not be your cup of tea if you are over forty and wash your hands regularly. Open Saturday and Sunday from 10 A.M. to 5:30 P.M.

CAMDEN LOCK

Camden High Street, NW1 (Tube: Camden Town)

PICCADILLY MARKET

For fifteen years now the craftsmen and hippies have been meeting on Fridays and Saturdays in the churchyard right on Piccadilly to sell a less-than-perfect-but-still-fun selection of sweaters, imports, and knickknacks. There are too many imports for me to feel great about this market, but you can't fault the location or the fun. I've been buying vintage clothing from the dealer in the far right-hand corner (if you are facing the church from the street); there are Aran sweaters and kilts and other touristy items, as well as the usual incense burners from Nepal. The market is not very big or even very good, but I love it and think it's worth a browse.

PICCADILLY MARKET

St. James's Church, Piccadilly, W1 (Tube: Piccadilly Circus)

Greenwich Markets

I stand very loud and very firm on this fact: there is simply no better Sunday than the one you will spend in Greenwich, SE10. I've outlined the way that I do it as a tour (see page 266). Since the town is small and the weekend markets dominate, you can probably figure it all out on your own. The markets are held both Saturday and Sunday. I have been on a Saturday and find that I slightly prefer the vendors on Sunday (they are elsewhere on Saturdays), but if you can't get here on a Sunday, a Saturday will help convince you that Greenwich is an essential part of the shopper's London.

There are several markets in Greenwich, so the idea is to spend the day going from one to the next. The fact that Greenwich houses museums, ships, and sights of historical interest means little to me, even if there's no time like Mean Time. If you want to combine culture and shopping, arrange your schedule accordingly.

CRAFTS MARKET

The Crafts Market is held under a covered roof

in the center of "downtown" and consists of rows of stalls selling merchandise much like at Covent Garden. The prices are slightly less than London.

BOSUN'S YARD

Around the corner from the Crafts Market, right at the waterfront, Bosun's Yard holds the overflow from the Crafts Market. It's a little too much for me: these are the dealers who just came back from Tibet and think they have something to sell, but it's a cute place and you can get an ice cream cone here.

CANOPY ANTIQUES MARKET

The scene of another one of Ian's and my many fights. He said, "You don't want to go to that market, it's very junky."

I said, "I know, it's my favorite market; I love junk."

You will not like this market if you don't like junk. This is of less standard quality than your average flea market or jumble sale. But I love it. The market sprawls for quite some bit; I enter at the far end—not where the truck says, "Beigels [sic] Sold Here."

The reason I enter from the far end is that this is where the jumble is; if you enter the first gateway, you have regular market stalls with new goods. I don't like these as much as the tat. The dealers back here specialize in vintage clothing (there's an entire shed of it), home decor from the 1950s, costume jewelry, and then junk.

GREENWICH ANTIQUES MARKET

Believe it or not, none of the above are the antiques market that Greenwich is famous for! The one that started all the fuss is on the high street, which means it's the first market you come to if you arrive by train, or the last market you come to if you arrive by boat and return by train.

This market is not huge, but it's packed with fun. The dealers farthest from the street specialize in vintage clothing. The quality of the merchandise here cannot be classified as junk; there may even be a few true antiques.

Take BritRail from Charing Cross Station any Saturday or Sunday for a town filled with markets.

GREENWICH MARKET
  Greenwich, SE10

Antiques and Collectibles Supermarkets

Antiques supermarkets have been created to give the smaller but established dealers a permanent place to set up and display their wares. They are covered shopping centers for antiques, collectibles, and junk. The fun is figuring out which is which. Very often the dealer stalls change, especially in these hard times; therefore I'm not really pointing out faves. Since the buildings are not going anywhere fast, I suggest you plow through. Don't forget that if you catch a rainy day in London town, an antiques gallery or supermarket can keep you busy for hours. The other advantage to shopping at a covered market is that very often other services are offered: There are repair shops at GRAYS, bureaux de change at ANTIQUARIUS and GRAYS, and places to eat at all of them.

GRAYS IN DAVIES MEWS, GRAYS IN DAVIES STREET

These two buildings, located on the opposite ends of the same block, house over 300 antiques stalls containing every variety of item, large and small. Davies Street conveniently intersects South Molton Street at one end and Brook Street at the other, placing it directly in the heart of the big-name-designer section of London. When you need a break from fashion, it is easy to breeze over to Grays and rest your eyes on some breath-taking antique jewelry, bound to coordinate with any purchase you have made on Bond Street. Don't miss the river tributary that runs decoratively through the basement of the Davies Mews building. The shops are open Monday to Friday from 10 A.M. to 6 P.M. only. You can grab a bite in the cute cafe on the lowest floor.

GRAYS

1-7 Davies Mews, W1 (Tube: Bond Street)
58 Davies Street, W1 (Tube: Bond Street)

ALFIE'S ANTIQUES MARKET

Alfie's is under the same ownership as GRAYS and houses another 150 stalls. It's a series of blue town houses now joined together higgledly-piggledly, so you weave around a lot when you shop. This is well worth the trip; prices are moderate and dealers will deal. Because the location is a tad offbeat, the dealers tend to be a little more funky, so you get high quality and some value. This is perhaps one of the best supermarkets for seeing a lot and feeling that you're getting good value. And if anyone can get that dealer down on the green glass 1950s necklace, I'm willing to pay £15, but not a tuppence more. Not far from the REGENT (the hotel, not the prince). Closed Sunday and Monday. Open Tuesday through Saturday from 10 A.M. to 5:30 P.M.

ALFIE'S ANTIQUES MARKET

13-25 Church Street, NW8 (Tube: Edgware Road or Marylebone)

ANTIQUARIUS

Located right on King's Road in Chelsea in the thick of several antiques venues, Antiquarius could be mistaken for a theater from the outside. In actuality it was constructed in an old snooker hall building dating way-back-when. With over 200 stalls, Antiquarius has gained a reputation for being the place to go for Art Nouveau and Art

Deco pieces of every variety, from jewelry to fur-
niture. There's also a very famous dealer (Sue
Norman) for blue-and-white porcelain. Open
Monday to Saturday from 10 A.M. to 6 P.M.

ANTIQUARIUS
135-141 King's Road, SW3 (Tube: Sloane
Square)

CHENIL GALLERIES

Chenil Galleries is more of a shopping arcade
with a long thin thrust to the floor pattern and a
swell chance to browse in good merchandise that
is not intimidating. They have an art gallery and
are known for being a good place to look for
antique medical instruments, as well as 17th-
and 18th-century paintings and smaller items.
There's a sensational dealer for costume jewelry.
Another one of the Chelsea galleries, this one
should be combined with your visit to ANTI-
QUARIUS. Open Monday to Saturday from 10 A.M.
to 6 P.M.

CHENIL GALLERIES
181–183 King's Road, SW3 (Tube: Sloane
Square)

BOND STREET ANTIQUES CENTRE

Like GRAYS, the Bond Street Antiques Centre
is located amid the finest in fashion and specializes in the finest of miniatures, porcelain, jewelry,
silver, and paintings. This one is a tad fancy for
my taste. Open Monday to Friday from 10 A.M. to
5:30 P.M.

BOND STREET ANTIQUES CENTRE
124 New Bond Street, W1 (Tube: Bond Street)

Antiques Neighborhoods

The best thing about antiques neighborhoods
is that the good shops stay for a long while and
they attract other shops, so that if one should

close or move, another comes in, and an area stays stable, more or less. High rents plague London, like any big city, but these neighborhoods are nuggets where you can just wander and gawk.

MAYFAIR

This is the most expensive part of London; the prices in the antiques shops reflect the rents and the unwritten law that objects displayed in windows must be dripping with ormolu. New Bond Street is the main source, but don't forget side streets such as Conduit Street, Old Bond Street, Vigo Street, and Jermyn Street. Mayfair is also headquarters for several auction houses, decorating firms, and big-time dealers. If you're just looking, make sure you're dressed to kill. If you're serious, you should probably have an appointment or a letter of introduction, or both. Don't miss GRAYS ANTIQUES MARKET (58 Davies Street), S.J. PHILLIPS LTD. (139 New Bond Street), MALLETT & SON (40 New Bond Street), and WARTSKI (14 Grafton Street). (Tube: Bond Street or Green Park)

CHURCH STREET/MARYLEBONE

Don't confuse this area with Kensington Church Street, which is an antiques area on the way to Portobello Road. This antiques area on the way to ALFIE'S ANTIQUES MARKET is not comparable to Portobello Road, but is fun nonetheless, and pretty much affordable. Forget it on Monday. Aside from Alfie's, there's the GALLERY OF ANTIQUE COSTUME & TEXTILES (2 Church Street), as well as SIMON TRACY (No. 18), BEVERLEY (No. 32), BIZARRE (No. 24), RISKY BUSINESS (two shops at Nos. 34 and 46), and PILLOWS (No. 48). This is kind of a funky neighborhood where you can wear casual clothes and not have to worry about the hoity-toity world. (Tube: Edgware Road or Marylebone)

COVENT GARDEN

The neighborhoods surrounding Covent Garden, from Charing Cross to The Strand and over to Leicester Square, are known as important haunts for those interested in antique books, used books, stamps, records, and also ephemera. There are some famous antiques stores sprinkled in here, and many vintage clothing shops, but it's mostly a papergoods neighborhood.

But wait: On Mondays there are two markets at Covent Garden, APPLE MARKET and JUBILEE MARKET, which is about 100 yards away from Apple Market. At Apple Market the stalls (which are normally devoted to craftspeople) are taken over by rather high-end antiques dealers. Jubilee Market is more open—many price ranges are available and there's more room for bargaining and fun. You may also find local publications about other markets and fairs at some of the dealers at Jubilee. I'm not talking hoity-toity antiques here, but you can have fun anyway. (Tube: Covent Garden)

KING'S ROAD

Don't ask me why transportation to King's Road is so difficult. The only way to get to all of the shops is to walk and walk some more. Or to keep flagging down the bus. The most interesting part of King's Road actually starts right at Sloane Square, but goes on and on to shops with numbers up in the high 500s. FURNITURE CAVE is the farthest away (No. 533), while DESIGNER'S GUILD (No. 277) is right in the thick of the chichi decorator part. There are several antiques malls here, and lots of showrooms. In terms of visual stimulation and the possibility of affording something nice, this neighborhood may offer the best combination of the right things. Other neighborhoods are cheaper, but this has a trendiness that can't be ignored. . . even in antiques. (Tube: Fulham Broadway)

LOWER SLOANE

I call the area including Pimlico Road, Ebury Road, and Lower Sloane Street simply Lower Sloane. It is an extension of Sloane Street, after you pass Sloane Square. Most of the dealers here are fancy, as is the clientele, but everyone is a tad more approachable than the high-end, don't-touch crowd. There are a lot of showrooms here, as well as antiques shops. If you're on Sloane Street, instead of turning to the right to get to King's Road, you walk straight and follow Lower Sloane Street to Pimlico Road. Convenient to cutting back to King's Road and Chelsea antiques shops. (Tube: Sloane Square)

FULHAM ROAD

There's lots of stuff in the Fulham area between the Gloucester Road tube stop and Brompton Cross, but within a special block or two of Fulham Road you'll find either an antiques shop or a decorator showroom behind every door. Look in at PETER LIPITEH (No. 120), TODAY'S INTERIORS (No. 122), MICHAEL FOSTER (No. 118), CHRISTOPHE GOLLUT (No. 116), COLEFAX & FOWLER (No. 110), JOHN STEFANIDIS (No. 253), and CLIFFORD WRIGHT (Nos. 104–106). If you keep walking you'll hit SOULEIADO (No. 171) and several other shops, and then Michelin House, which is where THE CONRAN SHOP has made history (No. 81). (Tube: South Kensington)

PORTOBELLO ROAD

I just love this Saturday market event (page 221), but don't think this is just a flea market scene or that Saturdays are the only day. Saturdays are the main event, but during the week, especially on Friday, the regular shops are open without the Saturday circus atmosphere. And yep, there is a ton to see, even on a weekday.

There are a few antiques markets here, with

many stalls and dealers, as well as some free-standing shops on Portobello Road and on Westbourne Grove. Get there via Pembridge Road to check out a few more shops (especially strong for vintage clothing), or by walking up the hill via Kensington Church Street, where there are a few more dealers. Check out CHELSEA GALLERIES (No. 76), ALICE'S (No. 77), and much, much more. Kensington Church Street includes KENSINGTON CHURCH STREET ANTIQUES GALLERY (No. 62). (Tube: Notting Hill Gate or High Street Kensington)

KENSINGTON CHURCH STREET

Shoppers please note that few of these stores are open all day—if at all—on Saturday, so despite the fact that you're a stone's throw from Portobello Road, Saturday is not really the day to combine these neighborhoods. Of course, a lot of serious Portobello Road dealers are open during the week (without the stalls and stands of Saturdays), and you can combine the two neighborhoods that way. The best way to do so is exit the tube at Kensington High Street, cross the street at the light and head slightly to your right before you zig up Kensington Church Street. You'll pass LANCER'S SQUARE (an American-style mall), on the right side of the street; Church Street will bend to the left as you go up the hill.

A zillion shops and a small gallery line Kensington Church Street. Many of the stores are the small fancy kind that make you nervous to even press your nose to the glass. The closer you get to Notting Hill Gate (at the top of the hill you are climbing), the more funky the stores get. The month of June can be tricky for shopping this area as most of the good stores exhibit at the important shows and close up shop.

OLIVER SUTTON (34 Kensington Church Street) sells only Staffordshire figurines; pressing your nose to the glass may suffice, as you can see quite a selection from the street. At No. 58 is a small gallery with very serious dealers in their tiny glass cubbyholes. JONATHAN HORNE (No. 66) is another famous dealer for pottery, tiles, and ceramics—also very serious. SIMON SPERO (No. 109) has more pottery.

Don't miss three little dealers in a row along Peel Street, who have Kensington Church Street addresses (it's a corner junction)—among them HOPE & GLORY (No. 131A), which specializes in royal porcelain memorabilia.

MOUNT STREET

This street begins, appropriately enough, with an AMERICAN EXPRESS office (No. 89), where you will undoubtedly have to go for more cash. It's sort of a two-block job, stretching from behind the Dorchester right to Berkeley Square, a sneeze from Bond Street. Here you can find a group of excellent antiques shops; my favorites on this street include JOHN KEIL (No. 25), KENNETH NEAME (No. 27), STAIR & CO. (No. 14); then you pass the Connaught to connect to more of Mount Street and BARLING OF MOUNT STREET (No. 112), BLAIRMAN AND SONS (No. 119), and JOHN SPARKS LIMITED (No. 128). (Tube: Green Park or Bond Street)

Books, Maps, and Autographs

The West End

MAGGS BROTHERS LTD.

Don't believe those ghost stories you hear about Maggs.

While it had been rumored for years that the Maggs mansion, built in 1740, was haunted, no ghosts were spotted during World War II, when fire-watch rules required at least one Maggs employee to sleep on the premises each night. Of course, the house next door was completely destroyed, and the one across Berkeley Square suffered heavy damage. . . . But there are no ghosts.

The only remaining mystery at Maggs is just how many books they have on hand. They've been accumulating since Uriah Maggs founded the firm in 1857, and not even their insurance company has been able to come up with a correct figure.

Such eccentricities are allowed any bookseller with an enormous collection of travel books, militaria, maps, illuminated manuscripts, autographs, and Orientalia. Maggs' travel section alone would fill the average bookstore with first-edition, on-the-spot reminiscences by the likes of Stanley, Livingstone, Robert Falcon Scott, and Admiral Byrd. Whenever the stock gets dangerously low, it is replenished by ten specialists who attend auctions around the world to keep current.

Maggs also boasts of a sizable autograph collection. Whether you're a bibliophile or not, you should visit Maggs to see just what a civilized delight book buying can be.

MAGGS BROTHERS LTD.
50 Berkeley Square, W1 (Tube: Green Park)

G. HEYWOOD HILL LTD.

If MAGGS is a showplace for books and autographs of the illustrious, nearby G. Heywood Hill on Curzon Street represents the cramped, Dickensian bookshop most visitors associate with literary London. For fifty years Heywood has been a beacon to authors, librarians, and collectors around the world.

Although space is limited, the shop is packed to the rafters with books that meet the standards of its knowledgeable staff. You won't find the newest Judith Krantz novel here, but employees know the stock and can lay hands on thousands of volumes quickly. Moreover, while antiquarian books pay the light bills, Heywood stocks contemporary books on a variety of subjects merely to satisfy its clients' needs. (It is also probably the only bookseller that will refuse to sell its clients books that don't meet its Olympian standards.)

The shop specializes in books on design, architecture, gardening, and the allied decorative arts. There's also an extensive collection of biographies and a subspecialty in literary criticism; Heywood's bookishness has attracted many writers as steady customers, including Evelyn Waugh, Anthony Powell, Nancy Mitford (who worked there during World War II), and other Waughs, Mitfords, and Sitwells for several generations.

This family feeling and the respect for the shop's high standards often give Heywood first crack at extensive private libraries. The location is right around the corner from the PARK LANE HILTON and the CONNAUGHT, off Berkeley Square.

G. HEYWOOD HILL LTD.
10 Curzon Street, W1 (Tube: Green Park)

Piccadilly

BERNARD QUARITCH LTD.
In October 1847, Bernard Quaritch came to London, determined to become a bookseller. He succeeded, attracting such clients along the way as Prime Ministers William Gladstone and Benjamin Disraeli, publishing Edward FitzGerald's *The Rubáiyát of Omar Khayyám*, and being eulogized by *The Times* as "the greatest bookseller who ever lived."

By this time, Quaritch has attained an international reputation. Boasting perhaps the largest stock of antiquarian books in London and thirty-two experts in fields as diverse as Arabic, bibliography, and psychiatry, Quaritch has an atmosphere that is quiet but not formal. The firm attends auctions on the Continent (sometimes bidding for the British Museum) and assembles collections that can run the gamut from Tibet to Henry James to rigging and shipbuilding.

Because of its size, Quaritch is able to airfreight its own crate of books to New York once a week; the contents are then sent separately to clients via UPS, bypassing the post office and possibly careless (and financially damaging) handling.

BERNARD QUARITCH LTD.

5-8 Lower John Street, Golden Square, W1 (Tube: Piccadilly Circus)

SOTHERAN'S OF SACKVILLE STREET

Sotheran's has been selling books since 1761 in York and has been established in London since 1815. Charles Dickens was a regular customer, and when he died, Sotheran's sold his library. The firm also purchased a number of volumes from Winston Churchill's library and was the agent for the sale of Sir Isaac Newton's library to Cambridge. The firm specializes in ornithology and natural science.

Books line the extensive perimeter of the ground floor, and the atmosphere is neat, formal, and as silent as a library. A lower floor is given over exclusively to antiquarian prints and maps, drawings by book illustrators such as Kate Greenaway and Arthur Rackham, sporting prints, and military and naval subjects. There's also an attractive private office in an adjoining building for private negotiations.

Sotheran's offers search service, handbinds serial publications such as the Bills and Acts of Parliament, restores books, and also maintains subscriptions to overseas periodicals for its customers.

SOTHERAN'S OF SACKVILLE STREET

2–5 Sackville Street, Piccadilly, W1 (Tube: Piccadilly Circus)

PHILLIPS SON & NEALE

Even though books are not on Phillips' weekly calendar (as are rugs, ceramics, furniture, and silver), the firm auctions books, maps, and autographs thirteen times a year and provides auction catalogs in these categories by subscription. Phillips' books generally cover English literature, militaria, modern first editions, and incunabula.

PHILLIPS SON & NEALE

101 New Bond Street, W1 (Tube: Bond Street)

Charing Cross Road

Visitors searching for 84 Charing Cross Road will be disappointed to find a record store, not the bookshop that inspired Helene Hanff's bestseller; nevertheless, the long street is filled with other, equally engaging book emporiums, all of which are open Monday through Saturday from 9 A.M. to 6 P.M.

FOYLE

Foyle is the largest bookstore in London, with over four million volumes in stock. It's as crowded as ever, but the somewhat lackadaisical staff has been replaced by earnest and mostly helpful college students. There are large children's and fiction sections on the main floor; upper floors are devoted to technical books; a small antiquarian library; and huge sections on hobbies, art, and commerce. The business section is particularly noteworthy. Hours: Monday to Wednesday, and Friday and Saturday, 9 A.M. to 6 P.M.; Thursday, 9 A.M. to 7 P.M. Closed Sunday.

FOYLE

119 Charing Cross Road, WC2 (Tube: Leicester Square)

ZWEMMER

Zwemmer has three stores in Charing Cross: (1) the Oxford University Press Bookshop, company store for one of the most respected publishers in the world; (2) a shop across the street devoted to the graphic arts—illustration, photography, etc. (there were three different books on Issey Miyake the last time we looked); and (3) a shop devoted to the fine arts (at 24 Litchfield Street). All three are open from 9:30 A.M. to 6 P.M. Monday to Friday and from 9:30 A.M. to 5:30 P.M. on Saturday.

ZWEMMER

Oxford University Press Bookshop, 72 Charing Cross Road, WC2 (Tube: Leicester Square)

ZWEMMER ART

24 Litchfield Street, WC2 (fine arts) (Tube: Leicester Square)

ZWEMMER BOOKSHOP

80 Charing Cross Road, WC2 (graphic arts) (Tube: Leicester Square)

FRANCIS EDWARDS

Francis Edwards is the leading antiquarian bookseller on the street and carries natural history and militaria. Open Monday to Friday from 9 A.M. to 5 P.M.

FRANCIS EDWARDS

48A Charing Cross Road, WC2 (Tube: Leicester Square)

EDWARD STANFORD

Stanford is a mecca for maps, charts, atlases, and travel books, not the reminiscences that MAGGS stocks, but rather the how-to variety. A particular specialty is guides for mountain climbers, skiers, and other outdoorsy types. Open Monday to Friday from 9 A.M. to 5:30 P.M, and from 10 A.M. to 4 P.M. Saturday.

EDWARD STANFORD
12–14 Long Acre, WC2 (Tube: Covent Garden)

CECIL COURT AND COVENT GARDEN
Cecil Court, a block-long street between Charing Cross Road and St. Martin's Lane, has some charming secondhand bookshops. Most are open from 9:30 A.M. to 6 P.M. Monday to Saturday. (Tube: Leicester Square)

Long Acre, the "Main Street" of Covent Garden, is also lined with bookstores on both sides of the road; it is a block from Cecil Court.

BELL, BOOK & RADMALL, No. 4: English and American first editions

PLEASURES OF PAST TIMES, No. 11: theater, music halls, juvenilia

TRAVIS & EMERY, No. 17: music, ballet, opera

FROGNAL, No. 18: law, economics, history, caricatures

ALAN BRETT, No. 24: *Vanity Fair* cartoons, topography, acts of Parliament

H.M. FLETCHER, No. 27: early English literature

More Books

DILLON'S

In London, Dillon's is to new books what HARRODS is to everything else. Consider that each year approximately 40,000 new titles are published in the English language. Dillon's has approximately 250,000 titles on hand at any one time. In September, the number actually increases to nearly 300,000, since Dillon's is near the University of London and must stock a vast variety of textbooks as well. While the vast majority of the stock is nonfiction, a quarter of Dillon's books are novels published in the last three years. Dillon's lays no claim to being a discounter, but its policy has led to rapid expansion.

There are now about fifty shops in the U.K.

DILLON'S
82 Gower Street, WC1 (Tube: Goodge Street)

THE BOOK BOAT
Sure you like books. After all, you're in London, the world's bookiest city, right? But here's the ultimate test: Would you, landlubber that you are, be willing to walk the plank to buy a book? If you want to test yourself, go to Greenwich and clamber aboard the Book Boat. Based on a tugboat moored in Greenwich harbor (and near the *Cutty Sark*), the Book Boat features children's books at the same prices you'll find at chains such as WATERSTONE'S and W.H. Smith. The fun is crossing a gangplank that must be lowered each morning, and then browsing for books while moored on the Thames. The gangplank can be crossed every day except Thursday from 10 A.M. to 6 P.M. Your kids will adore it.

THE BOOK BOAT
Cutty Sark Garden, Greenwich Church Street, SE10 (Train: British Rail from Charing Cross)

THE BUILDING BOOK SHOP
For design freaks, this is the last word. Just camp out and order in. This is a bookstore for the design trade, with specialty books for architects, designers, do-it-yourselfers, and the like. It's more industrial than crafts, but you'll find something for everyone. On Saturday they close at 1 P.M.

THE BUILDING BOOK SHOP
The Building Centre, 26 Store Street, WC1 (Tube: Goodge Street)

HATCHARDS
Looking for us in London? Stop by Hatchards at Piccadilly. I spend part of almost every day here. Far and away the most complete of the modern booksellers, the main Hatchards is in a town

house near FORTNUM & MASON, and is filled with just about everything. The store is owned by DILLON'S as a sort of boutique bookstore.

The children's book section is a good one— this is where we discovered *James the Red Engine*. They have an excellent travel book department.

All are open from 9 A.M. to 5:30 P.M. Monday to Friday and from 9 A.M. to 5 P.M. Saturday.

HATCHARDS

187 Piccadilly, W1 (Tube: Piccadilly Circus)

Harvey Nichols, 109 Knightsbridge, SW1 (Tube: Knightsbridge)

150-152 King's Road, SW3 (Tube: Sloane Square)

BERNARD STONE

Stone specializes in poetry, children's books, and whodunits, and has been called "addictive" for its seamless blend of rare and secondhand books, as well as a large selection of new stock. It's open from 10 A.M. to 7 P.M. Monday to Saturday.

BERNARD STONE

42 Lamb's Conduit Street, WC1 (Tube: Holbein)

WATERSTONE'S BOOKSELLERS

A chain, not so different from B. Dalton, but with a large selection of everything and many locations near the shopping areas you automatically gravitate to. A good shop for extra guidebooks (no one can survive in London without an A *to* Z), airplane-reading books, art books, etc.

WATERSTONE'S BOOKSELLERS

88 Regent Street, W1 (Tube: Piccadilly Circus)

99-101 Old Brompton Road, SW7 (Tube: Knightsbridge)

193 Kensington High Street, W8 (Tube: High Street Kensington)

121–125 Charing Cross Road, WC2 (Tube: Tottenham Court Road)

Collectors' note: Collectors of antiquarian books should also consult two new magazines devoted to the topic—*Driff's* and *Slightly Soiled*—which are available at SOTHERAN'S OF SACKVILLE STREET and the Cecil Court stores. Both carry news of auctions, sales, and book fairs, not to mention gossip about booksellers.

Collectibles

St. George he was for England
And before he killed the dragon
He drank a pint of English ale,
Out of an English flagon.

On our first visit to London, and several times thereafter, we were offered that very flagon each time we ventured off to check out the collectibles market. But after the first few not-so-convincing pitches we began to catch on. Shopping for the real thing in London is a tricky business.

As time went on we learned that:

- England is indeed a nation of shopkeepers.
- Many of the shops they keep are crammed with collectibles.
- Some of these collectibles are as real as St. George's flagon or that grand old American collectible, the Brooklyn Bridge.

The collectibles shops Mike lists in this section, on the other hand, have stood the test of time—they are the real thing. Some are famous, others are our personal finds. When we checked them last, they were fresh out of flagons (thankfully). Instead, they offered books as sensuous to the touch as they are titillating to the mind, dolls so beautiful that they brought a tear even to our cynical eye, and toy soldiers as spiffy as anything you'll see strutting around West Point. . . but these little metal guys are just a tad older than the West Point version.

While furniture, fountain pens, and fine art also are available here, and while we know full well that people are capable of collecting *anything*, I wanted to give you at least a small taste of the tempting collectibles London has to offer to those who know that London is the first city of the world for collectors.

Collectors of antiquarian books, maps, and autographs, please see page 232.

Coins and Medals

SPINK & SON LTD.

If you've yearned for those glitzy costume-jewelry medals, you'll all-out faint and go stark raving mad with delight when you see the original medals that the current fad was based on. Why was a man always so dashing in his uniform? Because of his medals, of course. And chances are, they came from Spink. Spink has tremendous stock in Orientalia, paperweights, and Greek and Roman coins, as well as an ample supply of early English hammered coins in gold and silver and milled pieces dating back to the late 1600s; however, as HAMLEYS is to toys, so Spink is to medals. Along with sheer size, Spink offers an expertise born of creating decorations for Great Britain and sixty-five other countries.

In addition to fashioning the medals, Spink also has world-class experience in mounting and displaying them, and even publishes a guide to wearing them. (Medals on your evening gown? Wear on sash, please. Medals on your safari jacket? Hmmmm.) The company also issues the monthly *Spink Numismatic Circular*, which includes large sections on medals, orders, and decorations. Hours: Monday to Friday, 9:30 A.M. to 5:30 P.M.

SPINK & SON LTD.

5–7 King Street, St. James's, SW1 (Tube: Green Park)

B.A. SEABY LTD.

Early coins bearing the likenesses of royalty from Corinth, Phoenicia, and Rome rub shoulders with tradesmen's tokens issued by coppers in Dover and fishmongers in Margate; each is presented with care, panache, and the necessary historical background.

The firm is deep in antiquarian coins, and that interest has led to sidelines such as collections of jewelry and copperplate from ancient Greece, Rome, and Jerusalem. Seaby publishes a magazine, the bimonthly *Coin & Medal Bulletin*, which is likely to contain scholarly pieces related to archaeological finds, as well as price lists of coins. Hours: Monday to Friday, 9:30 A.M. to 5 P.M.

B.A. SEABY LTD.

7 Davies Street, W1 (Tube: Bond Street)

FORMAN PICCADILLY LTD.

Forman specializes in medals, but also sells carved ivories made by soldiers and sailors, and other specialized antiquities. But it's the gorgeous colored ribbons and enamel medals that drew us into the shop, to peer hungrily into the large wooden case. If you brush up on your Russian, you can read the inscriptions on medals awarded by the czars. We're fond of Napoleonic medals, complete with ribbons or sashes.

FORMAN PICCADILLY LTD.

99 Mount Street, W1 (Tube: Bond Street)

ARMADA ANTIQUES

One of two important stalls in GRAYS ANTIQUES MARKET, Armada Antiques is crammed with militaria of all kinds. Armada Antiques (Stand 122) carries mostly edged weapons such as stilettos and sabers, but also has some medals. For the total effect, shop also at SEIDLER (Stand 120)—together these two fabulous dealers give you a nice overview.

ARMADA ANTIQUES

Grays Antiques Market, Stand 122, 58 Davies Street, W1 (Tube: Bond Street)

THE ARCHES

Soaring rents have forced small-time dealers out of Cutler Street, long a Sunday-morning fixture at the Petticoat Lane market; however, inexpensive coins still are available by the bagful at The Arches on Villiers Street, beneath the Charing Cross Road tube stop. This is where we got twenty coins from around the world for about $1.50. This is decidedly low-end, and major collectors will not be interested; however, the place is a lot of fun. In addition to coins, there are comic books, cigarette cards, military insignia, and used romance novels in this covey of little dealers nestled beside the tube station. Most proprietors are open Monday to Saturday from 9 A.M. to 6 P.M.

THE ARCHES

Villiers Street, WC2 (Tube: Charing Cross)

Collectors' note: In addition to the Spink and Seaby publications, there's also a periodical called *Coin Monthly*.

Scientific Instruments

TREVOR PHILIPS & SONS LTD.

A smaller version of ARTHUR MIDDLETON (see page 245), Philips carries gyroscopes, English drafting instruments, sundials, stethoscopes, and a selection of books about scientific instruments. The shop also carries miniature instruments, such as pocket botanical microscopes, pocket globes, and exquisite orreries—small clockwork representations of the solar system. Hours: Monday to Friday, 10 A.M. to 6 P.M.

TREVOR PHILIPS & SONS LTD.

75A Jermyn Street, SW1 (Tube: Piccadilly Circus)

STEPHEN O'DONNELL

An interest in navigation led O'Donnell to begin collecting and restoring sextants, spyglasses, and telescopes. By this time, his collection is extensive, as is a fairly new sideline in antique postage scales. The scales run from $150 to $1,000, while telescopes start at $250, and sextants run anywhere from $700 to $3,000. Hours: Monday to Friday, 10 A.M. to 6 P.M.

STEPHEN O'DONNELL

Grays Antiques Market, Stand 156, 58 Davies Street, W1 (Tube: Bond Street)

ARTHUR MIDDLETON

Located between Leicester Square and Covent Garden, this shop is chockablock with antique clocks, telescopes, surgical instruments, and early dental equipment, all in splendid condition. Even if you're not a collector, you'll enjoy the spit and polish of these fascinating pieces. Hours: Monday to Friday, 10 A.M. to 6 P.M.; Saturday, 11 A.M. to 5:30 P.M.

ARTHUR MIDDLETON

12 New Row, WC2 (Tube: Leicester Square)

Collectors' note: Collectors of scientific instruments should be aware of two specialty publications: *Rittenhouse Journal of the American Scientific Instrument Enterprise*, published by David and Yola Coffeen and Raymond V. Giordano, and *Bulletin of the Scientific Instrument Society*, published by the Scientific Instrument Society.

Stamps

Just as Nassau Street is home to dozens of stamp dealers in New York City, The Strand (and offshoots such as King Street and Cecil Court) is a magnet for philatelists in London. All the shops are in the Strand area, although we label some as in Charing Cross Road/Covent Garden—this is the same neighborhood and is an easy walk. (Tube: Charing Cross)

STANLEY GIBBONS LTD.

The shop has the largest collection of British Empire stamp material in the world as well as the most complete selection of stamp accessories—albums, tweezers, and perforation gauges—and its own well-researched catalogs.

Gibbons also sells extraordinary philatelic material. We were once shown an issued but unused full block of twelve of the Twopenny Blue with the original gum. Brilliantly colored and lettered "SG-TL" in the lower left- and right-hand corners (to prevent counterfeiting), this museum-quality piece was offered at a mere $20,000.

Such lofty material is viewed in private, secure surroundings on the second floor. On a more mundane level—the ground floor—Gibbons stocks a few topics such as birds and the Royal Family, and has specialists in first-day covers, plate blocks, precancels, overprints, color variations, etc. The firm gave up the coin and medal business several years ago but now carries a full selection of postcards and pertinent literature.

Gibbons is impossibly famous and therefore impossibly crowded—you may get less service, and they may not have what you are looking for. Don't be afraid to wander around the neighborhood and try the competition. Smaller and less-known dealers may be more fun.

STANLEY GIBBONS LTD.
399 The Strand, WC2 (Tube: Charing Cross)

DAVID BRANDON

The second in a row of three shops across from GIBBONS, Brandon has a large stock of classic material and is particularly up on postal history items of Great Britain and the Continent.

DAVID BRANDON
77 The Strand, WC2 (Tube: Charing Cross)

STRAND STAMPS

Three dealers operate as Strand and deal in

Commonwealth material. Even though GIBBONS has a larger stock in this area, the Strand dealers often come up with particular items from India or Australia that the big kid on the block doesn't stock. Moreover, Strand isn't pricey and is particularly patient with younger collectors. If you've gone to the trouble to seek the neighborhood, don't blow it now—you must stop in here.

STRAND STAMPS

79 The Strand, WC2 (Tube: Charing Cross)

Also try:

HARMER'S, 91 New Bond Street, W1 (Tube: Bond Street)

PHILLIPS SON & NEALE, 101 New Bond Street, W1 (Tube: Bond Street)

SOTHEBY'S, 34–35 New Bond Street, W1 (Tube: Bond Street)

SPINK & SON LTD., 5–7 King Street, St. James's, SW1 (Tube: Piccadilly Circus)

CHRISTIE'S, 8 King Street, St. James's, SW1 (Tube: Piccadilly Circus)

Collectors' and shoppers' note: All these shops are open Monday to Friday from 10 A.M. to 5 P.M. (GIBBONS opens at 9 A.M.) and the same hours Saturday, except for DAVID BRANDON (closed all day) and STRAND and Gibbons, which close at 1 P.M.

There are also several periodicals related to stamps, including *Stamp News*, and collectors also should keep in mind the large auction houses. PHILLIPS has a postage stamp auction nearly every Thursday, and CHRISTIE'S recently offered a collection that included proofs and essays from Bradbury, Wilkinson & Co., which has printed British stamps and bank notes for nearly 150 years.

Dolls and Toys

POLLOCK'S TOY MUSEUM

Nearly a hundred years ago, Robert Louis

Stevenson wrote, "If you love art, folly, or the bright eyes of children, speed to Pollock's." Thousands still do and find a treasure island of toys housed in two adjoining buildings overflowing with dolls, teddy bears, tin toys, puppets, and folk toys from Europe, India, Africa, China, and Japan.

Exhibits of mechanical toys and construction sets fill the lower floor of Pollock's Toy Museum, and the second story has exhibits of the paper "toy theaters" and cut-out actors and actresses that have fired the imagination of British children for generations.

In addition to the museum, there's a second Pollock's, a toy shop, set up in Covent Garden when the original was destroyed in the Blitz. The shop sells the theaters, popguns, and dolls, and there's no admission charge. The shop is open Monday to Saturday from 10 A.M. to 8 P.M.

The museum is at the corner of Scala and Whitfield streets, and is open Monday to Saturday from 10 A.M. to 5 P.M. Admission is 50p for adults and 20p for children and students. The museum also holds parties for up to thirty children.

POLLOCK'S TOY MUSEUM
1 Scala Street, W1 (Tube: Goodge Street)

POLLOCK'S TOY THEATRES
44 The Market, Covent Garden, WC2 (Tube: Covent Garden)

LONDON TOY AND MODEL MUSEUM

In a case devoted to dolls based on the Royal Family, a German-made Princess Elizabeth doll, from 1932, sits next to a Princess Anne doll made in 1953.

This royal rite of passage from child to queen is nearly overshadowed by other dolls at the museum—poured-wax dolls; bisque (china) dolls; a wax-headed Quaker lady in her original costume, from 1840; and a Topsy Turvy doll, which can be either white or black, depending on the owner's fancy.

In addition to dolls, the museum has 25,000 Matchbox and Corgi miniature cars, several working rocking horses, a collection of Paddington Bears, an entire room of toy trains, and a display of toy soldiers from Pierce Carlson (see page 250).

The latest addition is the Baywest exhibit, a computer-controlled model of 1,000 houses, 50,000 lights, a railway system, and a helicopter, and that requires a separate admission charge. There also are two smaller coin-operated versions by the same designer—a snow scene and a small town at twilight.

Hours: Tuesday to Saturday, 10 A.M. to 5:30 P.M.; Sunday, 11 A.M. to 5 P.M. Admission charge.

LONDON TOY AND MODEL MUSEUM

23 Craven Hill Road, W2 (Tube: Paddington)

Collectors' note: Doll & Toy World covers these collectibles on a monthly basis, as does Antique Toy World.

Toy Soldiers

UNDER TWO FLAGS

By the time toy soldiers became popular in America (during World War II), English children were celebrating the fiftieth anniversary of William Britain & Co. Britain went into the toy soldier business in 1893, creating a set of the Life Guards to honor Queen Victoria's forthcoming Diamond Jubilee in 1897.

Many Britain sets (including the first) are available at Under Two Flags on colorful St. Christopher's Place between Wigmore and Regent streets. . . just a stone's throw from Oxford Street and SELFRIDGES.

The store also offers inexpensive lead soldiers for do-it-yourself painters; a selection of military books; magazines and prints; bronzes; porcelains; and curios, such as a chess set made of toy soldiers.

Hours: Monday to Saturday, 10 A.M. to 6 P.M.

UNDER TWO FLAGS
4 St. Christopher's Place, W1 (Tube: Bond Street)

PIERCE CARLSON

There's a windowful of Britain soldiers at the LONDON TOY AND MODEL MUSEUM on loan from Pierce Carlson. He runs a retail shop near the British Model Soldier Society and also maintains a stall on Portobello Road for those collectors of the famous Britain brand.

PIERCE CARLSON
Portobello Road Market, Stall 27 (Tube: Notting Hill Gate)

Miscellaneous note: While there are specialty publications for almost every collectible, two British periodicals cover collectibles in general: *Collectors Mart* and *Collectors Gazette*. These are filled with ads for cigarette cards (the British equivalent of baseball cards), "advertiques" (specialty advertising paraphernalia, such as ashtrays), porcelain bottles of spirits, and pre-1960 boxed sets of Lego—with the original instructions, of course.

Enamels

HALCYON DAYS

For all you collectors of fine English enamels, it's time to go crazy. The Halcyon Days shop in London is small but loaded. You can find both antique English enamels and contemporary designs that include "paintings," clocks, picture frames, music boxes, sewing accessories, pens, etc. The prices are less expensive than in the U.S. Mail order is a cinch.

Best of all, once you buy an item, for years

afterward you'll be on the mailing list, and gorgeous brochures will come to you a few times a year—all with the London prices.

HALCYON DAYS
   14 Brook Street, W1 (Tube: Bond Street)

Comic Books

Yes, we know you outgrew these years ago, but there are collectors out there who are buying up nostalgic reminders of the good old days with the speed of (Zap!) the Flash. Like our teenage son Aaron.

Ten years ago, there were small comic-book departments in some of the better bookstores. Now, according to the comic cognoscenti, there are more than forty comic-book specialty stores in Great Britain, and a baker's dozen in London, each with a slightly different appeal.

FORBIDDEN PLANET

You're about to enter three strange worlds, one inhabited by aliens, a second in which fantasy princes and monsters reign supreme, and yet a third where comic-book characters rule, but that's not all. At Forbidden Planet you'll also find videotapes of all seventeen James Bond movies, trading cards from the original *Batman* movie, and the complete works of Al Capp (*Li'l Abner*). It's a comicoholic's dream. Where else would you find the unauthorized biography of *Superman* baddie Lex Luthor? The stock is vast, with some 10,000 different titles available. (Parents dragging kids should be aware that some are decidedly not for family consumption, such as *The Adventures of Johnny Condom*.)

While the emphasis is on new comic heroes, Dick Tracy, Superman, and Little Lulu are represented, as is, believe it or not, cowboy hero Tom Mix, who died forty years before current comic collectors were born. They also offer a limited stock of back issues. The shop also offers fantasy masks, an incredibly complete assortment of science fiction books and videos, and toys such as miniature versions of the original Starship *Enterprise*.

There are branches in Brighton, Glasgow, and Cambridge, and Forbidden Planet also sells most items by mail as well. The London shop is open 10 A.M. to 7 P.M. (8 P.M. on Thursday; 6 P.M. on Saturday).

FORBIDDEN PLANET

71 New Oxford Street, WC1 (Tube: Tottenham Court Road)

COMICS SHOWCASE

Despite its fantastic selection, FORBIDDEN PLANET can be a noisy, hectic place to shop. If you prefer to browse for that hard-to-find early *Batman* comic book in peace and quiet, you should know about Comics Showcase. The place is organized in aisles like a record shop and has early work by *Pogo*'s creator Walt Kelly. They also have early issues of *Dr. Who* and *Batman*. The staff is knowledgeable and will excitedly show you *Newsboy Legion*, an early work by Jack Kirby, who later did the *Fantastic Four*. Comics Showcase also has branches in Oxford and Cambridge.

COMICS SHOWCASE

76 Neal Street, WC2 (Tube: Covent Garden or Leicester Square)

GOSH!

Across from the British Museum on Great Russell Street is Gosh!, which dispensed with signs during the *Batman* craze and just hung an image of the Caped Crusader to attract passerby. Gosh! has a serene atmosphere very much in tune with museum goers. An employee confided, "We're dependent on the museum trade." As a result, you'll find, along with comics, complete histories of faded favorites such as *Captain Easy* and *Wash Tubbs* in eight volumes, and scholarly histories about cartoon strips and comic books. Gosh! is open daily, 10 A.M. to 6 P.M. Monday through Saturday and 1 P.M. to 6 P.M. on Sunday.

GOSH!

39 Great Russell Street, WC1 (Tube: Holborn)

THE TINTIN SHOP

If you know Thomson from Thompson and could pick the evil Rastopopoulos out of a police lineup, you'll be in heaven at this all-Tintin shop near Covent Garden. Tintin turned sixty recently, and his exploits have charmed children all over the world in over 50 languages—including Esperanto. The shop features all twenty-two Tintin adventures and other merchandise: drawing pads, unframed and framed posters. There's even an all-wool Tintin sweater if you're feeling expansive. If your kids have not yet discovered Tintin, now's the time.

THE TINTIN SHOP

34 Floral Street, WC2 (Tube: Covent Garden)

Cigarette Cards

Just as baseball cards became wildly popular in the U.S. beginning in 1981, so cigarette cards have become highly collectible in England. Sets that used to sell for $5 or $7 in 1986 are now fetching $10 or $12.

You might expect that cigarette card dealers would be proliferating; just the reverse is true. With more cards being held by collectors (and investors), the number of sets that used to turn over at flea markets and in antiques stores specializing in ephemera has decreased. One of the best shops specializing in cards is:

MURRAY & CO.

Murray & Co. has become the mecca for cigarette card collectors around the world. Since 1967, the company has published the only annual price catalog in the field. Murray has also been active reprinting valuable old sets (clearly marked *reprint*) and publishing its own checklists and books; a recent one, *Half Time*, covers English football (soccer) cards.

Murray has two shops in London, one on Cecil Court just off Charing Cross Road, the other in Hendon, served by the Hendon Central stop on the Northern Line. The Hendon shop has far greater stock in all respects, while the Cecil Court shop is more convenient to central London (less than a hundred yards from Trafalgar Square) and offers a brief overview of what's available. If you've got any idea at all of becoming serious about cigarette cards, however, the trip to Hendon is an absolute must. To save time for all concerned, come equipped with a list of the sets you want and their manufacturers' names.

MURRAY & CO.

20 Cecil Court, WC2 (Tube: Leicester Square)

51 Watford Way, Hendon Central, NW4 (Tube: Hendon Central)

Record Megastores: The Vinyl Solution

The London retail record scene is an accurate reflection of the record business itself: What was once a vital, creative maelstrom has become ho-hum and predictable, with a few giant megabuck companies dominating. Independent companies survive, if at all, by specializing. The three heavyweights—HMV, TOWER, and VIRGIN—have all the amenities and services you'd expect to find in a warehouse, but they do have mammoth selection, literally something for every taste. Virgin and HMV stores open at 9:30 A.M. and stay open until at least 7 P.M. Tower is even more accessible—9 A.M. to midnight. Finally, HMV and Virgin have a total of five stores on Oxford Street, making things ever-so-convenient.

HMV

150 Oxford Street, W1 (Tube: Oxford Circus)

363 Oxford Street, W1 (Tube: Bond Street or Marble Arch)

18 Coventry Street (Trocadero), W1 (Tube: Piccadilly Circus)

TOWER RECORDS

1 Piccadilly Circus, W1 (Tube: Piccadilly Circus)

62–64 Kensington High Street, W8 (Tube: High Street Kensington)

VIRGIN MEGASTORE

14–30 Oxford Street, W1 (Tube: Oxford Circus)

100 Oxford Street, W1 (Tube: Tottenham Court Road)

527 Oxford Street, W1 (Tube: Marble Arch)

RAY'S JAZZ SHOP

If what you're looking for relates to jazz, it's probably at Ray's Jazz Shop. New and used LPs and CDs, jazz books, magazines, and rare 78s. Some of the records are so rare that Ray's regularly auctions them off. Every month new records come up for auction, and bidders submit offers in person. The staff are more knowledgeable than employees in the jazz departments at the megastores, and very helpful. When a tourist asked to hear a used Billie Holiday CD, the manager sampled every cut on the compact disc to make sure it was all playable. You can wallow here in things jazz from 10 A.M. to 6:30 P.M. Monday through Saturday.

RAY'S JAZZ SHOP

180 Shaftesbury Avenue, WC2 (Tube: Tottenham Court Road)

TEMPLAR RECORDS

While rock, pop, and jazz fans have been unabashedly pro-compact disk, classical music lovers have often been astonished at CD prices.

There are classical CD bargains out there, however. Templar Records, an unprepossessing classical CD specialist, features the work of name artists for as low as $8, while double-disc operas run upwards from $30. Open 10 A.M. to 6 P.M. Monday through Saturday.

TEMPLAR RECORDS
   9 Irving Street, WC2 (Tube: Leicester Square)

Secondhand Records

   If the record you're looking for can't be found by browsing the specialty stores, there are always secondhand shops; however, such stores are almost as used as the merchandise they sell. They're generally dirty, dusty, and jumbled up. (We like that in bookstores, but hate it in record stores.)

   GRAMOPHONE EXCHANGE may have that record of "My Tears Have Washed 'I Love You' from the Blackboard of My Heart" you've been looking for all these years.

GRAMOPHONE EXCHANGE

   If you don't mind shopping for secondhand records in a place that's also devoted to Albanian trinkets, hit the Gramophone Exchange. It's covered with authentic dust, crammed full of records, and one of the house specialties is windup gramophones.

GRAMOPHONE EXCHANGE
   3 Betterton Street, WC2 (Tube: Covent Garden)

58 DEAN STREET RECORDS

   When was the last time you saw a store display devoted to Doris Day's records? If you answered "1958," you're halfway there. At 58 Dean Street, near Piccadilly Circus, you can check out Doris's greatest—"Que Sera Sera," and "A Guy Is a Guy,"—recorded before she was a virgin.

58 DEAN STREET RECORDS
   58 Dean Street, W1 (Tube: Green Park)

CHAPTER EIGHT

LONDON ON A SCHEDULE

Tour 1: Mayfair Mayhem/ Do-It-All-in-a-Day Tour

This is a complete tour of Mayfair with plenty of stops for real-people shopping, so don't be frightened away. Sure, lots of the stores on Bond Street and even Regent Street are out-of-bounds from a budget point of view, but I'm going to give you a little of everything, so hang on tight. Feel free to pop into stores you pass that interest you, as this trip will take you right by every store in London.

1) Begin at MARKS & SPENCER on Oxford Street, near Marble Arch. The British fondly refer to this store as "Marks & Sparks" or even "M & S." This is the only M & S branch that sells cashmere, so here's your first bargain tip of the day. Don't miss the basement, where you will want to buy ready-cooked foods in order to save money for clothes. I suggest the chicken *tikka*, followed by a tin of "Curiously Strong Mints." You may want to buy it now and keep it in your tote bag for a picnic lunch later. I do that all the time, honest.

2) Next, cross Orchard Street and explore SELFRIDGES, a great British example of one-stop shopping. Selfridges is a less glamorous version of HARRODS, but they do have a good Filofax department which is handily near their branch of THORNTON'S,

the mass candy marketeer that makes a toffee I am addicted to.

Don't miss MISS SELFRIDGE, young and kicky—perfect for the teen-and-twenties set. It's on the ground floor. So far, prices have been moderate.

3) Leaving Selfridges, go back onto Oxford Street. Proceed away from Marble Arch (turn left) on Oxford Street, then turn right onto South Molton Street. By the time you get to South Molton, you will have passed many street vendors selling London souvenirs. Prices are best on the street, so load up now.

4) Once on South Molton Street, inspect all of the shops. The most famous is BROWNS for high fashion; there's a Browns discount outlet at No. 45. There are a number of shoe shops here and some fabulous costume jewelry stores, including BUTLER & WILSON. There's also an antiques gallery if you are more interested in your home than your closet.

5) At the end of South Molton, take a left for a short block up Brook Street. Cross New Bond Street, visit HALCYON DAYS (14 Brook Street).

6) Retrace your steps back to New Bond Street and do both sides of New Bond and then Old Bond streets. You will find most of the major designer boutiques on these two streets. I suggest you spend some time in FENWICK, which is a small department store with moderately priced high fashion; it's the only store on Bond Street that I can afford. If you need a break, take a stroll through the ROYAL ARCADE (28 Old Bond Street), to BROWN'S HOTEL at 34 Albemarle Street. Stop in for a wonderful and classic tea, which will include tea sandwiches and scones. Consider a quick trip to MICHAELJOHN for

reviving aromatherapy (book ahead) or even a wash and blow dry.

7) Fortified and beautified, walk back through the Royal Arcade. Turn right and finish your shopping on Old Bond.

8) Then take a left on Piccadilly, a right through the PICCADILLY ARCADE, and again a right onto Jermyn Street. Jermyn Street is one of London's best-designed retail streets for men's items. Go down one side of Jermyn toward St. James's and then come back on the other side toward Piccadilly. Buy the man in your life a shirt at TURNBULL & ASSER (No. 71), or at HILDITCH & KEY. Walk to ALFRED DUNHILL, which is at the corner of Duke and Jermyn. At least look in the windows. FORTNUM & MASON is also here; don't miss the food hall toward the front of the store.

Go through the front of FORTNUM & MASON back out on Piccadilly and walk to your right directly to Piccadilly Circus and the entrance of LILLYWHITES, the sporting goods department store. Come around and leave the store on Piccadilly, walking back toward the BURLINGTON ARCADE. You can take in HATCHARDS, one of London's most famous bookstores, then cross over to the Burlington Arcade.

9) The BURLINGTON ARCADE is the prettiest covered shopping street in London. This arcade was built in 1819, and its atmosphere has remained delightfully British. The arcade is the only London area that maintains Regency rules of public conduct, prohibiting whistling, singing, or hurrying. Its 585-foot passage is watched over by two guards dressed in the ceremonial garb of officers of the 10th Hussars. Most of the thirty-eight shops sell mainly British goods from cash-

meres to linens to saddles. GIDDEN has handbags and leathergoods (and saddles) fit for a queen. They have several royal warrants to prove it.

If you get the feeling that I've sent you in a circle, yes, I have. The last part of the route has been a bit of a loop-de-loop. You aren't dizzy, are you?

10) Exit the arcade at the opposite end of where you entered, take a right onto Burlington Gardens, a left onto Savile Row (home of the famous Savile Row tailors), a right onto New Burlington Street, and then a left onto Regent Street. You have now entered another major shopping thoroughfare. Walk toward Oxford Street, to complete your full circle tour— don't miss HAMLEYS (No. 188), JAEGER (No. 204), AQUASCUTUM (No. 100), LAWLEY'S (No. 154), BURBERRYS (No. 165), REJECT CHINA SHOP (No. 134), and, finally, LIBERTY (Nos. 210–220). Collapse at the LANGHAM HILTON for tea, or maybe the week.

Tour 2: Knightsbridge Day Tour

1) Begin at HARRODS (Knightsbridge). Your visit here is optional—it's not un-American to bypass Harrods. I always swear I don't like Harrods, yet end up visiting several times on each trip to London. If you've never seen it, at least tour the food halls and, if you are looking for china or souvenirs, get them now.

If you've done it and the store unnerves you, do not feel obligated to try it again. Frankly, this place can be a zoo.

2) Go out of Harrods at the Brompton Road exit and walk to the right toward Knights-

bridge. Proceed on to HARVEY NICHOLS, a smaller and more fashionable department store (corner of Knightsbridge and Sloane Street), known for its great selection of designer fashions. If you are hungry, stop at the fifth floor coffee shop; you can browse the food halls after you've been fortified. Harvey Nichols is a lot easier to handle than Harrods; they have a very nice home furnishings floor.

3) Now you are ready to take the Sloane Street exit and walk toward Sloane Square. Sloane Street is a long, straight shopping avenue filled with fun, chic boutiques and all of Europe's big names from CHANEL to VALENTINO. Look out for Sloane Rangers, those trendy fashion yuppies who are wearing pearls with their Wellies.

4) You now have to make a choice: to stay in Knightsbridge or segue on to a different type of nearby shopping. You can cut back toward HARRODS from Sloane Square (or reverse the tour so you go to HARVEY NICHOLS and then Harrods) and get on Brompton Road heading toward Beauchamp Place and the major museums on Cromwell Road. This is a short walk and then you turn left on Beauchamp, which is lined with tony boutiques selling high-end Sloane Ranger designer togs from KANGA to BRUCE OLD-FIELD; there are three branches of REJECT CHINA SHOP.

5) If you want something funkier, continue on Sloane Street, where every big designer shop now has a branch. Turn right to get to PETER JONES, a big department store, and then turn right again on King's Road, where you can walk for a mile or two and see everything trendy in fashion and furnishings. I walk King's Road up into the 500 block; most peo-

ple will quit way before then. Hail a taxi to your next stop as there is no nearby tube stop.

Tour 3: Hot-to-Trot, Teeny-Bop London Tour

1) This is really a half-day tour for the afternoon, since many of these shops don't open until 11 A.M.

2) Take the tube to High Street Kensington, which is a central shopping drag—you will emerge from the underground right in the middle of a lot of stores, many of which specialize in the New Wave.

3) Look on both sides of the street at the small boutiques, jeans shops, the market selling used clothes, army surplus, and the like, and the now famous HYPER HYPER, where up-and-coming designers try out their creations. The KENSINGTON MARKET (Nos. 49–53) is an indoor den of dyed jeans and tie-dyed T-shirts and many leftovers from the 1960s, which are quite stylish now. (AMERICAN RETRO is on the basement level.) This is not for the Chanel customer. The market doesn't so much sell a look as it does pieces, so if you don't know what to do with those black studded things, this is not your kind of shop. There's also a branch of RED OR DEAD next to Hyper Hyper; there are some traditional stores mixed in here— don't be distracted by the likes of MOTHER-CARE and CRABTREE & EVELYN. It's a nice adventure to get a little of everything.

Your main thrill will be at HYPER HYPER (Nos. 26–40), which is a two-level (go downstairs) supermarket of booths maintained by the up-and-coming designers who walk on the wild side. Even if you buy nothing here, you will be able to tell your friends about it for years.

4) Have a taxi take you to ACADEMY at 188A King's Road, which is rather the heart of the area. King's Road is a street in transition, but it still has a lot of shops that sell the last word in new. Or weird. Academy is small but packs in the works of several up-and-coming designers. Prices can be surprisingly high.

5) Check out both sides of King's Road. Be sure not to miss DAVID FIELDEN (No. 137), EDINA RONAY (No. 141), HACKETT'S (No. 65), JONES (No. 71), and BOY (No. 195).

6) Walk along King's Road toward Sloane Square.

7) Catch the tube at Sloane Square and go to Piccadilly Circus. Once at Piccadilly, pull out your A to Z or a map, as the Soho area is a rabbit warren of tiny streets that weave behind Regent Street.

8) Tour Soho, taking in WORKERS FOR FREE-DOM (4 Lower John Street); ACADEMY (yes, again—this one is fancier) (15 Newburgh Street); and DRESSED TO KILL (13 Newburgh Street).

9) Wind your way onto Carnaby Street. Mixed in with the tawdry sex shops and tourist attractions, you'll find some cheapie stores selling black leather, floppy hats, bandanas, and tie-dye.

10) Take Beak Street (this street is the length of your driveway at home) from Carnaby Street to Regent Street, where you'll be in the heart of traditional London. If you still want New Wave, don't look when you walk by BURBER-RYS. Continue on Regent Street, passing all the hallmarks of British style, and end up at Oxford Circus, where you will turn right onto Oxford Street and walk one block to

DEPARTMENT X, *the* word on mass-produced trendiness.

11) Not tired yet? Great. Walk toward Marble Arch on Oxford Street, passing several department stores and souvenir shops. Be on the right-hand side of the street (if your back is to Oxford Circus) and take care to look for an itty-bitty street called Gees Court off St. Christopher's Place.

12) Turn right (the only possible choice) and note this two-block street, which is a virtual secret to those not in the know. The first block is called Gees Court, which is filled with stores. Most of them are chic and expensive, but WHISTLES has some rock-and-roll clothes. Wander two blocks till the stores stop, then cut back to Oxford Street. In another block, you'll be at MISS SELFRIDGE, which is maybe where you should have started. They have with-it clothes that aren't too weird or too expensive.

Now then, assuming you would only do this with a teen or two in tow, I want you to walk two blocks over from Oxford Street and Marble Arch and drag your teens into the Dorchester (on Park Lane), where you can take high tea. Teach them how to aspire to the upper-middle class while you stare at their Doc Martens.

Tour 4: Home-Is-Where-the-Heart-Is Tour

1) Put on those walking shoes. I'm going to march you around town like the Black Watch Guards. Leave your bagpipes at home, but take along any swatches you might have brought with you, or a notepad to write down things of interest as you pass by. If

you have business cards or credentials that admit you to the trade, bring 'em along. And don't forget the credit cards.

2) Take the tube to Knightsbridge, enter HARVEY NICHOLS the department store and take the escalator right upstairs to the home furnishings floor. Tour it slowly, taking mental notes. Then walk out of Harvey Nichols and onto Sloane Street. Ignore the fashion boutiques; this is a home furnishings tour. Turn left on Harriet Street, right off Sloane Street and walk right into the LAURA ASHLEY shop. This is a giant home-furnishings store now, and will give you many ideas. Be sure to check the bins for sale items. As you leave the store, walk along Sloane Street toward Sloane Square (and away from Knightsbridge).

3) Things will be dull for a few seconds but will warm up quickly as you get to JANE CHURCHILL at No. 135 and then the GENERAL TRADING COMPANY (No. 144), where the tabletop is particularly interesting.

4) Dive into PETER JONES, the department store, to check out sheets, duvet covers, bed linens, and trimmings, then come out of the store on the King's Road side and head to the right. King's Road is very long, and the design sources are far-flung (the reason I told you to wear sensible shoes). You'll pass several good antiques galleries on King's Road and should be quite warmed up for the chase by the time you hit DESIGNER'S GUILD, one of the two Tricia Guild shops. You'll be panting when you leave (it's so exciting), but don't miss the second shop a few doors farther down, where the fabrics are (No. 271 and No. 277).

5) OSBORNE & LITTLE has a showroom across the street (No. 304), and there are many

antiques shops here you'll want to browse. Keep on moving even if things get a little boring as the really chic stuff thins out. KNOBS & KNOCKERS has a shop at No. 385 for brass fixtures; T.F. BUCKLE at No. 427 has the reproduction fireplaces that are all the rage. Of course, you'll dive into the antiques galleries as you walk past them.

6) Cut over to Fulham Road, which parallels King's Road, and find yourself more or less in the mid-200 block. Walk or bus to that number if you're too tired to search. COLE-FAX & FOWLER has a branch at No. 110.

7) Continue toward Knightsbridge now, walking on Fulham Road, taking in SOULEIADO, THE SLEEPING COMPANY, DIVERTIMENTI, and maybe even SMALLBONE, where you'll see kitchens that will make you want to remodel right away. Finish up with a strong espresso at Michelin House, now known for THE CONRAN SHOP.

8) Restored from your coffee, go out the side door of THE CONRAN SHOP and head for Walton Street and more decorative shops (remember your trip to HARVEY NICHOLS? All the NINA CAMPBELL you didn't buy is still available at her shop on Walton Street), then wander into the Victoria and Albert Museum, where you'll find decorative arts that will inspire you in your design decisions. Learn to copy the best and you'll never go wrong.

Tour 5: Sunday Shopper's Delight

1) You are planning ahead for the perfect Sunday in London, so you have already been to a newsstand or kiosk because you have

realized that many of the Sunday sections of London's best newspapers are sold on Saturdays!

2) Order room service for breakfast (it *is* Sunday) or head for the RITZ, where the famous, famous dining room in London serves a formal breakfast every morning. Usually only hotel guests are here in the A.M. hours, so you won't have to deal with the same crowds who come to the Ritz for tea. While the full English breakfast costs about £12, you can get coffee and pancakes a la carte for less while you enjoy one of the best sights London has to offer: the very dining room you are sitting in.

3) Plan to be at the Westminster Pier any half hour after 10:30 A.M. to catch the boat to Greenwich. The cab fare from the Ritz is about £3, but if there's two of you, that equals the tube fare—and this is an extravagant Sunday.

4) Catch the boat to Greenwich. It takes almost an hour to get to Greenwich; there is commentary on the sights all the way to the Tower. After the lecture, the captain will pass the hat; £1 is fine for two of you. Commentary quits at the Tower, where some people on the boat will disembark. Not you. Now watch the Docklands go by as you drift downstream to town. The Greenwich Pier is right at the edge of downtown and couldn't be more convenient. There are public bathrooms there.

5) You may want to let the husband (and the kids) explore the two boats and museums here, the three-masted *Cutty Sark* and the tiny *Gipsy Moth*. In fact, Greenwich has so many sights—and a fabulous park—that you will have to make choices in order to fit in everything you require for the perfect

Sunday. If your time is limited, go right into the Victorian marketplace where a crafts show is taking place.

6) Finished with the craft market—and all the adjacent stores which are conveniently open—leave the covered market and cross over to Greenwich Church Street and find the Greenwich Tourist Information Office, a small storefront that sells certificates (20p each) for standing on the Time Line (this is home to Greenwich Mean Time) or for walking under the Thames in the Greenwich Foot Tunnel. Excellent gifts for kids. Check out the brochures (free) and see if there is an additional antiques show that day at Town Hall.

7) Across the street is Bosun's Yard, where there is another crafts market—this one is more crass (featuring more imports) than the excellent official market, but still worth a peek. As you leave and head up Greenwich Church Street toward High Road, you'll pass GODDARD'S EEL PIES, a very authentic English-style diner where your entire lunch won't cost more than £2. Don't miss the fresh homemade berry pie (with custard on top) for dessert.

8) Keep walking up Greenwich Church Street to CANOPY STREET MARKET, a meandering market that sprawls along and sells mostly junk. We think it's great junk, although our friend Ian disdains this particular market. It's certainly not for the Sotheby's crowd.

9) Turn onto the high street and take in the outdoor GREENWICH ANTIQUES MARKET: Used clothes are toward the rear. This is a pretty good place for used paperbacks if you need reading material for your travels and are horrified by the price of paperbacks (and all books) in Britain.

10) You are now half a block from Town Hall (it's that unattractive modern building with the clock tower), where there may be another antiques show. These usually charge admission (the other markets don't), but add to the fun of the day if you are feeling flush. Since you are now half a block from the train station, and probably have a good number of packages in hand, you can zip on home via train and end up at Charing Cross. Follow The Strand for two blocks to the SAVOY, where you can have high tea in one of London's fanciest hotels.

11) Refreshed? Good. Walk two blocks to Covent Garden, where the Sunday retail scene is happening.

12) Collapse!

SIZE CONVERSION CHART

Women's Dresses, Coats and Skirts

American	3	5	7	9	11	12	13	14	15	16	18
Continental	36	38	38	40	40	42	42	44	44	46	48
British	8	10	11	12	13	14	15	16	17	18	20

Women's Blouses and Sweaters

American	10	12	14	16	18	20
Continental	38	40	42	44	46	48
British	32	34	36	38	40	42

Women's Shoes

American	5	6	7	8	9	10
Continental	36	37	38	39	40	41
British	$3^{1}/_{2}$	$4^{1}/_{2}$	$5^{1}/_{2}$	$6^{1}/_{2}$	$7^{1}/_{2}$	$8^{1}/_{2}$

Children's Clothing

American	3	4	5	6	6X
Continental	98	104	110	116	122
British	18	20	22	24	26

Children's Shoes

American	8	9	10	11	12	13	1	2	3
Continental	24	25	27	28	29	30	32	33	34
British	7	8	9	10	11	12	13	1	2

Men's Suits

American	34	36	38	40	42	44	46	48
Continental	44	46	48	50	52	54	56	58
British	34	36	38	40	42	44	46	48

Men's Shirts

American	$14^{1}/_{2}$	15	$15^{1}/_{2}$	16	$16^{1}/_{2}$	17	$17^{1}/_{2}$	18
Continental	37	38	39	41	42	43	44	45
British	$14^{1}/_{2}$	15	$15^{1}/_{2}$	16	$16^{1}/_{2}$	17	$17^{1}/_{2}$	18

Men's Shoes

American	7	8	9	10	11	12	13
Continental	$39^{1}/_{2}$	41	42	43	$44^{1}/_{2}$	46	47
British	6	7	8	9	10	11	12

INDEX

ABOUT THE AUTHOR

Suzy Gershman is an author and journalist who has worked in the fiber and fashion industry since 1969 in both New York and Los Angeles, and has held editorial positions at *California Apparel News*, *Mademoiselle*, *Gentleman's Quarterly* and *People* magazine, where she was West Coast Style editor. She writes regularly for various magazines, including *Bride's* and *Travel and Leisure*; her essays on retailing are text at Harvard Business School. Mrs. Gershman lives in Connecticut with her husband, author Michael Gershman, and their son. Michael Gershman also contributes to the *Born to Shop* pages.

ABOUT THE PHOTOGRAPHER

Ian Cook is a British photographer based in London. A contributing photographer for *People* magazine, he has also worked as a reporter for British newspapers and periodicals and written numerous shopping and consumer information stories before joining the *Born to Shop* team.